The BP exhibition

Ming

50 years
that changed
China

The BP exhibition

Ming

50 years that changed China

Edited by
Craig Clunas and
Jessica Harrison-Hall

The British Museum

This book is published to accompany the exhibition at the British Museum from 18 September 2014 to 5 January 2015. Art Exhibitions China – principal Chinese contributor

Research supported by the Arts and Humanities Research Council.

 Arts & Humanities Research Council

First published in 2014 by The British Museum Press
A division of The British Museum Company Ltd
38 Russell Square, London WC1B 3QQ
britishmuseum.org/publishing

A catalogue record for this book is available from the British Library.

ISBN (cased) 978 0 7141 2477 3
ISBN (paperback) 978 0 7141 2484 1

Designed by Raymonde Watkins
Printed in Italy by Printer Trento S.r.l.
The papers used by The British Museum Press are recyclable products and the manufacturing processes are expected to conform to the environmental regulations of the country of origin.

Half-title page: Gold and gem encrusted hairpins (see fig. 55).
Frontispiece: Detail from a handscroll, 'Elegant gathering in the Apricot Garden' (see fig. 164).
Left: A blue-and-white wine vessel (see fig. 71).
Page 6: Detail from a gold pillow end encrusted with semi-precious stones (see fig. 98).
Pages 8–9: Carved red lacquer dish (see fig. 90).
Page 16: Detail from a handscroll, 'Lotus pond and pine tree' (see fig. 154).

 FSC MIX Paper from responsible sources FSC® C015829

CONTENTS

SPONSOR'S FOREWORD

Recent decades have been a time of rapid change in China. As a frequent visitor, I have been fascinated to see the country evolving as a global superpower. Connections through business, trade, diplomacy and cultural exchange have helped fuel China's growth and development. These connections are the same forces for change that were at work in China over half a millennium ago when the Ming empire emerged as a fifteenth-century superpower.

The surge of creativity that accompanied the early years of the new empire produced some of the most beautiful porcelain, paintings, sculpture, textiles, gold and jewellery ever fashioned by human hands. This special exhibition, which BP is proud to support, brings together an extraordinary range of objects to tell the story of a golden age for Chinese culture.

For over a quarter of a century BP has been helping to deliver the energy that supports China's economy and enhances China's energy diversification. We have built strong partnerships and forged close relationships in China – and cultural exchange helps to cement those bonds. We are grateful for the generosity of the many collections and institutions, in China and elsewhere, that are sharing so many of their most precious Ming artefacts with the world in this great exhibition.

Exhibitions such as this bring greater global understanding through shared knowledge and wonder. Such greater understanding is a precious investment in a global future. That is why BP has been a long-standing supporter of the British Museum, its series of China-related activities, and many other activities that widen access to the arts and culture worldwide.

Hundreds of thousands of people enjoyed the British Museum's *China: Journey to the East* touring exhibition between 2009 and 2012. My hope is that many will also appreciate and take great pleasure in *Ming: 50 years that changed China*.

Bob Dudley
Group Chief Executive BP

FOREWORD

The Ming dynasty that replaced the Yuan regime lasted 277 years, with a total of sixteen emperors and seventeen reigns beginning with the Hongwu emperor and ending with the Chongzhen emperor. The Ming dynasty was an extremely important period in China's late imperial society: on the one hand, traditional government, economics and culture reached great maturity; on the other, various new elements emerged, revealing a new sense of transformation towards modern society.

The exhibition *Ming: 50 years that changed China* organized by the British Museum and in partnership with Art Exhibitions China is unlike other exhibitions that aim to survey the whole history of the Ming dynasty. Instead, by focusing on artefacts from the period 1400 to 1450 (from the reigns of Yongle to Zhengtong), the exhibition highlights the developments and changes in early Ming China. On the whole, this period of the Ming dynasty enjoyed good government, a stable society, developments in production, and a powerful and prosperous state that could rival the heyday of Emperors Wen and Jing of the Western Han dynasty (206 BC–AD 9), and the Zhenguan and Kaiyuan eras of the Tang dynasty (618–906). Major historical events such as Zheng He's voyages to the Western Ocean, the building of the Forbidden City and the compilation of the Yongle encyclopedia all took place during this time. Ming China actively expanded its overseas contacts, while artists at the time absorbed diverse elements and styles, producing extraordinary works of art never seen before.

The exhibition *Ming: 50 years that changed China* will undoubtedly enrich audiences' understanding of China's historical development and social evolution, as well as enhance their comprehension of the skill and wisdom, and the thoughts and values of the Chinese people. I hereby express my appreciation to all those who contributed to this exhibition, and wish the exhibition every success!

Wang Jun
Director of Art Exhibitions China

FOREWORD

Understanding China's past is arguably more important today than at any other time in world history. *Ming: 50 years that changed China* offers a unique opportunity to understand a defining part of China's past, to re-examine the period in which Beijing was established as China's capital and when the Forbidden City, which remains a powerful symbol of China, was constructed. Chinese court life, military and cultural achievements, complex belief systems, and diplomatic and trading missions in this period (AD 1400–50) are explored through a diverse range of objects and paintings. It was an era of considerable stability, ambitious construction and extraordinary prosperity – a golden age of Chinese history that is celebrated in China itself but relatively little known outside the country.

This is essentially – and unavoidably – a tale of the powerful. Few traces exist today of the vast numbers of Chinese people who worked the land in this period to generate wealth and to produce rice, wheat, tea and cotton. These men and women are rarely mentioned in the texts that survive from the period and their modest possessions have mostly perished with them. However, the spectacular porcelains, lacquer, gold wares, jades, silks, jewellery and furniture that were made in workshops – some of them operating on an industrial scale – are eloquent testimony to the skill of the workers at this time. *Ming: 50 years that changed China* tells the history of the early Ming imperial courts and their global interactions, as emperors exchanged goods, staff and ideas with courts from Kyoto to Mogadishu. Ming China was a multi-faith, cosmopolitan society that was alive to the possibilities of global trade.

A century before Portuguese merchants began conducting direct European–Chinese trade in 1516, and nearly a century before Christopher Columbus sailed to America or Vasco da Gama navigated the Cape of Good Hope, Ming emperors deployed vast armadas to travel across the oceans. These ships brought luxury goods from China and exchanged them for local products, including speciality woods and spices. Research for the exhibition, led by Craig Clunas, Professor of the History of Art at Oxford University, and Jessica Harrison-Hall, Curator of Chinese Ceramics at the British Museum, has focused on the engagement of early Ming courts with societies beyond China's borders. By studying texts and surviving material objects and paintings that were mostly produced in the period 1400–50, the exhibition and accompanying book examine what Ming China absorbed from the outside world and what the outside world gained from encounters with China.

There were few direct contacts between Europe and the Ming court at this time, but luxury Chinese goods still made their way to Europe, and some of them were already antique by the time they were used in Europe. For example, Henry V, who triumphed at the Battle of Agincourt on St Crispin's Day 1415, had a funeral shield that was backed with Chinese silk. Similarly, European aristocrats made pilgrimages to the Holy Land and returned with Chinese porcelain, which they mounted in gold because they believed it had magical properties, such as the ability to detect poison. Renaissance artists painted images of rare Ming porcelain, depicting it as a material that was fit for presentation to God. We are particularly grateful to the J. Paul Getty Museum for lending, as the final piece in the exhibition, the painting by Andrea Mantegna (1431–1506) that shows the visit of the Three Wise Men, dressed in Eastern silks, to the newborn Christ child, bearing a Ming porcelain cup filled with gold.

Ming: 50 years that changed China has been made possible through the continued generosity of BP and the support for research by the Arts and Humanities Research Council. In total, thirty lenders have generously lent pieces from their collections and I would like to thank the museums, libraries and individuals who have temporarily parted with these items to make the ideas behind the exhibition a reality for the widest and largest possible audience. A sense of continuity between China's past and present has been intensified by the spectacular archaeological finds made in the past forty years and we would like to acknowledge the key role played by our major collaborator Art Exhibitions China, China's governmental organization for cultural exchange, by the Chinese Embassy staff here in London and by the Directors of the ten Chinese museums involved in the exhibition. We have had many years of fruitful collaboration with them all, and are particularly indebted to them for their help with this exhibition.

Neil MacGregor
Director, The British Museum

ACKNOWLEDGEMENTS

As collaborators and colleagues from the museum and university sectors, it has been a uniquely rewarding experience to work together since 2009 on this exhibition and on the research project that underpins it; we now have the extra pleasure of having very many individuals and institutions to thank. A project of this scale and complexity has involved teams of people in different countries, working in many different roles and disciplines. Above all we must thank the Project Curator Luk Yu-ping, who since joining the team in 2012 could not have made a greater or a more central contribution. The core team of authors for this book – Timothy Brook, Marsha Haufler and David Robinson – have been ideal collaborators, consistently generous with ideas, time and patience at the special demands of producing scholarship in the context of a major exhibition. Their commitment has been absolutely crucial to sustaining the whole enterprise.

The research project 'Ming: Courts and Contacts 1400–1450', funded by the Arts and Humanities Research Council of Great Britain, was launched in 2010 with a series of seminars held at the British Museum and at the University of Oxford, and we are grateful to all the participants in these early attempts to explain the project and hone its research questions: Richard Blurton, Robert Chard, Glen Dudbridge, Anne Gerritsen, Ros Holmes, Beth McKillop, Luisa Mengoni, Monica Merlin, Dirk Meyer, Laura Newby, Sarah Ng, Venetia Porter, Sascha Priewe, Jessica Rawson, Clarissa von Spee, Jan Stuart, Tian Yuan Tan, Hilde de Weerdt, Morgan Wesley, Frances Wood and Zhang Hongxing. We are also grateful to Anne Gerritsen and Stephen McDowell for an opportunity to present the project to a group of specialists gathered at the University of Warwick in June 2011, and to all of them for their feedback, criticisms and encouragement: Shih Ching-fei, Elizabeth Lambourn, Peter Jackson, Yuka Kadoi, Shane McCausland, Morris Rossabi and Ankeney Weitz.

In addition to all those listed above, for responding with suggestions and criticism and for support both in their areas of academic specialism and in many other ways, we would like to especially thank (at the British Museum) Ladan Akbarnia, Louise Chapman, Tim Clark, Gao Qing, Mary Ginsberg, Alexandra Green, Alfred Haft, J.D. Hill, Carol Michaelson, Nicole Rousmaniere, Helen Wang, Meixin Wang, and Michael Willis; as well as (from the University of Oxford) Vicky Brown, Clare Charlesworth, Peter Ditmanson, Barend ter Haar, David Helliwell, Jérôme Kerlouegan, Aileen Mooney, Christine Robertson, Shelagh Vainker and Rachel Woodruff. Other colleagues whose input is acknowledged with great gratitude include: Yu Hui, Zhang Rong, Geng Baocheng, Lu Chenglong, Li Zhongmou, Zhao Zhongnan (Palace Museum, Beijing); Yuan Wenqing (Hubei Provincial Museum); Feng Ming-chu, Ho Chuan-hsin, Lin Lina, Tsai Meifen, Yu Peichin (National Palace Museum, Taipei); Wang Cheng-hua (Academia Sinica); Rupert Faulkner, Julia Hutt, Anna Jackson, Ming Wilson, (V&A); Sara Chiesura, Graham Hutt, Ursula Simms-Williams, Hamish Todd (British Library); Tim Barrett, Stacey Pierson, Timon Screech (SOAS); John Moffatt (Needham Research Institute); Susan Bayly, Sally Church, Joe McDermott (Cambridge University); Regina Llamas (University of Bristol); Verity Wilson (RCA); Melanie Trede (University of Heidelberg); Kathlyn Liscomb (University of Victoria); Jennifer Purtle (University of Toronto); Yukio Lippit (Harvard University); Sarah Schneewind (UC San Diego); Dora Ching (Princeton University); Heechung Yang, Soomi Lee (National Museum of Korea).

We thank all the BM specialists who will enable the exhibition, conference and public programmes to reach their many and varied publics. Above all the Museum's Director Neil MacGregor has encouraged the collaboration, for the benefit of the widest possible audience, which lies at the heart of this enterprise; his support and his vision, as well as his keen critical eye, have made this a better exhibition than it would otherwise have been. As Keeper of Asia, Jan Stuart has worked tirelessly to move the project forward, and has been ever ready with help and advice. For the installation of the exhibition at the BM we would like to thank in particular Carolyn Marsden-Smith, Caroline Ingham, the designer Jonathan Ould, graphic designer Paul Goodhead, project manager Matthew Weaver, Elizabeth Bray, Kirsten Forrest and Mark Finch, loans co-ordinators Julia Evans and Jill Maggs, and interpretation managers Stuart Frost, Anna Bright, Iona Eastman and Nicola Freeman. Thank you to the photography department, especially John P. Williams, Kevin Lovelock and Claudio Mari. Lacquer, paintings, metal and ceramics conservators within the British Museum have worked tirelessly to conserve items for display, with especial thanks to Jin Qiu, Valentina Marabini, Carol Peacock, Joanna Kosek, Keisuke Sugiyama, Megumi Mizumura, David Green, Denise Ling, Loretta Hogan, Nicola Newman. We thank Senior Museum Assistant Kathryn Godwin and her team: Iestyn Jones, Lucy Carson, Xanthe Shrestha and Nina Harrison. At the British Museum Press, Coralie Hepburn, Kate Oliver, Axelle Russo-Heath, Ray Watkins and colleagues have done a wonderful job in producing this book. For all the hard work in marketing, broadcasting and press, as well as with the public programmes, we would like to thank: Charlotte Kewell, Patricia Wheatley, Hannah Boulton, Olivia Rickman, Nicola Elvin, Susan Raikes, Daniel Ferguson, Rosie Dalgado, Hilary Williams, James Trapp and all who work with them. At the British Museum Company we thank Roderick Buchanan and his team.

We are grateful above all to the lending institutions, which are listed separately in this volume. In this context, particular thanks go to the State Administration of Cultural Heritage of China, as well as to Art Exhibitions China and its Director Wang Jun, and Deputy Directors Yao An and Zhou Ming, together with their colleagues Zhao Gushan and Shang Xiaoyun. For preparations within China at AEC we thank: Shi Wanghuan, Gao Xiaoxu, Jiang Yutao, Qi Yue, Long Xiaofei, Chen Fenxia, Xu Liyi, Cui Yan, Qiu Xiaoyong, Jiang Qun, Wang Jichao, Ren Zhuo. We also acknowledge with gratitude the advice and support of Xiang Xiaowei, Minister Counsellor of the Embassy of the People's Republic of China, London.

Many museums were visited or worked with in the early stages and this did not lead to loans, but the collaboration has fuelled the project in other ways. We are particularly grateful to colleagues from: National Silk Museum, Hangzhou, Jingdezhen Ceramics Museum, Jingzhou Museum, Tibet Museum, Lhasa, Wudangshan Museum; Museum of Fine Arts, Boston, Art Institute of Chicago, Cleveland Museum of Art; Baur Foundation, Geneva, Guimet Museum, Paris, Pierrre Uldry Collection at the Rietberg Museum, Zürich; Institute for Research in Humanities, Kyoto University.

Picture research by Luk Yu-ping and Axelle Russo-Heath has been vital for book and exhibition, and has drawn upon the goodwill of many individuals, not all of whom can be thanked by name; particular thanks go to Roderick Whitfield and Malcolm McNeil, who helped with pictures in special circumstances. Translation work by Luk Yu-ping and Malcolm McNeil has been a great asset. For help with due diligence research, thanks go again to Luk Yu-ping, Malcolm McNeil, Jean Martin and Dominic Jellinek. For help with reading the manuscript and providing useful comments thanks are gratefully offered to Rose Kerr, Regina Krahl, Jan Stuart and many others. Colin Sheaf and Rosemary Scott have also provided important information to help with this project; as have a host of volunteers.

The mistakes that remain are entirely the responsibility of the authors, who wish to record their gratitude for special support to Verity Wilson, to Martin, Beatrice, Alexander and Eleanor Keady; and also to Helen Valuks.

Without the generous arts sponsorship of BP, projects on this scale simply could not be achieved. For this support we will always be very grateful.

Craig Clunas and Jessica Harrison-Hall, August 2014

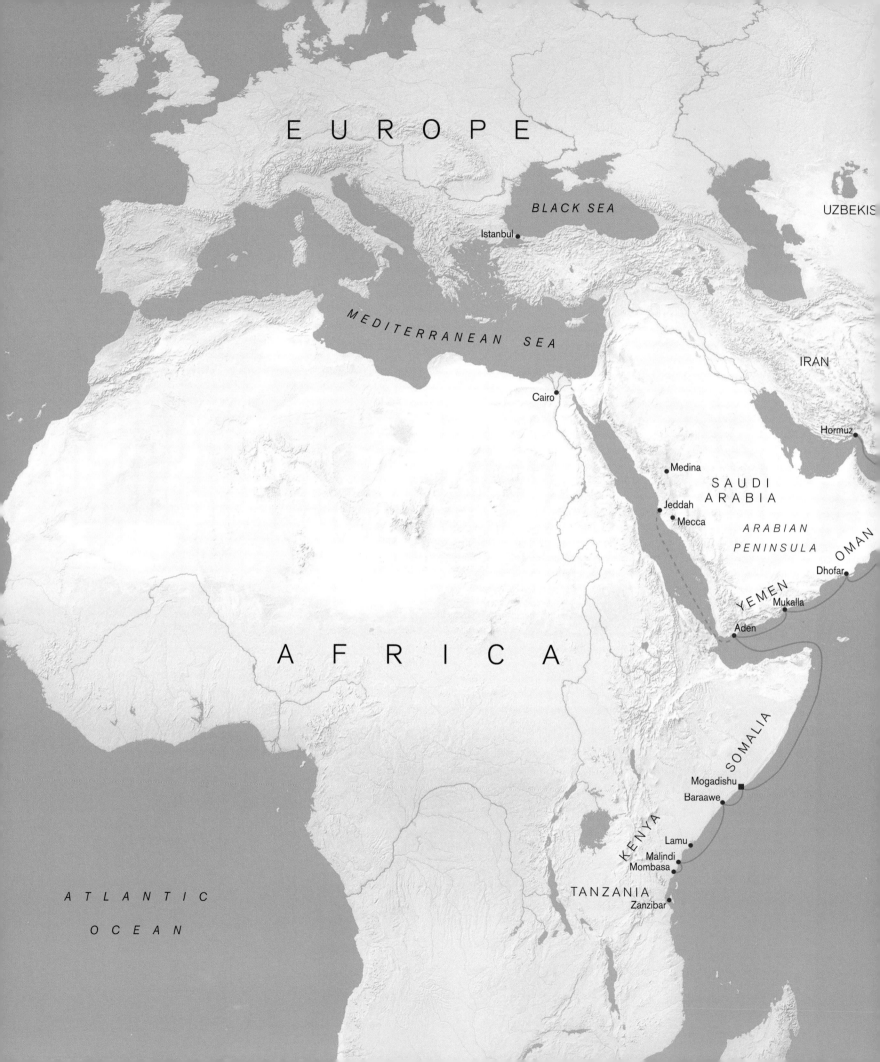

EUROPE

BLACK SEA

Istanbul

MEDITERRANEAN SEA

UZBEKIS

IRAN

Cairo

Hormuz

Medina

SAUDI
ARABIA

Jeddah
Mecca

ARABIAN
PENINSULA

OMAN

Dhofar

YEMEN

Mukalla

AFRICA

Aden

SOMALIA

Mogadishu

Baraawe

KENYA

Lamu

Malindi
Mombasa

TANZANIA

Zanzibar

ATLANTIC

OCEAN

SIBERIA

MONGOLIA

ASIA

GOBI DESERT

THE STEPPE

Amur

Songhua

HEILONGJIANG

Tyr

LIAONING

Hami

XINJIANG AUTONOMOUS REGION
(XINJIANG UYGUR ZIZHIQU)

Samarkand

GHANISTAN

QINGHAI

CHINA

TIBET AUTONOMOUS REGION
(XIZANG ZIZHIQU)

HIMALAYAS

NEPAL

PAKISTAN

New Delhi

Yellow River

Xuanfu
Datong

Tumu Fort
Juyong Pass

Mount Wutai ▲

Taiyuan

Xi'an

Kaifeng

Grand Canal

Liaodong Peninsula

Dalian

SHANDONG

Beijing ■

NORTH KOREA

Seoul

SOUTH KOREA

Jeju Island

JAPAN

Mount Wudang ▲

SICHUAN

Yangtze

HUBEI

Mount Zhong ▲

Nanjing

Suzhou
Liujiagang

Jingdezhen

Shanghai

Hangzhou

Taihe County

Changle

Quanzhou

Xiamen

Okinawa

Ryūkyū Islands

GUJARAT

INDIA

BANGLA-DESH

WEST BENGAL

Chittagong

MYANMAR
(BURMA)

YUNNAN

LAOS

Red River Delta

VIETNAM

Nanning

PACIFIC OCEAN

Kozhikode (Calicut)

Cochin

Quilon

SRI LANKA

Galle

Nicobar Islands

Andaman Islands

THAILAND

Ayutthaya

CAMBODIA

Qui Nhon

PHILIPPINES

Strait of Malacca

Kelantan

BRUNEI

Sulu

Banda Aceh
Semudera

Sumatra

Pahang
Malacca

MALAYSIA

Borneo

INDONESIA

INDIAN OCEAN

Palembang

Java

Surabaya

N

Zheng He's main route

Subsidiary route

Locations mentioned in the book   Istanbul ●

0   500   1000 miles

0   500   1000   1500 kilometres

CHRONOLOGY OF THE MING DYNASTY

Reign title	Reign period	Family name	Temple name
Hongwu 洪武	1368–1398	Zhu Yuanzhang 朱元璋	Taizu 太祖
Jianwen 建文	1399–1402	Zhu Yunwen 朱允炆	Huidi 惠帝
Yongle 永樂	1403–1424	Zhu Di 朱棣	Chengzu 成祖 or Taizong 太宗
Hongxi 洪熙	1425	Zhu Gaozhi 朱高熾	Renzong 仁宗
Xuande 宣德	1426–1435	Zhu Zhanji 朱瞻基	Xuanzong 宣宗
Zhengtong 正統	1436–1449	Zhu Qizhen 朱祁鎮	Yingzong 英宗
Jingtai 景泰	1450–1456	Zhu Qiyu 朱祁鈺	Daizong 代宗
Tianshun 天順	1457–1464	Zhu Qizhen	Yingzong 英宗
Chenghua 成化	1465–1487	Zhu Jianshen 朱見深	Xianzong 憲宗
Hongzhi 弘治	1488–1505	Zhu Youtang 朱祐樘	Xiaozong 孝宗
Zhengde 正德	1506–1521	Zhu Haozhao 朱厚照	Wuzong 武宗
Jiajing 嘉靖	1522–1566	Zhu Houcong 朱厚熜	Shizong 世宗
Longqing 隆慶	1567–1572	Zhu Zaihou 朱載垕	Muzong 穆宗
Wanli 萬曆	1573–1620	Zhu Yijun 朱翊鈞	Shenzong 神宗
Taichang 泰昌	1620	Zhu Changluo 朱常洛	Guangzong 光宗
Tianqi 天啟	1621–1627	Zhu Youxiao 朱由校	Xizong 熹宗
Chongzhen 崇禎	1628–1644	Zhu Youjian 朱由檢	Sizong 思宗

1 A SECOND FOUNDING
MING CHINA 1400–1450

Craig Clunas

No place is superior to Nanjing as an imposing and beautiful capital site.
Yet no place surpasses Beijing for having broad, deep terrain and steep
secure passes which will firmly protect the level, broad plan forever.

YANG RONG (1371–1440), COLOPHON TO 'THE EIGHT VIEWS OF BEIJING'[1]

ONE DAY IN THE EARLY MING

Some time early in the year 1414, an otherwise unknown Chinese twelve-year-old boy named Xie Dingzhu went out into the woods near his home with his mother; they were probably gathering firewood. They were in north China, in Guangchang county, in the province of Shanxi, up near the border garrison city of Datong. It would have been cold; perhaps it was snowing. In the woods they were attacked by a tiger, which sank its jaws into the (unnamed) mother, but was beaten off by the valiant though doubtless terrified child. The woman lived to tell the tale, which was passed up through the ranks of the empire's network of governing officials, finally reaching the desk of the Yongle emperor himself on the fifth day of the third month of the twelfth year of his reign (25 March 1414). The emperor, a man who appreciated violent action, praised the boy, rewarding him with paper banknotes, a quantity of rice and a flag to be hung outside his door proclaiming his bravery. At this point, Xie Dingzhu, his mother (and the still-hungry tiger) pass out of history and beyond our knowledge.[2]

This apparently insignificant little story, illuminating for an instant a moment of fear and panic in China six hundred years ago, actually tells us quite a lot about the Great Ming empire and what it was like to live there. It concerns ordinary people, the vast peasant majority whose lives are largely unrecorded in any history book, yet it is written down in the most formal and prestigious of official historical texts, the *Veritable Records (Shilu)* of the Yongle reign. It merits this commemoration not because Xie Dingzhu was brave, but because he was 'filial' (the Chinese word is *xiao* 孝, meaning devotion and service to parents). He saved the life of his mother, and thus lived out an instance of one of the highest virtues of the ethical and moral system we now call 'Confucianism', by which all in this vast empire were to be governed. It tells us that a network of information and control, a huge literate bureaucracy run on documents, could connect even a dangerous wood on the northern frontiers to the all-powerful ruler in his capital. Xie Dingzhu, we are told, lived in a certain county, in a certain province, part of the network of administrative structures that blanketed the whole huge empire. It tells us that even ordinary boys from 'the people' had names that were worthy of record, but that the names of grown women were usually not. It tells us about the value of rice (a rare luxury to all but the rich in the dry north), and of a paper currency, which demonstrated the state's attempts to exercise control

over trade and wealth. Finally, it tells us that there were still tigers in those woods, perhaps leading to a number of encounters that did not turn out so fortunately. Ironically, when tigers and their cubs feature in the art of the period (fig. 1) it is *they* who can stand for filial piety, the absolute duty owed by a child to a parent. But they can have another meaning, as a critique of the rapaciousness of some officers of imperial government, the ever-present threat that hung over the heads of the masses, and a bad example to the educated class that filled the ranks of magistrates and prefects who governed in Guangchang and represented the power of the Great Ming there.[3]

DYNASTY, EMPEROR, REIGN

While the brave boy Xie Dingzhu is not a famous figure, the Yongle emperor (r. 1403–1424) who rewarded him is one of the most renowned rulers in Chinese history. The complexities of naming a Ming emperor can be challenging to the modern understanding. 'Ming' (明), the name of the dynasty that ruled China from 1368 to 1644, is not the name of the imperial family, but a title meaning 'Bright', 'Luminous' or 'Shining'. It was chosen by Zhu Yuanzhang (1328–1398), the founder of the dynasty (fig. 2), who had spent nearly two decades in arms against the Mongol emperors of the Yuan dynasty (1279–1368) – who had ruled all of China between

FIG. 1

Zhao Ruyin (趙汝殷)
(fl. 1436–49), 'Tigers in windy
woods' (*Fenglin qunhu tu*
風林群虎圖)

This is a detail from a very long handscroll of tigers, one of many early Ming artworks to feature these powerful beasts, which were at that time widely distributed throughout the Chinese countryside. Tiger painting was a speciality of Zhejiang province, where Zhao Ruyin lived and worked.

Handscroll, ink and colours on silk
1441
China
h 33.2 cm, w 794.2 cm
National Palace Museum, Taipei

FIG. 2

Anonymous, 'Portrait of the Hongwu emperor' (*Ming Taizu zuoxiang* 明太祖坐像)

This life-size ritual portrait of the powerful founder of the Ming dynasty, who reigned from 1368 to 1398, was created for use in the ancestral rites of the imperial family.

Hanging scroll, ink and colours on silk
c. 1400
Nanjing
h 268.8 cm, w 163.8 cm
National Palace Museum, Taipei

1279 and 1368 – and against all other contenders to succeed them. The title possibly had religious associations for him and his closest advisors, taken from then current un-orthodox Buddhist ideas about a 'Prince' or 'Lord of Brightness', a longed-for saviour from all sorts of feared apocalyptic disasters.

Most early Chinese dynastic names (such as Han, Tang or Song) are the names of places; the Mongol Yuan dynasty broke with this tradition, since 'Yuan' means 'Primal', or 'Originary'. Choosing a dynastic name that was a quality rather than a place was thus in a sense a mark of continuity between the Yuan and the Ming, and one that was to become standard for the rest of Chinese history down to the twentieth century. It is just one of many ways in which the new dynasty sought to follow the precedents of its simultaneously admired and feared predecessor.

The Ming empire was ruled by a family, the members of which had a surname and given names just like their subjects. In the same way as Xie Dingzhu was a member of the Xie family (family names come first in Chinese), with the given name 'Dingzhu', so his sovereign, the Yongle emperor Zhu Di (1360–1424), was a member of the Zhu family. A reigning emperor was referred to as *Jin shang* (今上), meaning 'Present Majesty'; more formally (and in his presence) he was *Tian zi* (天子), 'Son of Heaven', acclaimed with the wish that he might live 'Ten Thousand Years!' (*Wan sui* 萬歲).

At the accession of each emperor, a reign title, made up of two Chinese characters, was chosen and publicly promulgated. Although their meanings may sometimes seem obvious to us now (and may have done so to some at the time), reign titles invariably carried complex allusions to the Confucian classics and were picked with great care. The very first Ming reign period, *Hongwu* (which literally means 'Vast Military Power'), was clearly chosen by the dynastic founder to celebrate his overthrow of the Mongols, just as that of his successor, *Jianwen* (literally 'Establishment of Civil Culture'), was meant in some sense to provide a balancing principle. The reign period was the principal way by which the sequence of years was measured; so the Anno Domini year of 1403 in the Ming empire largely overlapped with the first year of *Yongle* (the literal meaning is something like 'Perpetual Joy'), to be succeeded by Yongle 2 (1404), Yongle 3 (1405) and so on.[4] It was thus in the twelfth year of Yongle, or 1414, that the encounter with the man-eating tiger of Guangchang county took place.

In earlier Chinese history emperors had often changed their reign periods, sometimes more than once. The Ming, however, began the practice of, in general, having only one reign period per emperor, making the ruler and reign period effectively synonymous. Reign periods began only with the lunar New Year (rather than with the death or accession of individual emperors). Thus it is that we speak today of 'the Yongle emperor' (fig. 29), whose reign of twenty-two years from 1403 to 1424 is the first of the four covered here. His personal name, Zhu Di, is hardly ever seen in Ming sources and would almost never have been uttered in his lifetime. As a mark of his status far above that of other mortals, an emperor's personal name was taboo and never used by his subjects; nor could it be used in writing. The same prohibition extended to the name of his eldest son, Zhu Gaozhi (1378–1425), who

enjoyed the briefest of Ming reigns as the Hongxi emperor (fig. 30), ruling from 7 September 1424 to his death nine months later on 29 May 1425; the Hongxi reign period, meanwhile, ran on from 20 January 1425 to 7 February 1426 (from one lunar New Year to the next).[5] On his death, every Ming emperor was given a posthumous title, by which he was generally known subsequently; that of the Hongxi emperor was Renzong, 'Benevolent Ancestor'. He, like all emperors, also received a longer and more fulsome title for the most formal occasions; in his case it was nothing less than 'Respecter of Heaven, Embodiment of the Way, Pure in Sincerity, Perfect in Virtue, Extensive in Culture, Dominant in Militancy, Standard of Sageliness, Thorough in Filial Piety, Luminous Emperor'.[6]

The son of this paragon of all the virtues, Zhu Zhanji (1399–1435), reigned in turn as the Xuande emperor from 1426 to 1435 (fig. 31), to be succeeded by the first child emperor of the Ming, Zhu Qizhen (1427–1464; fig. 32). Zhu Qizhen is unique among Ming emperors in having two reign periods: Zhengtong (1436–1449) and Tianshun (1457–1464). The hiatus of seven years is due to his long period of house arrest following his eventual release (in 1450) by the Mongols who had defeated and captured him in 1449 (see below), during which time his half-brother Zhu Qiyu (1428–1457) ascended the throne as the Jingtai emperor (1450–1456).

The shattering of a major Ming army by the Mongol foe at the Battle of Tumu Fort on 3 September 1449, the death of many of the dynasty's most senior military commanders, and the unprecedented capture of the emperor, were traumatic events that affected the course of Chinese history in many ways (see Chapter 3, p. 119). They shocked contemporaries into looking at the world through different eyes, sharpening divisions between 'Chinese' and 'non-Chinese', and putting an end to a tradition of activist military leadership by Ming rulers: never again to the end of the dynasty in 1644 would the emperor lead his army into battle in person.

By 1449 the heroic age of the Ming founding some eighty years earlier was passing beyond human memory; those who could recall the reign of its charismatic and terrifying founder, the Hongwu emperor Zhu Yuanzhang – a man of the most humble origins who had led the armies that ended the Mongol rule of the Yuan dynasty over China – were becoming few and far between. Although official commemorative activities and rituals continued unabated, neither his great-grandson, the Xuande emperor, nor his great-great-grandson, the Zhengtong emperor, can have had any personal memory of their formidable ancestor. However, there were still men around them who did.

Huang Huai (1367–1449), who died in that very fateful year of 1449, was the last Grand Secretary (one of the group of men at the apex of the imperial bureaucracy) who would have had memories of the Hongwu reign; he passed the highest of the civil service examinations (see Chapter 4, pp. 184, 188) in its penultimate year, 1397.[7] He then served as an official at the court of the second Ming ruler Zhu Yunwen (1377–1402), grandson of the founder, who reigned as the Jianwen emperor from 1399 to 1402. That unfortunate ruler's reign came to an end in another bloody and violent trauma, when his uncle Zhu Di emerged as the victor from a three-year civil

FIG. 3

Bronze bell, from the Dazhong (Great Bell) Monastery, Beijing, 1420

Weighing around 46 tonnes and measuring 5.5 metres high, this huge bell is capable of creating a sound audible 50 kilometres away. Cast on its surface is a section of the Buddhist text *Sūtra of the Names of the Buddha*, those names being 'recited' by the bell each time it is rung.

FIG. 4
Scenery of Taihe county, Jiangxi province

The prosperous south of the Ming empire continued to provide a high proportion of its senior officials even after the capital was moved to Beijing. Taihe county produced many of the most powerful figures in the empire in the years 1400–50.

A SECOND FOUNDING: MING CHINA 1400–1450

war, seized the throne and was proclaimed as the Yongle emperor. Although the Jianwen emperor almost certainly perished in the burning imperial palace as his uncle's troops stormed his capital of Nanjing, rumours of his survival, and pretenders to his identity, plagued the dynasty for years. One of the very last men to claim to actually be the Jianwen emperor was captured, tortured and died in prison in 1447, only two years before the battle at Tumu.[8]

The four reigns of the usurper Yongle – shortlived Hongxi, urbane Xuande and boy Zhengtong emperors – spanning the years 1403 to 1449 (and coincidentally almost exactly matching the first half of the fifteenth century AD), are therefore bracketed between two wars, two acts of violence that had significant effects on the course of China's history. The first brought the Yongle emperor to power and seemed, in a way that harked back to the often bloody succession struggles of the Mongol imperial clan, to say that prowess in war (often waged against one's closest relatives) was a prerequisite of rulership. The second led to the conclusion that military adventures could be the road to disaster. But the years in between these wars were in fact times of relative stability both for China's rulers and for its masses of the ruled.[9] The latter numbered perhaps 85 million at this period, making the Ming empire by far the most populous state in the world at that time.[10]

Just as with China today, everything about Ming-period China was on a grander scale than that of its contemporaries. Compared to the Timurids then ruling in west and central Asia, or other contemporaries such as the Ottomans, or the Delhi Sultanate – never mind Poland–Lithuania, or the Holy Roman Empire, or the French and English kingdoms, or the Aztec and Inca empires of the western hemisphere – Ming China was on a large scale. It had a greater land area, bigger cities (and *more* big cities), bigger armies, bigger ships, bigger palaces, bigger bells (fig. 3), more literate people, more religious professionals; and it produced more books, ceramic dishes, textiles and spears than any other state on earth at that time. It covered numerous ecological zones and varied environments, from the subtropical to the steppes, from the lush (fig. 4) to the arid. Encompassing a population that was diverse in language and culture as well as well as in religion (see Chapter 5), the Ming empire required a highly sophisticated level of organization to hold it together as the largest polity on earth at that time.

FIG. 5
**Shang Xi (商喜) (fl. 1426–35),
'Guan Yu capturing Pang De'
(*Guan Yu qinjiang tu* 關羽擒將圖)**

This scene from ancient history links
the victories of Guan Yu (162–220)
with the martial prowess of the Ming
emperors, under whom he was
worshipped as a war god and patron
of the dynasty.

Hanging scroll, ink and colours on silk
c. 1426–35
Beijing
h 200 cm, w 237 cm
The Palace Museum, Beijing

IMPERIAL FAMILY AND IMPERIAL PRINCES

Yet despite its variety, the Ming empire held together, under the rule of one family,
the most populous state the world had ever seen. Although there was at least one
attempt in the period to repeat the success of Zhu Di and overthrow a reigning emperor (when the Xuande emperor was threatened in 1426 by the revolt of *his* uncle
Zhu Gaoxu (1380–?1429), Prince of Han), and although peasant rebellions con-
vulsed the provinces of Fujian and Zhejiang in the late 1440s, as environmental
conditions worsened (see p. 41) and starvation loomed, still there were no serious
possibilities of the empire splitting apart. The Zhu family rule seemed firm, and
indeed survived both the coming to the throne of a child in 1436, and his subsequent
violent removal from it by a Mongol army.

Emperors feature largely in the extensive written record of the Ming period,
but we should remember that they were only the leading members of an extended
family that had many branches, and numbered many men and women. The practice
of polygamy meant that some Ming emperors had extensive numbers of legitimate
children. The Ming founder had thirty-six sons and sixteen daughters, while the
Yongle emperor had four sons and five daughters, the Hongxi emperor had eleven
sons and seven daughters, and the Xuande and Zhengtong emperors only one son
and two daughters, and eight sons and eight daughters respectively.

By Ming law, instituted as unchangeable by the founder, those sons not
designated as crown prince and heir were established as *qinwang* ('Princes of the
Blood') and granted extensive estates far from the imperial capital, on which they
were sent to live. Princes were thus simultaneously removed from the centre of
imperial power while serving to validate and exemplify that power throughout the
vast empire. The Hongwu emperor had anticipated his sons acting as 'a fence and
a screen' for the original imperial capital of Nanjing, commanding extensive military
forces destined primarily for defence against the defeated but still formidable
Mongols. Yet, paradoxically, the entrusting of military power to close relatives was
in itself a feature of Mongol rule, and one of many ways in which the organizational
structures, as well as the charisma, glamour and style of the descendants of Chinggis
Khan (*c.* 1162–1227), continued to be meaningful to early Ming rulers.[11] The Mongol
Great Khans of the Yuan dynasty (1279–1368) had ruled over an unprecedently
large land mass stretching deep into inner Asia; they had even attempted (though
ultimately failed at) the conquest of Japan and Indonesia. The *pax Mongolica* had
extended for a time right across the Eurasian landmass, allowing the transfer of
people, technologies and artistic and philosophical ideas as never before in history.
But at the same time their rule in China was often resented, particularly by educated
elites who viewed them as cultural inferiors. Even after the final overthrow of the
Yuan by Zhu Yuanzhang among others, the Mongols remained a powerful military
threat to the early Ming. Numerous campaigns were fought against them (see
Chapter 3), most successfully by Zhu Di, Prince of Yan, who initially launched
his rebellion from the old Yuan capital of Daidu (later Beijing). Part of his justification
for doing so was a series of moves by his nephew, the Jianwen emperor, aimed at

reducing the autonomy of princes such as himself. Zhu Di's success taught him the lesson that heavily armed relatives were indeed (as the Jianwen emperor had feared) a potential threat to the throne, and he systematically reduced the military capacity of his own surviving brothers and their heirs, a process continued by his immediate successors.

By 1441, when Prince Zhuang of Liang (1411–1441) was buried on his extensive estates in Hubei province, the presence in his tomb of armour and weaponry (figs 117 and 118) was purely symbolic. The Ming princes thereafter played a major

FIG. 6
Shang Xi (商喜) (fl. 1426–35), 'The Xuande emperor on an Outing' (*Ming Xuanzong xingle tu* 明宣宗行樂圖)

The imperial hunt was a key activity of the early Ming court. Here its fifth emperor, who was passionate about the pastime, is surrounded by eunuchs, officials and guardsmen, while magically auspicious black-and-white animals appear in the background.

Hanging scroll, ink and colours on paper
c. 1426–35
Beijing
h 211 cm, w 353 cm
The Palace Museum, Beijing

role as landowners in local society, but (barring two later rebellions in the early sixteenth century) a less prominent one in national politics. Still, the fact that a Ming prince who led no actual troops was buried with his weaponry underscores the extent to which a distinct military style and ethos captured by the Chinese term *wu* (figs 5 and 6) remained prominent at both the imperial and the regional courts in the years from Yongle to Zhengtong (see Chapter 3, pp. 143, 148). The reduction of aristocratic and princely power, and the rise of an ethos of civil culture (*wen*: see Chapter 4, pp. 188, 192) were only two of the many ways in which the Ming empire of 1449 differed from that of 1403, and in which decisions taken in this era affected the course of China's history in subsequent centuries.

CAPITAL CITIES AND CAPITAL PROJECTS

Numerous changes and developments during the Ming period set the pattern for China's development down to the modern era. Particularly significant was the Yongle emperor's decision to move the capital from Nanjing, in the rice-growing and economically vibrant lower Yangtze Delta, to Beijing, in the more arid wheat- and millet-growing north of China. The capital has remained there ever since, with the exception of the years 1927–49, when the Republic of China situated its capital (in deliberate homage to the Ming founder) back in Nanjing. The northern city (known under the Mongols as Daidu) had been the Yongle emperor's powerbase as Prince of Yan prior to the civil war, and he clearly felt safer there, as well as better situated to lead an aggressive and forward policy against the remaining power of the 'Northern Yuan' Mongols of the steppe and desert zone.

The new capital, designed as one part of a system of dual seats of imperial power, was the most long-lasting of the huge and expensive construction projects that, alongside military campaigns undertaken to both the north and south on a grand scale, have led historians to see the Yongle reign as a 'second founding' of Ming China.[12] As early as 1404, 10,000 households were ordered to be moved to Beijing from Shanxi province, to populate the new capital.[13] But it was to be a long process. In 1406 preparations were begun for palace buildings and walls.[14] The following year a large body of artisans (including some 7,000 prisoners captured in the attempt to incorporate what is now northern Vietnam into the Ming empire) was assembled to work on the massive construction project.[15] In April 1409 the emperor felt secure enough to visit Beijing for the first time in his reign, and to mount from there the first of a series of major campaigns against the Mongols.[16] By 1412 key members of the bureaucracy had made their homes there, and we have a record of Grand Secretary Xia Yuanji (1366–1430) taking his mother on an outing to see the 'Turtle Mountain' New Year display of fireworks and lanterns at the Meridian Gate.[17]

There may well have been opposition, however, to the move of the capital, which by going against the explicit wishes of the dynastic founder risked both the wrath of Heaven and the charge of being 'unfilial', disobedient to parental command. A painting such as the 1413 'Eight Views of Beijing' by the court artist Wang Fu (1362–1416), inscribed with poems praising the imperial choice of the new capital location, illustrates how all the cultural powers of imperial propaganda needed to be mustered in defence of the decision (fig. 7).[18] So too does the trumpeting of 'auspicious responses', signs of Heaven's blessing on the emperor and dynasty, such as the normally muddy Yellow River running clear, the appearance of two heads of grain on one stalk and the presentation of marvellous beasts from distant lands (see Chapter 4, p. 181).[19] It was in 1414 (a particularly cold year, perhaps explaining the tiger's desperation for food) that the bravery of the boy Xie Dingzhu was brought to the emperor's notice.[20] The righteous actions of subjects were themselves signs of a realm that was well governed, which helps us to understand why this event was deemed worthy of recording.

The *Veritable Records* for that same month (the third of the year) give us a sense of quite how much governing the Ming empire took, as the Yongle emperor also dealt with such matters as a request to establish schools to inculcate Confucian values in a tribal area of remote Yunnan.[21] On the thirteenth day of the month he ordered his son the crown prince (still resident in the 'official' capital of Nanjing) to announce to Heaven and Earth, to the Ancestral Temple, and to the Altars of Soil and Grain his departure on another campaign, and to 'supervise the realm' in his absence.[22] The emperor felt secure enough to campaign against the Mongols in the company of his fifteen-year-old grandson, Zhu Zhanji (later reigning as the Xuande emperor), of whom he seems to have been particularly fond.[23]

On the way to confront the Mongol host, the emperor passed by Taiyuan, seat of the Prince of Jin (his nephew), where he reprimanded the prince, and ordered his officers to 'instruct him in virtue'.[24] The princely household of Jin descended from Zhu Gang (1358–1398), third son of the Hongwu emperor and *elder* brother of the

FIG. 7
Anonymous after Wang Fu (王紱), 'Eight Views of Beijing' (*Beijing bajing tu* 北京八景圖)

This long handscroll was painted as part of the project to justify the move of the imperial capital north to Beijing, after the violent overthrow of the Jianwen emperor (r. 1399–1402). It carries numerous inscriptions praising Beijing's location and historical associations with past rulers.

Handscroll, ink on paper
c. 1414
h 42.1 cm, w 2006.5 cm
National Museum of China

successful usurper Zhu Di (hence with an arguably equal or better claim to legitimacy). Their huge palace, like those of other senior princely houses, was filled with the gifts that flowed between the central imperial and regional courts, including works of art once in the Yuan collections that are among some of the most famous of all surviving Chinese paintings (fig. 8).

Having dealt with his dangerous relative, by the twenty-fifth day of the third month the Yongle emperor was at Xuanfu, a frontier garrison town, where the chronicle captures him at ease in his tent, telling war stories for his grandson, who we are told delighted all with the acuity of his answers, and was acclaimed by the assembled officials as 'certainly a future Son of Heaven of Great Peace, the fortune of your house and your people!'[25] The legitimacy and continuity of their line were never very far from early Ming emperors' calculations (and, of course, it was under the reign of the Xuande emperor himself that this praise of his virtue was recorded in the *Veritable Records* of his grandfather's reign, completed in 1430).[26]

There were many practical as well as ideological problems to be solved in the move of the capital to Beijing. Ming China was an agrarian empire, in which the vast majority of the population worked the land as peasant farmers (some owning their own land, some the landless tenants of the rich, the group from whom the educated officials of the state were drawn), and where the wealth of the state, its very viability in fact, depended on extracting the surplus from agriculture through taxation. The richest arable land lay in the south, around the original capital of Nanjing. One crucial achievement of the Yongle emperor for China's long-term development, therefore, was the completion of restoration work in 1415 on the Grand Canal (fig. 9), the vital artery that brought rice north to Beijing to feed court and armies alike; now it no longer needed to make the more dangerous, and more costly, journey by sea.[27]

Through the latter part of the 1410s and into the early 1420s, more symbolic and practical acts signalled that Beijing was now meant,

FIG. 11

Early twentieth-century view of the city wall of Beijing

The vast Ming walls of Beijing stood virtually intact until their demolition in the mid-twentieth century. They provided both symbolic and actual protection for court and capital.

at least by its lord, to be the Ming empire's primary capital for ever. In 1416, for example, stone tablets were set up to record the names of those who passed the imperial examinations that gave entry to the bureaucracy;[28] in the same year the first sacrifices were made at the vast new imperial tomb complex in the hills outside the city.[29] By 1417 the emperor dwelled in Beijing permanently; he sacrificed there to his ancestors and received lavish embassies, the largest of which arrived in 1420 from the other Asian superpower of the day, the Timurid empire of Iran, Afghanistan and central Asia.[30] By 1421, when sacrifices to Heaven, the most solemn of Ming court ritual observances, were held in Beijing for the first time, and the printing of licences to trade in salt (a government monopoly and a major source of revenue) was transferred there, the move must have seemed definitive.[31] But in the very same year a huge fire destroyed three of the new palace buildings, leading some officials who were unreconciled to the move to protest – opposition that cost at least one his life and some their careers.[32] So some, at least, may have rejoiced when in 1425 the new Hongxi emperor decided to contradict his father's wishes and move the primary capital back to Nanjing, a move cut short only by his premature death.[33] That decision in turn was rescinded by his son, the Xuande emperor, who moved his residence back again to Beijing (and campaigned from there in person against the Mongols like his grandfather), but who retained terminology that showed that formally, at least, Beijing was only a 'temporary capital'. Some objects made in Beijing during his reign, such as a golden pomander dated 1432 (fig. 58), still carry the formula 'following the imperial chariot' (*sui jia*). Only in 1441 was the 'temporary' label definitively removed from the titles of Beijing offices and ministries, closing the argument finally.[34] The Beijing city wall was finally completed in 1445 (fig. 11), just in time to deter the Mongols from following up the advantage of their victory at Tumu in 1449.[35] Now it was in Beijing that the imperial elite would definitely bestow their patronage and create their memorials, such as the Zhihua Monastery (figs 12 and 13), founded in 1444 by the eunuch favourite Wang Zhen (d. 1449), who himself perished on the ill-fated Tumu expedition.[36]

EUNUCHS AND THE WEALTH OF THE EMPIRE

As a eunuch Wang Zhen was one of a class of men who were viewed with distaste by members of the bureaucracy, and who have in general received nothing but scorn from history. Eunuchs – a term used for any male castrated in childhood or adulthood to enable them to serve in specific roles in imperial or princely courts – served the emperor's meals, washed and dressed him, guarded his wives, undertook journeys and delivered messages at his command, undertook diplomatic missions, handled his personal correspondence and wrote out documents in his name.[36] They served entirely at the emperor's pleasure, were answerable only to him, and were hence potentially an alternative source of power and authority to the men who populated the complex official structures of ministries and bureaus. The 'evil eunuch' is a stock figure of Chinese history, always available to be blamed for catastrophes (Wang Zhen,

FIG. 12
Hall of the Zhihua (Transformation of Wisdom) Monastery, Beijing, 1440s

Founded by Wang Zhen (d. 1449), the eunuch favourite of the Zhengtong emperor, this Beijing monastery is one of the best-preserved complexes of early Ming building in China.

FIG. 13
Ceiling from the Hall of Great Wisdom of the Zhihua Monastery, Beijing, 1440s

This painted wooden ceiling was removed in the 1930s from the Zhihua Monastery, which was at that time in a poor state of repair. It is evidence of the quality of craftsmanship available to both court and private patrons in early Ming Beijing.

Philadelphia Museum of Art, Gift of Mr and Mrs Joseph Wasserman, 1930

FIG.14 ABOVE

Main hall of the Fahai (Sea of the Law) Monastery, Beijing

Built between 1439 and 1441 on the western outskirts of the imperial capital, this exquisite small Buddhist temple was founded by Li Tong (d. 1453), a senior eunuch of the imperial court, and decorated by court artists.

FIG. 15 RIGHT

Wall painting from the main hall of the Fahai (Sea of the Law) Monastery, Beijing, unknown artists

The murals of the Fahai Monastery's main hall are the finest surviving early Ming religious wall paintings, and give a sense of the artistic talent available to patrons with court connections in the new imperial city.

for example, posthumously took most of the blame for the Tumu defeat). But they were also sources of cultural patronage, especially for religious institutions such as the Fahai Monastery in the Beijing outskirts (fig. 14), home to some of the finest surviving Ming wall painting (fig. 15), almost certainly executed by artists of the imperial court.

Eunuchs acted as key imperial agents in distributing the lavish patronage expended by the Yongle emperor and his successors on major religious sites, such as the Buddhist complex at Mount Wutai in Shanxi province (fig. 17) and the Daoist temples on Mount Wudang in Hubei (fig. 16); in 1405 both of these sites were the recipients of the emperor's significant benefactions (see pp. 226, 238).[38] Despite tensions and jealousies, the idea that eunuchs were necessarily in a state of perpetual conflict with the other powerful figures around the emperors is an inaccurate one. In the debates that took place at the imperial court around the value and profitability of the great series of state-sponsored oceanic voyages, which distinguished the Yongle and Xuande reigns (see pp. 259,

FIG. 16 ABOVE
View of Mount Wudang, Hubei province

The Daoist pilgrimage site of Mount Wudang was the centre of the cult of Zhenwu, the Perfected Warrior, a god to whom the Yongle emperor was particularly devoted, believing him to have been responsible for his victory in the civil war of 1399–1402. He and subsequent Ming rulers lavished patronage on the mountain and its numerous temples.

FIG. 17 RIGHT
View of Mount Wutai, Shanxi province

Located in Shanxi province southwest of Bejing, the Buddhist pilgrimage site of Mount Wutai (Five Terrace Mountain) is believed to be the terrestrial abode of Mañjuśrī (Ch. Wenshu), the Bodhisattva of Wisdom, one of the Four Great Bodhisattvas, recognized since the Tang dynasty (618–906) as a special protector of emperors and the nation.

271–4), there is no sense that they were a bad idea *because* they were led (at imperial command) by a eunuch, the redoubtable commander Zheng He (1371–1433). He set sail in the very same year, 1405, in which Mount Wudang, centre of the cult of the warrior god Zhenwu, became the object of sustained imperial attention; both voyages and temple building depended on eunuchs as the ever-ready agents of the imperial will.

Despite the fact that we know very little about Zheng He personally, the bare facts we have do give an insight into the complexity and diversity that marked the years of the Yongle and Xuande reigns (see also pp. 211, 214–20). He was by birth a Muslim, though in adulthood this did not prevent him from patronizing other religious traditions as well. The origins of his family lay in western Asia; they had come to China's southwestern province of Yunnan as part of the flow of peoples that marked the Yuan Mongol hegemony of the fourteenth century. He was hence a native of a region only loosely integrated into the Chinese world under previous dynasties, but definitively absorbed by the Ming. Indeed, it was in the years 1400–50 that China's southern borders were fixed where they have remained down to modern times, and in those same years that many of China's 'national minorities' in that diverse region (fig. 18) received the names by which they are still known in Chinese today.[39]

Captured and castrated as a child when Ming armies overran forces loyal to the Yuan in 1381, Zheng He served Zhu Di when the latter was still a regional prince, and accompanied his master in the long campaign that led to the imperial throne. As a Muslim eunuch exercising military command in a princely court, Zheng He is both an 'eccentric' figure in the higher reaches of Ming society (all of his identities were minority ones), and also a reminder that the 'normality' of the early Ming (like that of many empires) was a fluid and plural one, where many possibilities existed, and many alternative scenarios might have played themselves out. If the Hongxi emperor had lived longer and transferred the capital back permanently to the Lower Yangtze Delta, it seems less likely that the language of Beijing would have established itself today as the national spoken standard for Chinese, the form of speech we call *putonghua*, or 'mandarin'.[40] If the Zhengtong emperor had not come to the throne as a small child, which interrupted for over a decade the continuation of the activist military style of emperorship practised by his father, then perhaps the eventual dominance of the Ming elite by a civil bureaucratic ethos, rather than an aristocratic military one, might not have happened in exactly the way it did. These, like the decision to suspend the major oceanic voyages, are contingencies that give rise to fascinating, if ultimately unprovable, histories of the counter-factual.

Yet there were equally important changes taking place in China between 1400 and 1450 that owed less to human agency, and indeed were beyond the grasp of individual rulers and statesmen at the time. These years saw China's definitive engagement in a pan-Eurasian economy, which rose and fell as one under the impact of climactic and economic disaster from the 1430s (see pp. 40–41). They also saw the definitive establishment from the 1430s of an economy based on silver traded by weight, the initiation of an 'age of silver' encompassing a Chinese world of goods and trade which remained a major part of the global economy down to the nineteenth century (see Chapter 6, p. 279).[41] Furthermore, only in recent years have historians started to accommodate new awareness of environmental and ecological change in our understanding of the past. The Great Ming of the Yongle, Hongxi, Xuande and Zhengtong emperors was much less populated than the China we know today. However, the land must have been impacted by the density of its population, and the recovery of that population's growth after the disastrous wars following the overthrow of the Mongol Yuan, the civil wars between contending successors to them, and the war to overthrow the Jianwen emperor. It was in the early fifteenth century that elephants became extinct in China's southwest, retreating into what is now Burma, Thailand, Laos and Cambodia. In 1393 the military unit stationed at Nanning in deep southern Guangxi was able to present elephants to the court for the last time (making the miraculous white elephant sent in tribute from Annam in 1414 all the more marvellous). Attacks by tigers, such as that suffered by Xie Dingzhu and his mother, also in 1414, may possibly have reflected the decline of their usual prey following human pressure on their habitat.[42]

It was not just Heaven's favour, as signalled by the appearance of miraculous beasts and apparitions in the skies, that allowed the Yongle emperor to pursue the costly projects of his 'second founding'. His reign was marked by relatively benign weather conditions, which provided wealth through taxes on agriculture, and by an expansion of mining for the metals (copper and silver) used in trade as currency.[43] These were the

頭目寶圭由德勝

FIG. 18
Anonymous, 'The Chieftain Baoguiyoudesheng' (*Toumu Boguiyoudesheng* 頭目寶圭由德勝)

This image of a chieftain from the southern borderlands of the Ming empire was created by an anonymous court artist to record the facial features and dress of an exotic visitor to court, one whose presence was evidence for the reach of Ming power to the edges of the known world.

Album leaf, ink and colours on paper
1400s
h 44 cm, w 31 cm
The Palace Museum, Beijing

medium of exchange used to expand commerce by China's merchants, who were by then making more use of the abacus, a device crucial to life in China from this time (its first appearance in a printed book is in one that was originally published in the Xuande period, fig. 19).

An equally important innovation of this period, which played a central role in commercial life down to the twentieth century, was the *huiguan*, a lodging, place of business, and social and religious centre for merchants from a specific province. The earliest evidence for a *huiguan* comes from the 1420s–30s, when the merchants of Anhui province established the first one in Beijing.[44] Other changes to commercial life were taking place in these decades too. The paper currency (fig. 243) with which the Yongle emperor had rewarded Xie Dingzhu for his bravery was already fading in value, and trusted by few, while the huge demand elsewhere in Asia for Chinese copper

FIG. 19

Newly Compiled Illustrated
Four-Word Glossary (Xian bian
xiang si yan), 1436

First printed in the Xuande reign
(1426–1435), this anonymous primer,
designed to teach the characters of
the Chinese language, is possibly the
world's earliest children's book. The
page illustrated includes the hierarchy
of 'four types of people' into which Ming
society was in theory divided: scholars,
peasants, craftsmen and merchants.
Women are conspicuously absent.

Woodblock-printed book
1436
h 19 cm, w 31 cm
Columbia University Library

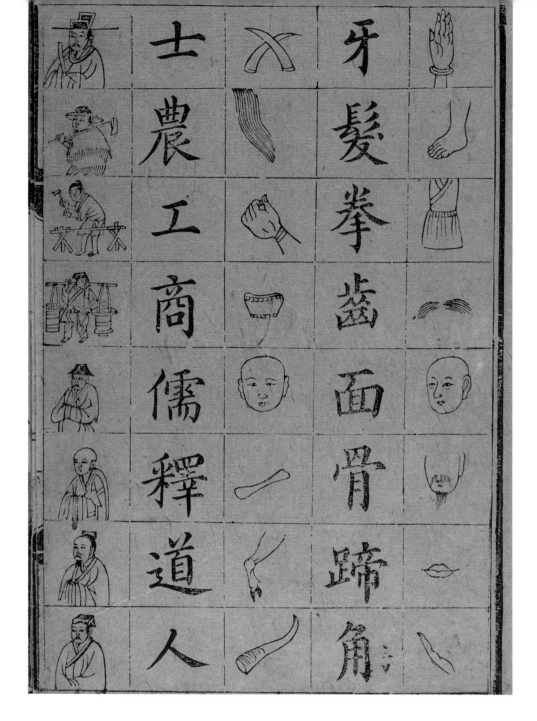

coins led to their outflow from the Ming (see Chapter 6, pp. 276–8). This put more
and more emphasis on silver, used by weight as the principal medium of exchange
(fig. 242); its purchasing power increased greatly in this period despite government
attempts to restrict its use.[45] In the final years of the Xuande reign the state accepted
the reality of the situation and in practice allowed silver to be used as the medium of
exchange for all transactions. In 1436 the court finally lifted the long-standing and
utterly futile ban on the use of copper coinage in private trade (although no new coins
were cast by the imperial government in the Zhengtong reign itself).[46]

Thankfully, silver flooded into China from western Eurasia to buy luxuries such
as porcelain, but above all silk textiles, exported in large quantities to the Islamic world,
from Bengal to Gujarat to Cairo, where the Mamluk silk industry went into a decline
as a result of Chinese imports (see Chapter 6, p. 281). In 1404 in Samarqand, the

Spanish ambassador to the Timurid court Ruy Gonzáles de Clavijo (d. 1412) observed a caravan of 800 camels from China bearing musk, gems and spices alongside silks, 'the finest in the whole world', and marvelled: 'The goods that are imported to [Samarqand] from Cathay indeed are the richest and most precious of all those brought hither from foreign parts, for the craftsmen of Cathay are reputed to be the most skilful by far beyond those of any other nation'.[47]

However, as early as 1420 Grand Secretary Xia Yuanji was worrying about the costs of prestige projects such as the Zheng He voyages, costs which it became harder to meet as some mines began to be worked out, as the long and expensive attempt to subdue Vietnam (a source of precious metals) was abandoned in 1427, and as hostilities with the ethnic groups of the southwest in the 1430s and 1440s curtailed mining there.[48] At the same time, the forces of nature turned against the Ming empire, as the middle decades of the fifteenth century turned particularly cool (possibly related to a series of major volcanic eruptions). The government of the boy Zhengtong emperor, therefore, inherited a confluence of economic and environmental pressures that were intimately linked.[49] While Ming intellectuals at the time blamed the evil influence of eunuchs such as Wang Zhen (who had personal interests in mining operations), they could not know that the grinding to a halt of economic activity that they experienced in the 1440s was a global, or at least a trans-Eurasian, crisis: the entire northern hemisphere was experiencing bad climatic conditions and 'a serious monetary contraction'.[50] The connectedness that seems so obvious to us now was not entirely visible to those who lived through it.

A CONNECTED EMPIRE

Some aspects of early fifteenth-century China's connectedness were, however, very visible. It was manifest, for example, in an ethnically and religiously diverse population, particularly in Beijing, with its three major mosques (the Flower Market, Inner City and Ox Street Mosques) and maybe as many as 100,000 Muslims, many of whom had family ties to western Asia. Diversity was also evident in the continued presence within the empire's borders of large military formations of loyal Mongols, whose dress styles and fondness for the hunt continued to influence fashions at court. The complex interaction between Han Chinese and steppe cultures can also be seen in attitudes towards women and their proper conduct. On the fifth day of the twelfth month of the twelfth year of Yongle (15 January 1415), a number of women who had maintained their chastity, refusing to remarry when their husbands died young, were awarded honours by the court for their adherence to strict Confucian notions of proper womanly conduct. These women (unlike the mother of Xie Dingzhu) *are* named, one of them being Madame Liu, the Chinese daughter-in-law of a Ming military commander from the Jurchen ethnic group with the very Mongol name of Peiyashi Tiemuer. When her dying husband urged her to marry again, she replied (and her words are recorded in very vivid Chinese), 'What are you saying? When the husband dies all die; if you don't believe me, let me go first', and promptly hanged herself.[51] This extreme adherence to the idea of a widow's chastity was no isolated case. No fewer than sixteen

FIG. 20
Sesshū Tōyō, 'Winter', from
Landscapes of the Four Seasons

The Buddhist monk Sesshū Tōyō was the leading painter of the Muromachi period (1337–1573) in Japan. In 1468–9 he visited Ming China as part of a trading mission organized by powerful lords of the Ōuchi clan. The set of *Landscapes of the Four Seasons* was possibly executed in China, and shows Sesshū's engagement with the art he would have seen there.

Hanging scroll, ink and colours on paper
1468–9
h 70.6 cm, w 44.2 cm
Tokyo National Museum

of the Yongle emperor's concubines were buried with him – whether voluntarily or under duress we cannot say. But by 1450, in one of the many changes that mark the early fifteenth century, manners were softening, and such mass suicides of imperial and royal women, seen now by Confucian theorists as a hangover from the increasingly alien culture of the 'barbarian' Mongols, were no longer practised.

Peiyashi Tiemuer's care for the commemoration of his daughter-in-law's adherence to strict Confucian morality, just like the eagerness of the tribesmen of Yunnan for Confucian schooling, the spread of Chinese weights and measures throughout Southeast Asia, the use by the Korean court of the Ming calendar, and the continued preference of a liberated Vietnam for Ming commentaries on the Confucian classics,[52] demonstrate the power of the Ming empire, at least as far as its rulers saw it, to set standards of civilization for the whole world. So too did the attractiveness of the Ming to visitors from the adjacent states of Korea, Japan (fig. 20) and Vietnam, where the educated shared a common literary culture based on the written Chinese language and on the canon of literature composed in it (figs 147–50). The many 'tribute bearers' (for so they were understood, though in truth their motives were more often trade) from further afield were similarly seen as the proof to the whole known world of the power of the Ming example (see Chapter 6, p. 265).

Yet at the same time the Ming emperors of the early fifteenth century were keenly aware of the presence of other powers, some of which also had aspirations to inherit the Mongol claims to world empire. In 1418 a white horse was presented by a Ming embassy to the Timurid ruler, possibly commemorated in a painting made in China but preserved now in Istanbul (fig. 21). This demonstrates an understanding, strengthened through the numerous embassies that passed between Beijing and Samarqand in these years, that both courts shared a culture of military prowess and devotion to hunting that descended from the heirs of Chinggis Khan.[53] The Ming state maintained an extensive apparatus of translators to service its diplomacy with the world of western Asia. Although Chinese archives retain little evidence of their activities, a letter written in Chinese and Mongol (fig. 22) in the name of the 'caretaker' Jingtai emperor to the ruler of a small state in what is now southern Iran is a precious piece of evidence that well into the fifteenth century Chinese emperors could communicate, when they needed to, in languages other than Chinese.

This reminder that the evidence we have for this formative period of China's history, for all its richness and complexity, is still far from complete, underlines the necessity for a fresh look at what we do have from the years from the Yongle emperor's victory in 1403 to the Zhengtong emperor's defeat in 1449. This period is long overdue a thorough re-examination, enlightened by new archaeological finds, new directions in scholarship and China's new position in the world. Magnificent recent archaeological discoveries, for example, such as the tomb of Prince Zhuang of Liang, have brought into better focus the role of the imperial aristocracy, too long ignored by historians influenced by the agendas of the official class who dominated the written record.[54] The exhibition *Ming: 50 years that changed China* is the first to give due weight to the princely element of Ming culture. It is also the first to examine early fifteenth-century China in terms of its links with a wider Eurasian world, not in terms of 'Chinese influence', but based on an understanding of the complex flows of people, goods and ideas that underlay its connectedness to its neighbours and beyond, and which was, for example, key to the development of the Chinese diaspora throughout the Asian-Pacific world.[55] That connectedness is based in many cases on a common heritage in the world empire of the Mongols. Here the Mongol Yuan rule is seen, in another new understanding of the age, not as an alien force that was expelled definitively in 1368. It is instead viewed as the source and inspiration for the Great Ming era, which drew strength and vitality from China's multiple interactions and engagements with the world around it.

FIG. 21 BELOW

Anonymous, 'Horse with Chinese grooms'

This Chinese painting, preserved in an album of painting and calligraphy made for the Persian prince Bahram Mirza (1517–1549) in the mid-sixteenth century, may relate to the gift of a white horse by the Ming emperor to a Timurid ruler in 1418. It is one of several Chinese paintings of the early Ming preserved in the Bahram Mirza album.

Colours on silk
c. 1418
h 39.9 cm, w 28.2 cm (grooms); h 49 cm, w 30.4 cm (horse)
Topkapi Palace Museum, Istanbul

FIG. 22 RIGHT

Edict written in Chinese and Mongolian 1453

This diplomatic document produced at the Ming court, written in Chinese and Mongolian, grants sixteen bolts of variously coloured silks to Yanglirgi, the minor ruler of the city of Lar, in modern Iran.

Ink on paper
1453
h 51 cm, w 172 cm
Topkapi Palace Museum, Istanbul

2 COURTS
PALACES, PEOPLE AND OBJECTS

Jessica Harrison-Hall

Fierce beasts from the extreme west,
Pace back and forth in the imperial gardens.
Their claws and teeth are truly fierce and agile,
Their fur and bones singularly imposing.

YANG RONG (1371–1440), 'POEM ON AN OUTING TO LONGEVITY HILL', 1428[1]

IMPERIAL MING PALACES – FROM NANJING TO BEIJING

Nanjing, situated on the banks of the Yangtze River, was from 1368 the first Ming capital and home to the imperial court. It was established by the dynastic founder and maintained as a capital by his son and grandson until 1421, when Beijing became the official capital.[2] Today there are just a few physical remains of Nanjing as a Ming capital city. These include the tomb of the first Ming emperor and his wife;[3] sections of the Ming city wall; stone pillar bases and tiles from the roofs of the palace;[4] figures from the tomb spirit way of the Sultan of Brunei, 'Abd al-Majid Hasan (1380–1408) (see Chapter 6, p. 276); and architectural fragments from imperially sponsored religious buildings (figs 189 and 190).[5]

An extremely rare painting represents the cosmopolitan palace of Nanjing as it would have appeared in the fifteenth century (fig. 24).[6] A group of envoys from Joseon Korea is shown leaving the imperial city in a small boat, seen off by members of the Ming court. We can identify Nanjing from comparison with earlier woodblock-printed maps (fig. 23). The Nanjing palace was extended and lost its symmetry as the outer palace wall was adapted to accommodate the flow of the river and the local terrain.[7] The imperial court buildings are easily identified as they follow the same layout, architectural style and colour scheme as the later Forbidden City in Beijing.

After the civil war, which brought the Yongle emperor to power in 1402, a new monumental imperial palace was constructed in Beijing (fig. 25) and for a while Nanjing and Beijing functioned as two equal capitals. This dual system is noted in an edict of the Hongxi emperor of 1425: 'Those from the offices of the Six Ministries in Nanjing who should receive imperial mandates should receive the same ones as those from the capital [Beijing]' (fig. 27). Officials travelling between the two capitals could go by barge along the Grand Canal, a journey that took forty days.[8] For the period 1403 to 1449 Beijing could be described as a great building site, except during the long bitterly cold winter months each year when construction was all but impossible. Timber came from Sichuan, Shanxi, Jiangxi, Hunan, Hubei and Zhejiang, while tile works and brick factories were set up locally in Beijing (not in the palace to avoid the risk of fire), supplying hundreds of thousands of baked bricks and glazed tiles. Almost nothing of the early fifteenth-century palace can be seen in the Forbidden City in Beijing today, as the city has been so extensively rebuilt, redecorated and added to over the centuries. Most of the original structures were made of wood, and fires were commonplace.

FIG. 23

Woodblock-printed map of the Ming imperial capital at Nanjing

This Ming-dynasty map shows Nanjing's asymmetrical city walls and the city's position on the banks of the Yangtze River. The Nanjing imperial palace was the blueprint for the Forbidden City in Beijing, with grand halls arranged on a north–south axis, and other buildings placed on the sides, surrounded by a wall.

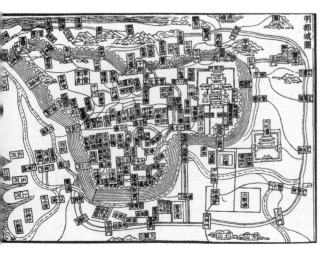

FIG. 24 BELOW AND OVERLEAF
**Anonymous, 'Seeing off Korean
envoys returning to their country'
(*Song jo cheon gaek gwi guk si
jang do* 送朝天客歸國詩章圖)**

This is the earliest known painting of
Nanjing as a capital city. Nanjing was
chosen by the Ming founder, the Hongwu
emperor (r. 1368–1398), to be the
official capital and it remained so until
1421. Nanjing was a cosmopolitan city.
Texts describe the arrival and departure
of visiting dignitaries by boat, but images
of such visits are rare. Korean scholars
believe that this painting was executed
at the Joseon court painting bureau
in the Korean capital city, Hanseong.
Details such as the turtle-shell-
patterned curtain on the boat look
distinctly Korean rather than Chinese.

Hanging scroll, ink and colours on silk
c. 1451–1600
Hanseong (modern-day Seoul), Korea
h 103.6 cm, w 163 cm
National Museum of Korea, Seoul
Bon 13265

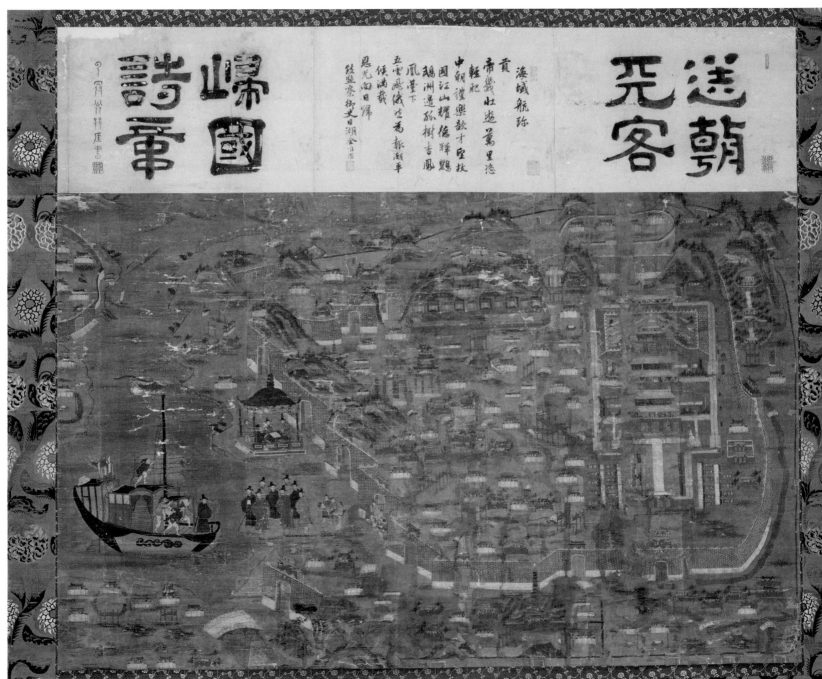

Anonymous, 'Portrait of an official in front of the Beijing imperial palace'
(*Beijing gongcheng tu* 北京宮城圖)

FIG. 25 OPPOSITE

THIS SET OF BUILDINGS, known popularly as the Forbidden City, was the political centre of the Ming empire, a site for imperial audiences and banquets, and the home of the ruling monarch and his family. After years of planning, work began in earnest on its construction in 1417. The Yongle emperor (r. 1403–1424) built the palace, modelled on the layout of the palace at Nanjing, by expanding and refurbishing the old Yuan-dynasty palace abandoned when the Mongols were defeated. Beijing became the main capital from 1421, in which latter year the palace buildings were badly damaged by fire; the new city was not completed until 1445.

In this painting an unidentified official is shown in court robes, holding an official tablet and posing in front of the palace complex, which is surrounded by billowing clouds. These only half reveal the distinctive red-walled buildings with their yellow-glazed roofs, stone courtyards and marble bridges, and yet the gold names on blue boards on each of the buildings and gateways leave the viewer with no doubt as to the location. On account of the bird's-eye view, we can see past the grand front halls (indicated by the drum and bell) and right up to the veiled-off buildings and the emperor's private quarters at the back. The official's proximity to the actual quarters of the Son of Heaven indicates that he himself enjoyed great prestige.

During the Ming period the imperial palace in Beijing was the world's largest walled complex, extending over a square kilometre. Forced labourers built the brick-faced city wall, with nine fortified gates to protect the capital. It was completed in 1445 in the Zhengtong reign. Timber came from the provinces of Sichuan, Shanxi, Jiangxi, Hunan and Hubei, and Zhejiang. Tile and brick factories were set up locally in Beijing. Labourers were gathered from all over China, but 7,000 prisoners of war from northern Vietnam

FIG. 26
The Forbidden City, Beijing

The late Qing-dynasty arrangement – with the main buildings along a north–south axis, the emperor's residence at the back and numerous other buildings at the sides – is consistent with the design of the early Ming palace and other royal residences across China.

were also sent to work there. The Chief Architect was a eunuch from northern Vietnam whose Chinese name was Ruan An (d. 1453). Furnishings came from workshops across China and from international tribute.

The painting is not unique: a number of other extant works, including one in the National Museum of China and one in the Nanjing Museum, show the imperial palace in Beijing with different officials standing in front.

Hanging scroll, ink and colours on silk
Signed Fengxi (豐溪); seal in relief 'Seal of Zhu Bang'
(*Zhu Bang zhi yin* 朱邦之印); seal in intaglio
'Sleeping soundly without dreams leisure seal'
(*Hanhou wumeng xian zhang* 酣齁無夢閒章)
c. 1480–1580
Image h 170 cm, w 110.8 cm; with mount h 204 cm, w 114 cm
British Museum, London 1881,1210.087

FIG. 27

The Hongxi emperor, Zhu Gaozhi (朱高熾) (1378–1425), 'Imperial edicts of the Hongxi emperor' (*Zhu Gaozhi xingshu* [*chi yu*] 朱高熾行書敕諭)

These hand-drafted notes are on paper decorated with a design of gold orchids. The first edict lists personnel appointments, which testifies to the level of personal involvement in government of the early Ming emperors. The emperor's reign period lasted for just a year, from 20 January 1425 to 7 February 1426. While still crown prince, he often acted as a regent in Nanjing when his father, the Yongle emperor, was leading military campaigns in the north. It is particularly interesting that the Hongxi emperor involved himself in the details of bureaucracy as his father had advised him to do so: 'Even though the secretaries handle the documents you must read them all yourself. Thus may you know the hardship of the official so that one day you may be a ruler of men'. The Hongxi emperor's edict reads:

To the Ministry of Personnel by imperial decree: Promote Huang Huai to Junior Guardian and Minister of Revenue, continue as Grand Secretary; Yang Shiqi continue in his previous position, promote to Minister of War; Jin Youzi also continue in his previous position, promote to Minister of Personnel. All are given three salaries and granted imperial mandates. Grant the late Vice Supervisor of the Household of the Heir Apparent Zou Ji, Admonisher, Junior Guardian, confer [upon him] posthumous title and grant [him] imperial mandate. Those from the offices of the Six Ministries in Nanjing who should receive imperial mandates should receive the same ones as those from the capital. Promote Gu Pu to Minister of Revenue in Nanjing, Wei Shou Minister of Rites in Nanjing, Tang Zong Chief Minister of the Court of Judicial Review in Nanjing, as decreed. On the fifth day of the first month of the first year of the Hongxi reign [24 January 1425].

敕吏部：黃淮升少保、戶部尚書，學士如故；楊士奇前官如故，升兵部尚書；金幼孜亦前官如故，升吏部尚書。俱支三俸，給授誥命。已故少詹事鄒濟、贊善述贈太子少保，賜謚，授誥命。南京六部等衙門，應得誥命者俱與在京官同。古樸升南京戶部尚書，蔚綬南京禮部尚書，湯宗南京大理卿，故敕。洪熙元年正月五日。

The second edict reads:

To the Ministry of Personnel by imperial decree: In haste compose the imperial mandate to the Grand Mentor Duke of Qianguo, to be conferred together on the sixteenth day. Without delay, the Minister knows about it. Zhu, on the fifth day of the first month.

[Translated by Luk Yu-ping]

敕吏部：太傅黔國公誥命作急撰寫，十六日一同頒給，不可有誤，卿其知之。朱 正月五日。

Ink on gold decorated paper
Dated 1425
Nanjing
Image above h 26.4 cm, w 14.8 cm; image below h 26.1 cm, w 14.3 cm;
mounted together h 36.1 cm, w 71.8 cm
The Palace Museum, Beijing

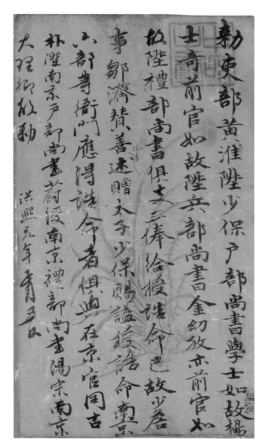

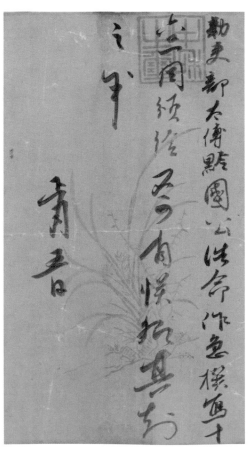

DESCRIPTIONS OF THE IMPERIAL COURTS

Visitors came to the courts from across the world. A diplomatic mission sent from the Timurid ruler Shahrukh (r. 1409–1447) to the Ming court of the Yongle emperor included the artist Ghiyath al-Din, who kept a diary of his journey, detailing all he witnessed during a five-month-long sojourn in China (fig. 220).[9] On arriving in Beijing in 1420, he described 'a city of inordinate magnitude, made all of stone', probably referring to the stone courtyards, bridges, building platforms and walls. Also, because 'they were still in the process of building, 100,000 scaffolds were fastened to the city walls'.[10] In fact, the gate the diplomats were planning to go through was not completed, so they had to be diverted.

Like other foreigners visiting Beijing, Ghiyath al-Din was struck by the quality of Chinese artefacts within the palace and the fine detailing of the architecture. He described the vast and regular cut-stone courtyards of the imperial palace, which could hold 100,000 people at a time; the special pathways for the emperor; the palaces and halls with their pillars the colour of turmeric; gilded furniture; incense burners and yellow silk throws. Five live elephants flanked their path on either side. He concluded that 'the masters of stone cutting, carpentry, painting and tile-making of that region have no peers'.

EMPERORS

At the centre of the imperial court were the members of the ruling family. Arguably the most powerful of the early Ming emperors, whose tenure in office had the greatest impact, not just on court life but on the structures of imperial rule, was the Yongle emperor.[11] A centralizing autocrat, he wanted to re-create the Yuan Mongol empire and its successful domination of the region. As part of this project of universal rulership, the Yongle emperor was receptive to accommodating a diverse range of staff within the palace; he ate imported food such as Korean rice cakes, Jurchen duck and 'Muslim pancakes';[12] listened to music from other cultures;[13] and commissioned exotic furnishings in non-Chinese forms for his palace. His own jewellery included imported gems. In one portrait (fig. 29) he holds a gold belt (see fig. 249) inlaid with imported jewels in one hand, perhaps signifying his control over the foreign supplies of these luxuries.[14] The carpets beneath the throne equally incorporate elements of Central Asian, Tibetan and Islamic art. The Yongle emperor is described by Ghiyath al-Din as follows: 'He was of medium height with neither large nor small features, with two or three hundred facial hairs so long that they had been knotted into three or four plaits.' His son, the Hongxi emperor (fig. 30), ruled for just nine months before he died suddenly in 1425 aged forty-seven. Had he reigned for longer, he would have permanently transferred the capital back to Nanjing; he urged his son, the Xuande emperor, to do so. Moving the capital had been a controversial decision and there were still people who would have preferred Nanjing as the capital.

The Xuande emperor (r. 1426–1435) (fig. 31) was as an aesthete, a collector and patron of the arts who has left behind poetry and accomplished paintings of

FIG. 28
Detail of carpenters from the *Scripture of the Jade Pivot*, c. 1403–24

Little visual evidence survives of early Ming China's extensive agricultural population and manual workforce. This image shows carpenters with long hair worn in buns, preparing building materials in clearly divided roles – trimming the timber with an axe, splitting it into planks and transporting it. All the men wear shoes and light clothing.

Woodblock-printed, ink on paper
Each page: h 34 cm, w 12 cm
British Library, London ORB 99/161

his own (figs 152–4). When his father, the Hongxi emperor, died unexpectedly, the court was still officially in mourning for his grandfather. The Xuande emperor had admired and been a favourite of his grandfather, the Yongle emperor, accompanying him on military expeditions to the Mongolian frontier. When emperor himself, he led his own troops into battle on successful campaigns against individual Mongol leaders. His continuation of the Yongle emperor's policies was crucial in establishing the capital in Beijing and in determining the style of government: he buried his father in the grounds of the Ming tombs (fig. 10) that had been built by the Yongle emperor outside Beijing rather than in Nanjing where the first Ming emperor was buried; he continued to sponsor the voyages to the Middle East and Africa that had been initiated by the Yongle emperor (see Chapter 6, p. 259); and he completed the construction of the Forbidden City. In this way, he further legitimized his grandfather's reign and the transfer of the capital to Beijing.[15]

The Zhengtong emperor (r. 1436–1449) came to the throne as a child (see Chapter 1, p. 38). His mother, grandmother and a council helped him to rule initially, but as he entered adulthood he was influenced by leading bureaucrats and palace eunuchs such as Wang Zhen (fig. 212). Lacking his forebears' judgement, his attempt to follow their example and lead his men into battle ended disastrously with his capture at Tumu Fort in 1449. His official portrait (fig. 32) is markedly different from those of his Ming predecessors, being much less of an individual's likeness and more

FIG. 29 OPPOSITE
Anonymous, 'Official portrait of the Yongle emperor' (*Ming Chengzu zuoxiang* 明成祖坐像)

Hanging scroll, ink and colours on silk
c. 1424
Probably Beijing
h 220 cm, w 150 cm
National Palace Museum, Taipei

FIG. 30 ABOVE LEFT
Anonymous, 'Official portrait of the Hongxi emperor' (*Ming Renzong zuoxiang* 明仁宗坐像)

Hanging scroll, ink and colours on silk
c. 1425
Beijing
h 111.2 cm, w 76.7 cm
National Palace Museum, Taipei

FIG. 31 ABOVE RIGHT
Anonymous, 'Official portrait of the Xuande emperor' (*Ming Xuanzong zuoxiang* 明宣宗坐像)

Hanging scroll, ink and colours on paper
c. 1436
Beijing
h 215.8 cm, w 171 cm
National Palace Museum, Taipei

FIG. 32

Anonymous, 'Official portrait of the Zhengtong emperor' (*Ming Yingzong zuoxiang* 明英宗坐像)

Zhu Qizhen (1427–1464) was the only Chinese emperor to rule twice. His first reign period was called Zhengtong (1436–1449) and his second was Tianshun (1457–1464). In between his half-brother ruled as the Jingtai emperor (1450–1456).

Hanging scroll, ink and colours on silk
c. 1464
Beijing
h 208.3 cm, w 154.5 cm
National Palace Museum, Taipei

of a generic imperial image. Instead of being viewed from the side looking slightly to the left or right, he is positioned to face the front. His capture by the Mongols in 1449 tested the strength of the dynasty. In fact, the Ming dynasty survived and continued for another 200 years. The decision not to retreat south and return the capital back to Nanjing but to maintain it in the north in Beijing helped shape the China we know today.

EMPRESSES AND IMPERIAL WOMEN

Although Ming emperors could have many partners – an empress, consorts of various ranks and concubines – they had just one principal wife. Imperial women played a vital role in securing the dynasty through childbirth and dynastic continuity, as well as performing imperial and state rituals.[16] To prevent too strong a concentration of power in other rival families, which might threaten the stability of the dynasty, early Ming emperors chose their partners from a variety of families and geographical areas, often selecting women from middle- and lower-middle-class military households. This policy led to a degree of social mobility and to a mixture at court of elite and popular culture; it also brought together foreign and Han Chinese women. Some relatives of imperial women also gained positions at court.

The principal wife of the Yongle emperor, Empress Renxiaowen, Xu Yihua (1362–1407) (fig. 33), was the well-educated daughter of Xu Da (1332–1385), an important general and one of the closest confidants of the Ming founder. She entered the Nanjing palace at the age of ten and was trained by Empress Ma (1332–1382), who was the Hongwu emperor's principal wife. In 1376 she married the future Yongle emperor and in 1380 accompanied her husband to his princely palace in Beijing. Her biography records that while her husband was away from Beijing, pursuing the throne in the civil war that brought him to power, she organized the defence of the city. After the civil war she played an essential role in both legitimizing the Yongle emperor's position and confirming the court's role as the centre of intellectual activity, even publishing a number of works in her own name, including in 1407 *Exhortations to promote good deeds by Empress Renxiao of the Great Ming* (fig. 37). Whether the empress herself actually wrote the text, or whether it was simply authored in her name, its existence reveals the assumption that a woman of the imperial family was not only expected to act as an example of moral standards to the whole realm, but was also presumed to be literate enough to express them in prose. An extract from the text reads: 'Those families who accumulate goodness must have an abundance of blessings. Those families who accumulate its opposite must have an excess of misfortune. Those who bequeath goodness to their descendants will prosper. Those who bequeath disaster will cease to exist.' This book was distributed to officials throughout the empire and also presented abroad, transmitting Chinese ideas beyond China's frontiers to Korea and Japan.[17]

Empress Xu died in Nanjing halfway through the Yongle reign but the emperor did not appoint another empress, even though he went on to have children with other consorts. He pronounced that she should not be buried in Nanjing, demanding

Empress Xu (1362–1407), *Exhortations to promote good deeds by Empress Renxiao of the Great Ming*

(*Da Ming Renxiao huanghou quanshan shu* 大明仁孝皇后勸善書)

FIG. 37 OPPOSITE

EMPRESS XU, also known as Empress Renxiao, was the principal wife of the Yongle emperor. She was married to him for thirty-three years. She is said to have written this book that was distributed in 1407, the year of her death. This earthy book encouraged good deeds. At its heart is the premise that good deeds will be rewarded and bad deeds will not go unpunished. Each chapter starts with proverbs and quotations that are supported by historical anecdotes. Chapter 1 includes the maxim 'Those who bequeath goodness to their descendants will prosper. Those who bequeath disaster will cease to exist ...'. Chapter 19 is devoted to the topic of jealousy condemning women who indulge in slander and secret evil-doing. The eclectic religious content of this book combined Confucian, Buddhist and Daoist teachings quite naturally together. It helped to establish *quanshanshu* (books to promote good deeds) as a popular literary genre.

This was one of several books published under Empress Xu's name. These legitimized her imperial line and healed rifts caused by the civil war that brought her husband to power. Empress Ma, the founding Ming emperor's wife and the Yongle emperor's mother, also published texts to cement her position. Other books said to be written by Empress Xu include *Gujin lienü zhuan* (*Biographies of illustrious women past and present*) published in 1403 and *Neixun* (*Household instructions*) issued in 1404. The latter was intended as a textbook for her own children but was circulated widely after her death. The preoccupation of the early Ming emperors with correct behaviour of court ladies was connected to their efforts to prove themselves rightful rulers. They sought to establish Ming ladies' court etiquette and to spread this behaviour to vassal states.

Texts printed at the Ming courts were promulgated within China but also internationally. In 1404 copies of *Biographies of illustrious women* were presented to the Joseon king at the behest of the Yongle emperor. In 1408 the Ming Court presented copies of a biography of Empress Ma as well as copies of the *Exhortations* to the Joseon crown prince. Queen Sohye (1437–1504), surname Han, of the Joseon court published her own *Lessons for the inner chambers* in Classical Chinese in 1475 based on Empress Xu's works. Calendars, morality books and Confucian classics with commentaries were given by the Ming to other courts including in Thailand, Japan and the Ryūkyū Islands (modern-day Okinawa). Several of these books were still in circulation at the end of the dynasty in the 1600s.

Empress Xu's brothers had divided loyalties in the civil war that brought her husband to power. Her elder brother Xu Huizi (1368–1407), Duke of Weiguo, was loyal to the Jianwen emperor, while her younger brother Xu Zengshou (d.1402), posthumously Duke of Dingguo, was executed by the Jianwen emperor for assisting the future Yongle emperor. The heirs to both dukedoms added their names to this book, the *Exhortations*, showing their loyalty to the Yongle emperor. Empress Xu also praises her father Xu Da in the text, one of the founding Ming emperor's most important generals. As well as being endorsed by her nephews – her brother's heirs – her book was endorsed by her three sons. The future Hongxi emperor added formal texts while his younger brothers, the Princes of Han and Zhao, wrote less formally, lamenting the death of their mother. Then all of the important military and civil officials in the realm who had read and praised the book are listed.

Woodblock printed, ink on paper with imperial seal impression and yellow silk cover
Juan 5 and 6
Imperial edition, published in Nanjing, 1407
h 36.8 cm, w 22.7 cm
The Muban Foundation Collection

嘉言

儒

天之所助者順也。人之所助者信也。○惟天無親。克敬惟親。○皇○無

親惟德是輔。○天畏棐忱。○敬之敬之。天惟顯思。命不易哉。無曰高高在

上。陟降厥士。日監在兹。○敬天之怒。無敢戲豫。敬天之渝。無敢馳驅。○民

人無恐。故明神降之觀其德政。而均布福焉。○得天者高而不崩。得人者

甲而不可勝。○天之履高而聽卑。○聖人法天。天亦助聖。○天道無親常

與善人。

釋

存心佛法當蒙福祉。○克誠可以感鬼神。惟德能以動天地。○為人豪

貴國王長者。從禮事三寶中來。○眾生俏善。以清淨心。歸佛法僧命終生

天。○歸依佛。不墮地獄。歸依法。不墮餓鬼。歸依僧。不墮傍生。○三寶護世

間我今頭面禮。六道諸眾生。今盡為歸依。○若人知敬佛。及佛弟子眾現

世人讚歎後世生天上。○大覺之慈至極之聖。聞名致敬。則勝業肇於須

史。憑心想化。則妙果成於曠劫。

FIG. 38

Anonymous, 'Amusements in the Four Seasons' (*Siji shangwan tu* 四季賞玩圖)

Here the emperor, his court ladies, young children and palace eunuchs are shown enjoying life, watching and performing seasonal rituals within the Beijing palace. Unlike the official imperial portraits that were meant to be seen primarily by the imperial family, this genre of painting was produced in multiple versions and circulated among elite officials from the Xuande reign onwards. The inscription at the end of this painting is dated 1484, but the seasonal activities depicted also took place in the Xuande era.

Handscroll, ink and colours on silk
Xuande to Chenghua periods, c. 1426–1484
Beijing
h 35 cm, w 780 cm
Private Collection

the entourage of the Ming founder, and Korean kings continued to send women and eunuchs as tribute to both the Yongle and Xuande emperors. One of the Yongle emperor's senior consorts was a Korean woman, Consort Gongxianxian, called Lady Gwon (1391–1410), daughter of Gwon Yeong-gyun. She was installed in 1409 and died while accompanying the Yongle emperor on a military expedition against the Mongols. Another Korean woman, known in China as Consort Kang Hui Zhuang Shu Li, daughter of Han Yeong-jeong, was one of thirty beauties forced to commit suicide and buried with the Yongle emperor to serve him in the afterlife.[18] As well as the emperor's partners, the court housed Korean chambermaids, cooks, singers and dancers. Eunuchs were dispatched to the Korean king to demand healthy teenage virgins from civil and military families, as well as from families of ordinary soldiers. Korean in-laws of the Yongle emperor all had houses in Nanjing. Korean tribute girls were sent to the Xuande emperor in 1427 and 1428, but after his death fifty-three Korean women were allowed to return home.

COURT LIFE

The noise within the Forbidden City must have been extraordinary. When the Yongle emperor appeared in public 2,000 singers sang in harmony praising him, and 'drums, cornets, cymbals and bells' sounded.[19] The fact that the 510 people who constituted one Timurid embassy in 1420 could be accommodated in the 'post house' (*yamkhana*) of the palace gives us a sense of the scale of the buildings and the numbers of visitors that could easily be absorbed.[20]

The palaces included areas dedicated to pleasure and to official business. There are no paintings showing the Yongle emperor within his palace, but a new genre of imperial painting was pioneered in the Xuande emperor's reign at his

FIG. 39

Anonymous, 'The Xuande emperor watching quails fighting' (*Ming Xuanzong dou anchun tu* 明宣宗斗鹌鹑圖)

This painting shows the Xuande emperor seated on a lacquer chair within the gardens of the imperial palace. In front of him is a square red lacquer table ornamented with a gold design, upon which is placed a circular lacquer tray filled with sand. Two beardless eunuchs have released a pair of small fighting quails into the sand ring. On either side of the emperor are four bearded men holding birds in red silk bags ornamented with gold thread or in box cages. Two further eunuchs attend to the birds. Quail were conditioned to fight and their feathers were treated to afford them extra protection. The birds were kept hungry before a small amount of seed was scattered in the middle of the ring or tray. When they were released from their bags or cages, they fought over the grain; each bout lasted about 15 to 30 minutes before a victor was declared. This form of sport, in which bets are placed on the winning bird, is still played in India and Afghanistan today.

Hanging scroll, ink and colours on silk
c. 1426–35
Beijing
Image: h 67 cm, w 71 cm;
with mount: h 248 cm, w 99 cm
The Palace Museum, Beijing

instigation. This featured images of the emperor at leisure: engaged in palace amusements (figs 39 and 127); hunting (figs 6, 121 and 124–5); taking part in spring outings; and enjoying the palace through the four seasons (figs 38 and 85). This genre of painting continued to be popular in the Chenghua emperor's reign (1464–1487) and later. Such images of a court at leisure were perhaps intended to reassure the viewer that the empire was at peace and in good hands. Other paintings show the court enjoying the lantern festival and the emperor's private zoo.[21] Exotic animals, which could be viewed from the Fengtian Gate in the Forbidden City, came to the palace gardens through gift exchanges between rulers understood in the Ming as 'tribute' (see p. 260). Many of these creatures, such as the elephants (fig. 232), leopards, lions and giraffes (figs 218 and 219), must have found north China's climate quite unsuitable. One lion was personally delivered by its keeper as a diplomatic gift from the son of the Timurid ruler Shahrukh in 1420. Such tribute continued on a smaller scale in the second half of the fifteenth century, and a lioness was presented as late as 1483.[22]

FIG. 40

Tomb model of a carriage

This model carriage was buried in the brick tomb of Zhu Yuelian (1388–1409), Crown Prince of Shu. There is a seat and footrest inside the carriage, and removable steps for the crown prince to climb into or alight from the carriage. The figures buried alongside this carriage formed part of a procession or guard of honour of almost 500 figures. During the early fifteenth century princes would have travelled in these kinds of carriages, but by the middle of the century they were increasingly confined to their regional palaces and extensive grounds. Their movement to other regional courts was also restricted to guard against any conspiracy between different princes.

Earthenware with coloured glazes,
brown lacquer, gilded handles
c. 1400–9
Sichuan
h 70 cm, l 78 cm, d 34 cm
Sichuan Museum, excavated from
the tomb of Zhu Yuelian, Crown Prince of Shu,
at Fenghuangshan, Sichuan province

PRINCELY COURTS

Princes represented the emperor across China in locations remote from the central imperial court. These princes had a unique status in Ming society, particularly in the cities where they resided. Many placed themselves above the law, behaving as tyrants towards local officials, seizing women for their households, and confiscating land and commercial assets. In the early Ming regional courts were military strongholds theoretically guarding China's borders, but they were also cultural centres providing patronage for art, architecture, publishing and music. Quite apart from the imperial courts in Beijing and Nanjing, the princely or regional courts would have taken up vast areas of the cities in which they were based. For example, in the city of Xi'an in modern Shaanxi province the Prince of Qin's estate occupied one quarter of the whole city. A reconstruction shows that it was built along the lines of the Forbidden City, with up to 863 individual halls, as well as extensive gardens, grounds and summer palaces. The palaces also contained ritual spaces – temples and family shrines, as well as altars for making offerings to improve the weather or harvest (see Chapter 5, p. 225), and to guard against natural disasters.

About ten undisturbed princes' tombs from this period have been discovered.[23] The prevalent Chinese belief that the deceased would need to have access in the afterlife to the material culture that they enjoyed in their lifetime, led to large quantities of objects, either actual possessions or miniature models (as, for example, in the case of people such as guards and servants), being placed in tombs. The tombs of imperial princes are thus lavishly furnished, far beyond a standard available to even the wealthiest. Little remains of the princely estates above ground, but the underground tombs of the Princes of Shu (fig. 41) suggest how they must have looked, with brick or stone floors, open rectangular halls with coloured pillars and glazed earthenware roof tiles. The massive tomb doors of Prince Zhuang of Liang's tomb enable us to imagine the grandeur of the palaces, while the wooden tomb figure procession of Prince Huang of Lu evokes the vast numbers of people who would have dwelled and worked within these courts.

PRINCE HUANG OF LU

Prince Huang of Lu, Zhu Tan (1370–1389), the tenth of twenty-six sons of the Ming founder, was sent from Nanjing to his seat in Yanzhou, in Shandong province, aged fifteen.[24] He died aged just nineteen after swallowing a potion designed to extend his life, as he dabbled in Daoist elixirs and the pursuit of immortality. He was the first of the regional princes to die in his father's lifetime, and so great care was taken over

FIG 41

Underground tomb of the Crown Prince of Shu, c. 1409

Zhu Yuelian (1388–1409), Crown Prince of Shu and eldest son of Zhu Chun, Prince of Shu, was buried at Fenghuangshan in Sichuan, in a tomb that resembled an underground palace. It was painted in red and gold with green glazed tiles, with similar structures above ground.

FIG. 42

Tomb model of a carriage

Each son of the Hongwu emperor, including Prince Huang of Lu (1370–1389), in whose tomb this carriage was found, had his own estate, staff and substantial army. Princes were given enough land to produce a substantial income through agricultural cultivation, and they were also given salaries from the imperial central court in the form of rice, paper money, textiles, salt, tea and horsefeed. In addition to these staples, they were presented with luxury goods, such as gold and jewels, direct from the capital. Princes came to court when summoned and would travel in carriages such as this one, escorted by their staff and guards. They were instructed to come separately in an attempt to prevent them plotting together. Imperial audiences became far less frequent as the fifteenth century progressed. This carriage has a small chair inside for the prince and would have been pulled by a team of horses. He was also buried with a second smaller carriage, perhaps for his wives.

Painted wood, lacquer, gold and paper
c. 1389
Shandong
h 53.5 cm, l 83.7 cm
Shandong Museum, excavated from the tomb of Zhu Tan, Prince Huang of Lu at Yanzhou, Shandong province

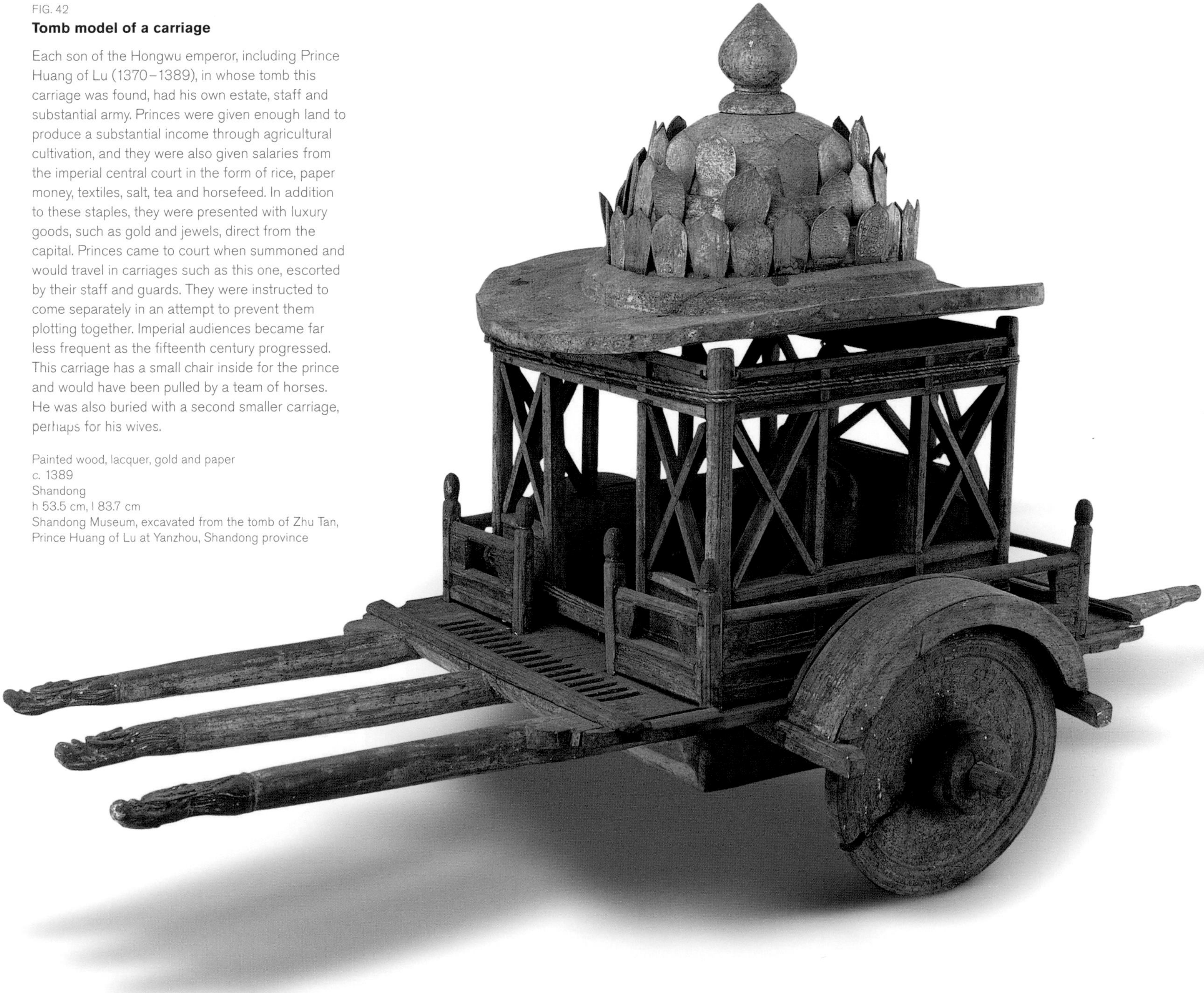

FIG. 43
Tomb figure of a eunuch

This tomb figure of a eunuch with black hat, and brown and green robe was placed within a guard of honour, arranged in a procession. In total, 500 earthenware figures with coloured glazes were unearthed from this brick tomb. The tomb figures re-created the realm in which the prince had lived and signalled to both the populace and to the spirit world his status as a member of the ruling imperial household.

Earthenware with lead-fluxed glazes
c. 1409
Sichuan
h 32.0 cm
Sichuan Museum, excavated from the tomb of Zhu Yuelian, Crown Prince of Shu, at Mount Fenghuang, Sichuan province

his burial. In April 1390 the Hongwu emperor refused to let civilians, who should have been busy farming, work on the tomb construction: instead the labour was carried out by soldiers.

Zhu Tan's well-preserved tomb furnishings present him as a cultured young man who liked to read literature, compose poetry, play chess (fig. 167) and the zither (fig. 166), and admire antique Chinese paintings: there are two Song-dynasty (960–1279) paintings and one from the Yuan dynasty (1279–1368) included in his tomb, which demonstrate his interest in collecting art. They have seal impressions that show they were once in the imperial Mongol collection, then transferred to Nanjing after the fall of the Yuan dynasty and establishment of the Ming. In 1970–71 archaeologists excavated Zhu Tan's tomb, situated in a most auspicious place according to Chinese geomancy at the foot of Jiulong Hill, between Qufu (birthplace of Confucius, 551–479 BC) and Zoucheng (birthplace of Mencius, 372–289 BC, the most important 'Confucian' philosopher of the ancient past after the Sage himself). The tombs of his two wives, only one of which has been excavated, are on either side. Altogether more than 2000 items were recovered.

PRINCE ZHUANG OF SHU

The tomb of Crown Prince Zhuang of Shu, Zhu Yuelian (1388–1409), eldest son of the first Prince of Shu, Zhu Chun (1371–1423), and grandson of the Hongwu emperor, is located south of Mount Fenghuang, in a suburb of modern-day Cheng-du in Sichuan province. Although partially robbed in the past, it still revealed many treasures when excavated in 1970. The tomb was constructed as an elaborate underground palace, painted in red and gold with green-glazed tiles resembling similar now-vanished structures above ground.[25] The carved stone sculptures of the spirit way – civil and military figures as well as animals – echo the figures that line the spirit way at the imperial tombs in Beijing (see Chapter 6, p. 276). Five hundred ceramic tomb figures were interred with the prince, their distinct costumes – representing military figures, musicians, grooms and palace servants – providing a glimpse of the scale and diversity of palace life.

Both the tombs of the Crown Prince of Shu and Prince Zhuang of Liang contained weapons, perhaps to remind those who buried him and the dead of their original role as protectors of the imperial clan. Iron weapons are particularly hard to preserve, but the presence of a Japanese-style iron sword with a sheath of red lacquer patterned with gold and an iron bow with a bronze string (modelled on a central Asian weapon) reflect both the court's all-pervading military culture and their interest in foreign things.

PRINCE ZHUANG OF LIANG AND LADY WEI

Prince Zhuang of Liang, Zhu Zhanji (1411–1441) was grandson of the Yongle emperor, ninth son of the Hongxi emperor and brother of the Xuande emperor. He died of an unspecified illness in the reign of his nephew, the Zhengtong emperor, aged just thirty. Receiving the title Prince of Liang in 1424, in 1429 he went to his state in

FIG. 44
Marriage certificate for a princess

This gilded silver document is a marriage certificate for Lady Wei, wife of Prince Zhuang of Liang, ruler of one of the regional courts in Hubei province, central China. She was buried with this document to identify her to the bureaucrats who were then believed to govern the afterlife. It reads:

On the day jiayin, third day after the beginning of the seventh month renzi, in the year guichou, the eighth year of the Xuande reign [1433], the emperor's edict states: I, following the regulations of Taizu, the High Emperor, when enfeoffing princes must select virtuous women as their match. My brother, Prince of Liang, has come of age. You of the surname Wei, daughter of Wei Heng, now receives this gold plaque that establishes you as the consort of the Prince of Liang. You must be reverent and cautious in the ways of a wife, and assist the family and state from within with respect!

[Translated by Luk Yu-ping]

維宣德八年歲次癸丑七月壬子朔越三日甲寅,
皇帝制曰: 朕惟太祖高皇帝之制封建諸王必選
賢女為之配。朕弟梁王年已長成. 爾魏氏. 乃
南城兵馬指揮魏亨之女, 今持授以金冊立為梁
王妃爾. 尚尊謹婦道內。 助家邦敬哉!

Gilded silver with incised inscription
Dated 1433
Beijing
h 23 cm, w 9.1 cm, d 0.4 cm
Hubei Provincial Museum, excavated from the tomb of Zhu Zhanji, Prince Zhuang of Liang, and of Lady Wei at Zhongxiang, Hubei province

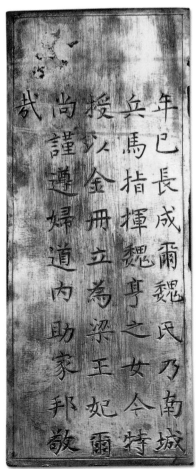

modern Zhongxiang city in Hubei province, leaving his brother's court in Beijing to make the long overland journey of more than seven hundred miles. He was the first and last Prince of Liang as he had no male heirs and the title died with him. His first wife was Lady Ji, the daughter of a military officer who commanded a unit based in nearby Anhui. She died childless in 1428. His second marriage in 1433 was to Lady Wei, daughter of a Nanchang cavalry commander Wei Heng. She gave birth to two daughters.[26]

Lady Wei begged to 'follow the prince into death'. Suicide was common practice in the imperial clan in the early Ming (see Chapter 1, pp. 41–2) but by the mid-fifteenth century this practice had been abandoned, wives being no longer required to die when their husbands did.[27] After Lady Wei passed away in 1451, the prince's tomb was reopened and she was interred. As there were no sons to inherit their wealth and the Wei family may have wished to demonstrate their imperial connections, the tomb goods were spectacular, including many gold vessels, as well as male and female jewellery. Between 2001 and 2002 archaeologists recovered 5,100 items from the tomb, including 120 gold objects. Other surviving tomb furnishings included items of silver, jade, porcelain, pottery, bronze, iron, pewter, lacquer, bone and horn.

Imperial and princely courts were bonded through family ties and interacted through rare audiences granted by the emperors initially in Nanjing or latterly Beijing. The tombs of both the Prince Huang of Lu and the Crown Prince of Shu included model carriages in wood and earthenware respectively (figs 42 and 40). The full-size versions would have been used to convey princes around their estates, and to make the occasional journeys to the central court. Such journeys to the capital were far less frequent after the 1420s as the Yongle emperor wanted to avoid plotting between the members of the regional courts, to safeguard his and his successors' power (see Chapter 1, p. 27).

FIG. 45
Crown

Crowns were part of the official regalia given to princes when they were sent off to their regional kingdoms by the emperor. This crown is made up of a woven bamboo base, with elaborate semi-precious stone beads sewn on to the dome. A gold pin would have secured the crown to the prince's hair bun. This example was excavated from the tomb of Prince Huang of Lu (1370–1389) in Shandong. The remains of a similar crown have been found in the tomb of Prince Zhuang of Liang (1411–1441) in Hubei, showing that this type was part of the official regalia given to the princes when they were sent off by the emperor to their regional court, and that the style remained the same throughout the early Ming period. This and the nine-tasselled crown (fig. 48) were both well preserved as they were stored in a large red lacquer box.

Leather, woven bamboo, lacquer, semi-precious stones and gold
c. 1380
h 21 cm, w 31 cm
Shandong Museum, excavated from the tomb of Zhu Tan, Prince Huang of Lu at Yanzhou, Shandong province

COURTLY COSTUME AND JEWELLERY

Ming princes, their wives and children represented an imperial presence in the regions and their costumes echoed those of the emperor. The princes received salaries and luxury gifts from the emperor to maintain their palaces and staff. Costumes and jewellery were strictly governed by imperial sumptuary laws. Certain fabrics, colours and designs were reserved for court costume to identify the wearer as a member of the imperial household. An imperial edict issued in 1403 banned the general populace from wearing certain fabrics such as gold embroidery, figured gauzes, brocaded damasks and other fine silks. They were also forbidden from wearing particular colours, such as yellow, which was reserved for the court. All early Ming emperors were painted in yellow official robes decorated with dragons for their imperial portraits. As a representative of the emperor in the regions, princes wore yellow dragon robes, too; Prince Huang of Lu, for example, was buried with several yellow silk robes bearing dragon motifs (fig. 54). Both Ming court dress and the court dress of Joseon Korea[28] were influenced by Mongol formal costume (figs 53 and 54). For official duties princes wore jewelled crowns (figs 45 and 48), or official hats (fig. 50), ornate jade (fig. 51) or bejewelled gold belts (fig. 249), as well as dangling sets of jade pendants (fig. 52).

Empresses wore impressive clothes of investiture – a headdress ornamented with nine dragons, symbolizing imperial power, and four phoenixes, representing imperial marital harmony, twelve large and twelve small flowers on stalks (fig. 56) and

FIG. 46
Head ornament

Court goldsmiths produced this thinly beaten gold headdress with relief ornament, which imitates the larger bead-decorated leather examples, excavated from the tombs of the Prince Huang of Lu and the Prince Zhuang of Liang, in shape and decoration. In the early Ming period, Chinese aristocrats wore their long hair swept up and tied back into buns. This gold headdress would have fitted over the piled hair and been secured by a gold hat pin, which went through the side holes horizontally. The manufacture of gold objects was tightly controlled by the central imperial court and the use of gold was restricted to the imperial family and high officials.

Gold
c. 1400–50
Nanjing or Beijing
h c. 10.2 cm
British Museum, London, purchased with the help of public subscription from the George Eumorfopoulos Collection, 1938,0524.247

FIG. 47
Hat-top ornament

This hat-top ornament is decorated with a finely worked jade dragon set into a gold base, with tubes for holding tail-feathers festooned with polished gemstones mounted in gold. Mongol noblemen wore this style of ornament stitched onto their hats like a top knot; we can see such ornaments depicted in portraits of Mongol Yuan emperors. Early Ming court culture absorbed many aspects of Mongol Yuan court culture, including its costume and jewellery styles. This is the largest example ever discovered, though the cloth hat on to which it would have been stitched has not survived burial.

Jade, gold, semi-precious and precious gems
c. 1424–41
Nanjing or Beijing
h 6.3 cm, d 6.6 cm
Hubei Provincial Museum, excavated from the tomb of Zhu Zhanji, Prince Zhuang of Liang, and of Lady Wei at Zhongxiang, Hubei province

FIG. 48
Nine-tasselled crown

Each regional prince would have had a crown like this one; unfortunately only two have survived today and this is by far the best example. It was excavated from the tomb of Prince Huang of Lu in Shandong. The gold pin through the top would have secured the crown to the prince's hair and the holes on either side are for fastening a chin strap. Jade rings dangle on either side to protect the ears. The suspended bead curtain created a pleasant tinkling sound as the prince moved about. It is strung with nine beads across; the emperor's crown was larger and had twelve beads across and twelve down. Similar crowns worn by deities and historical figures in earlier paintings and murals would have been familiar to the early Ming people: thus when they saw the prince wearing this crown they would have connected the new imperial family with ancient deities. The construction of the crown also includes elements of cosmic significance referring to the circular heavens and square earth.

Leather, woven bamboo, lacquer, jade, gold with semi-precious stones rethreaded on silk threads
c. 1380
Nanjing
h 18 cm; the board is l 49.4 cm, w 23.5 cm; tube diam. 17.6 cm
Shandong Museum, excavated from the tomb of Zhu Tan, Prince Huang of Lu at Yanzhou, Shandong province

FIG. 49 ABOVE

Wide-brimmed hat

This black hat is softer, more flexible and therefore more informal than the rigid official crowns. Hats for different occasions were included in the young Prince Huang's burial to provide him with appropriate costumes for all eventualities in the afterlife. No other hat of this type survives, but the *Great Canon of the Yongle Reign* (*Yongle da dian*) includes illustrations of such headgear. This type of tall crowned hat later became popular in Korea through contacts between the Ming and Joseon courts. Although the hat is original, the woven bamboo brim is a replacement, as only the outer hoop survived burial.

Woven bamboo and silk
c. 1389
Nanjing
h 17 cm, w 41 cm
Shandong Museum, excavated from the tomb of Zhu Tan, Prince Huang of Lu at Yanzhou, Shandong province

FIG. 50 ABOVE RIGHT

Official hat for a prince

Princes' costumes relate closely to imperial robes, but they were dictated by elaborate sumptuary laws. Hats and robes were changed with the seasons, but also according to the official or non-official nature of the princes' activities. An official portrait shows the Hongxi emperor dressed in a similar hat. Archaeologists discovered this rare silk gauze hat in 1970–71 in Zou County, Shandong province, in the tomb of Zhu Tan, Prince Huang of Lu. He would have worn this hat, which resembles a scholar's cap, for official duties. The winged back section is detachable.

Woven bamboo and silk
c. 1389
Nanjing
h 22.5 cm, w 15.5 cm
Shandong Museum, excavated from the tomb of Zhu Tan, Prince Huang of Lu at Yanzhou, Shandong province

ornaments decorated with precious stones (fig. 55). For ordinary occasions empresses wore a headdress with a single dragon and a pair of phoenix hairpins (fig. 57). Court ladies wore beautifully worked ornaments; bracelets were gold or jade, set with gems, pearls and kingfisher feathers. Robes were made in various colours and embroidered with dragons and phoenixes, again symbolizing the emperor and empress respectively, and belts were made of jade and gold.

The imperial court controlled the manufacture of gold jewellery and ornaments for its members. Craftsmen worked in precious metals, in a department called the *Yinzuoju* (literally 'Silver Workshop' or 'Jewellery Service'). Beautifully worked jewellery was presented by the central imperial court to male and female members of the regional courts on special occasions, such as the taking up of office or marriage. The similarity between some of the objects in the different princely tombs, and the presence of inscriptions revealing that they were the products of the *Yinzuoju*, suggests that they were high-quality gifts from the imperial workshops, which were centrally manufactured for official purposes. Princes were not allowed to receive direct foreign tribute, so the foreign gems and gold found in their tombs by archaeologists must also have been gifts of the central imperial court. The diversity of other tomb contents reflects the personalities and preoccupations of the tomb occupants themselves and their families.[29]

Far fewer representations of early Ming imperial women survive than of their male counterparts. From texts and surviving images of aristocratic women we can reconstruct the princesses' appearance, with their high-piled hair bedecked with gold and gem-encrusted hairpins (figs 55–7), spiralling bracelets and bangles (fig. 60).

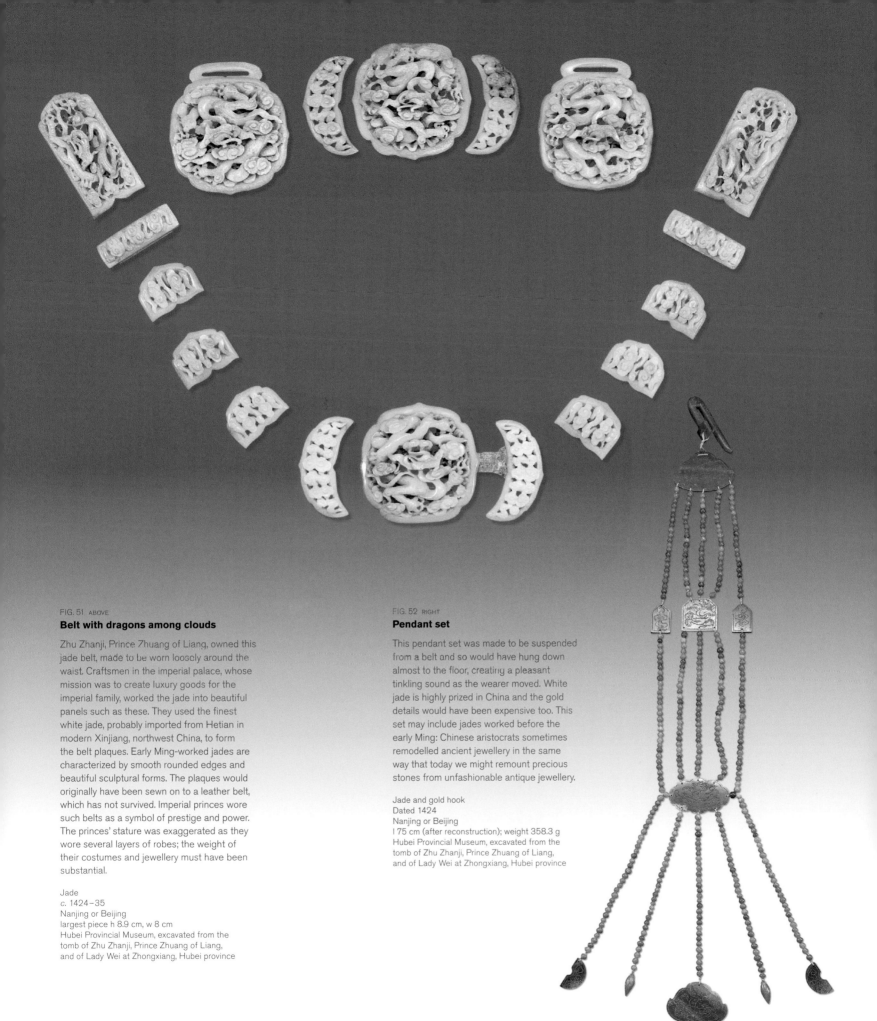

FIG. 51 ABOVE

Belt with dragons among clouds

Zhu Zhanji, Prince Zhuang of Liang, owned this jade belt, made to be worn loosely around the waist. Craftsmen in the imperial palace, whose mission was to create luxury goods for the imperial family, worked the jade into beautiful panels such as these. They used the finest white jade, probably imported from Hetian in modern Xinjiang, northwest China, to form the belt plaques. Early Ming-worked jades are characterized by smooth rounded edges and beautiful sculptural forms. The plaques would originally have been sewn on to a leather belt, which has not survived. Imperial princes wore such belts as a symbol of prestige and power. The princes' stature was exaggerated as they wore several layers of robes; the weight of their costumes and jewellery must have been substantial.

Jade
c. 1424–35
Nanjing or Beijing
largest piece h 8.9 cm, w 8 cm
Hubei Provincial Museum, excavated from the tomb of Zhu Zhanji, Prince Zhuang of Liang, and of Lady Wei at Zhongxiang, Hubei province

FIG. 52 RIGHT

Pendant set

This pendant set was made to be suspended from a belt and so would have hung down almost to the floor, creating a pleasant tinkling sound as the wearer moved. White jade is highly prized in China and the gold details would have been expensive too. This set may include jades worked before the early Ming: Chinese aristocrats sometimes remodelled ancient jewellery in the same way that today we might remount precious stones from unfashionable antique jewellery.

Jade and gold hook
Dated 1424
Nanjing or Beijing
l 75 cm (after reconstruction); weight 358.3 g
Hubei Provincial Museum, excavated from the tomb of Zhu Zhanji, Prince Zhuang of Liang, and of Lady Wei at Zhongxiang, Hubei province

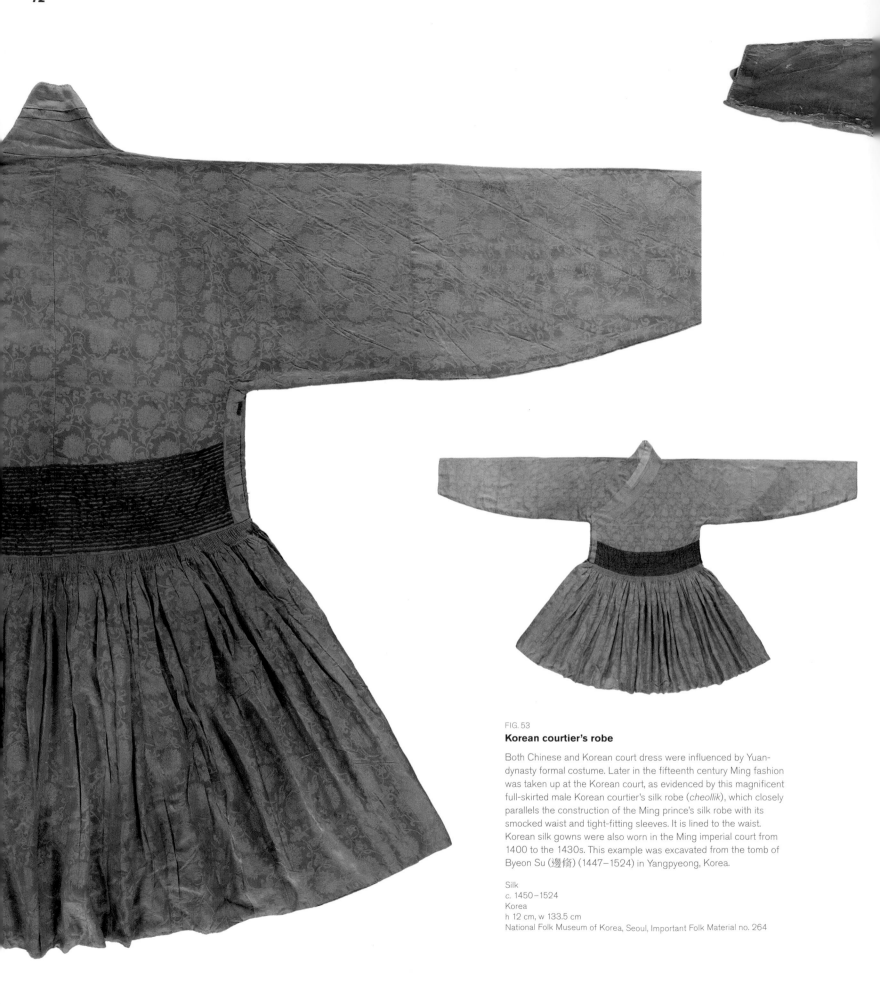

FIG. 53
Korean courtier's robe

Both Chinese and Korean court dress were influenced by Yuan-dynasty formal costume. Later in the fifteenth century Ming fashion was taken up at the Korean court, as evidenced by this magnificent full-skirted male Korean courtier's silk robe (*cheollik*), which closely parallels the construction of the Ming prince's silk robe with its smocked waist and tight-fitting sleeves. It is lined to the waist. Korean silk gowns were also worn in the Ming imperial court from 1400 to the 1430s. This example was excavated from the tomb of Byeon Su (邊脩) (1447–1524) in Yangpyeong, Korea.

Silk
c. 1450–1524
Korea
h 12 cm, w 133.5 cm
National Folk Museum of Korea, Seoul, Important Folk Material no. 264

FIG. 54

Ming prince's 'dragon robe'

Zhu Tan, Prince Huang of Lu, was buried with this silk costume and six other 'dragon' robes. The upper sleeves are integral to the bodice, which is tight-fitting with a side fastening, and it has a full, pleated skirt. Research has shown that, when new, the silk outfit would have been bright yellow, with paler yellow rising dragons woven through in a raised pattern on the front, back and shoulders. Yellow silk was reserved for the imperial family to wear. The prince's undergarments would probably have been made of cotton. Cotton, mulberry (on which silk worms fed) and tea were the main cash crops of the early Ming.

Silk
c. 1389
Nanjing
h 130 cm, w 110 cm
Shandong Museum, excavated from the tomb of Zhu Tan, Prince Huang of Lu at Yanzhou, Shandong province

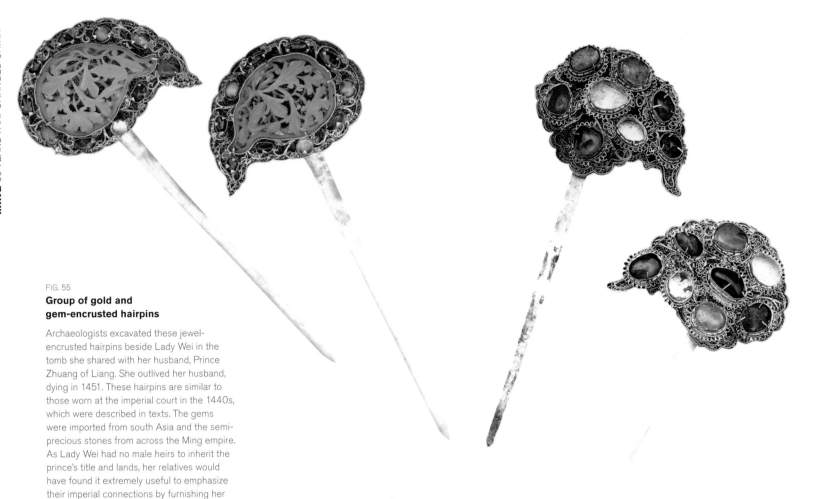

FIG. 55

Group of gold and gem-encrusted hairpins

Archaeologists excavated these jewel-encrusted hairpins beside Lady Wei in the tomb she shared with her husband, Prince Zhuang of Liang. She outlived her husband, dying in 1451. These hairpins are similar to those worn at the imperial court in the 1440s, which were described in texts. The gems were imported from south Asia and the semi-precious stones from across the Ming empire. As Lady Wei had no male heirs to inherit the prince's title and lands, her relatives would have found it extremely useful to emphasize their imperial connections by furnishing her tomb with such lavish goods, including many gold vessels and sumptuous jewellery.

Gold, jade, precious and semi-precious stones
c. 1403–51
Nanjing or Beijing
Max. l 20.5 cm
Hubei Provincial Museum, excavated from the tomb of Zhu Zhanji, Prince Zhuang of Liang, and of Lady Wei at Zhongxiang, Hubei province

FIG. 56

Gold flower-shaped hair ornament

This hair ornament, made of concentric leaves of beaten sheet gold, was excavated from the tomb of Lady Wei. Its craftsmanship indicates that is was made in the imperial workshop in Nanjing or Beijing, supervised by the eunuch craft agency – the Jewellery Service. Stylistically, it relates to earlier gold jewellery made in north China for ladies of the Liao (907–1125) court. Members of the imperial clan distinguished themselves from other grand families by the scale, quality and quantity of their treasures.

Gold
c. 1424–41
Nanjing or Beijing
h 13.4 cm, w 10 cm
Hubei Provincial Museum, excavated from the tomb of Zhu Zhanji, Prince Zhuang of Liang, and of Lady Wei at Zhongxiang, Hubei province

FIG. 57 OPPOSITE

Pair of gold filigree phoenix hairpins

These two finely worked hair ornaments were excavated in 2001–2 from the tomb occupied by Lady Wei. The delicate details of the phoenix would have moved and caught the light when Lady Wei walked, attracting attention and admiration. Similar phoenix filigree hairpins have been excavated in a Jin-dynasty (1115–1234) context in Beijing, perhaps indicating that these examples followed antique models.

Gold
c. 1403–51
Nanjing or Beijing
Max. l 24 cm, weight 95 g
Hubei Provincial Museum, excavated from the tomb of Zhu Zhanji, Prince Zhuang of Liang, and of Lady Wei at Zhongxiang, Hubei province

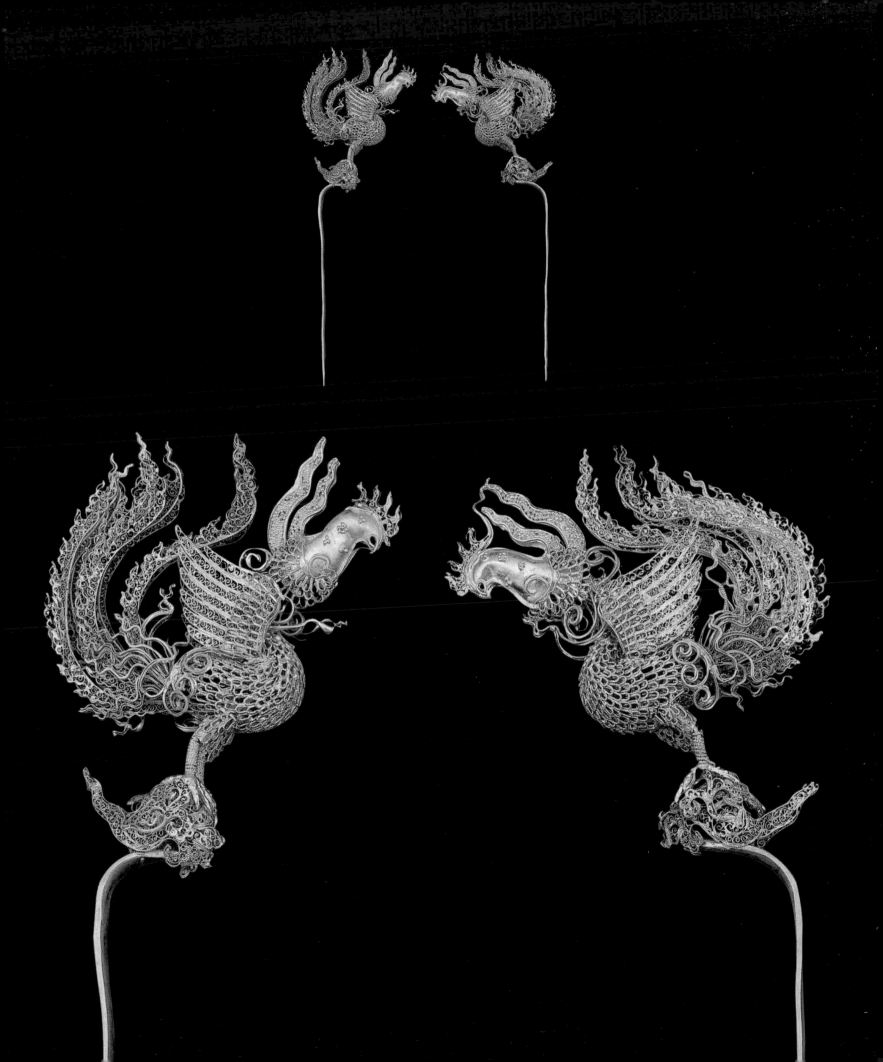

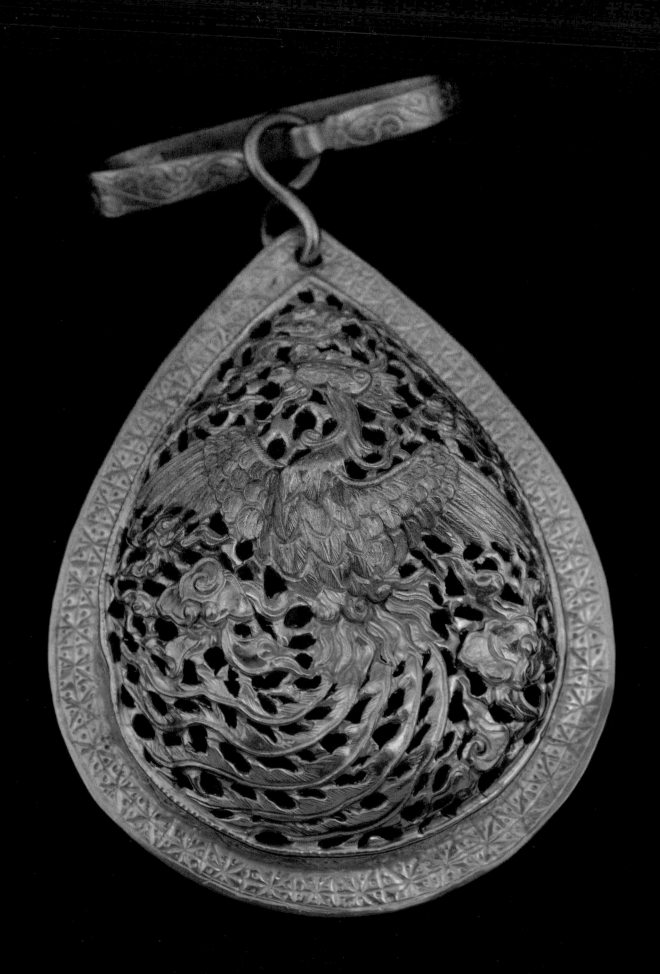

FIG. 58 OPPOSITE
Perfume container

Archaeologists excavated this gold ornament from the tomb occupied by Lady Wei. It is finely worked and decorated, with an openwork design of a phoenix with five streaming tail-feathers – an emblem of an imperial woman. It was meant to be worn with a princess's ceremonial robes. The container, which would have held fragrant incense, was made to be worn at the waist, suspended from a hook that carries the inscription: 'Made by craftsmen from the Jewellery Service, following the imperial carriage [i.e. travelling with the emperor between Nanjing and Beijng] during the twelfth month of the seventh year of the Xuande period [1432], from 70 per cent pure gold, [weighing] one *liang* and nine *qian*' (隨駕銀作局宣德柒年拾貳月內造柒成色金壹兩玖錢). Similar ornaments have been excavated from other aristocratic women's tombs. The Xuande emperor may have presented it as an engagement gift to Lady Wei on her marriage to his brother, Prince Zhuang of Liang.

Gold
Dated 1432
Yinzuoju (the Jewellery Service) as it followed the court between Nanjing and Beijing
h 14.2 cm, w 7.8 cm; weight 72.4 g
Hubei Provincial Museum, excavated from the tomb of Zhu Zhanji, Prince Zhuang of Liang, and of Lady Wei at Zhongxiang, Hubei province

FIG. 59
Pair of gold earrings

More than twenty sets of ornaments were excavated at the joint tomb of Prince Zhuang of Liang and Lady Wei, including earrings and hairpins. These earrings are made of gold and further ornamented with imported turquoise.

Gold and turquoise
c. 1424–51
Nanjing or Beijing
h 6 cm, w 5.8 cm
Hubei Provincial Museum, excavated from the tomb of Zhu Zhanji, Prince Zhuang of Liang, and of Lady Wei at Zhongxiang, Hubei province

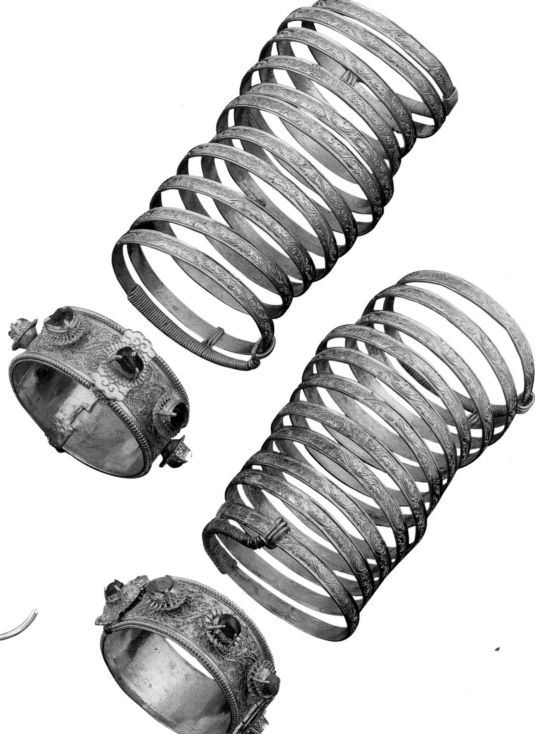

FIG. 60
Pair of gold spiral arm bangles and bracelets

Excavators discovered this pair of bracelets and arm bangles in 2001 in a lacquered wooden box placed inside the coffin of Lady Wei. Such precious jewellery would have been produced in the eunuch-run craft workshops of the central imperial palace. They were perhaps bestowed on Lady Wei as a marriage gift from her brother-in-law, the Xuande emperor, or from Prince Zhuang of Liang's father, the Hongxi emperor, or his mother, Empress Zhang.

Gold, semi-precious and precious gems
c. 1424–51
Nanjing or Beijing
l 12.5 cm and 13.8 cm, w 6.5 cm and 6.7 cm
Hubei Provincial Museum, excavated from the tomb of Zhu Zhanji, Prince Zhuang of Liang, and of Lady Wei at Zhongxiang, Hubei province

EUNUCHS AND OTHER PALACE WORKERS

Eunuchs, recognizable in Ming paintings by their lack of facial hair, were employed in a number of functions within the imperial and princely palaces (fig. 43; see also Chapter 1, p. 34).[30] Twelve offices administered by eunuchs served the court with responsibilities for 'personnel, accoutrements, regalia, horses, temple offerings, food, seals, credentials, palace maintenance, apparel, communication and ceremonial affairs'.[31] Although the first Ming emperor decreed that eunuchs should not be educated, during the Xuande reign young eunuchs were taught within the palace and by 1450 elite palace eunuchs had a well-balanced education and were knowledgeable in the histories and classics. In turn, eunuchs served an important role in educating the princes and palace women. They also gradually came to take over the duties of female palace musicians and eventually dominated Ming palace music.[32] By 1446 eunuchs' positions became hereditary, so they were able to pass on their responsibilities to brothers or nephews.

Eunuchs were ethnically diverse. The Yongle emperor employed Mongol, central Asian, Jurchen, Vietnamese, Korean and Chinese eunuchs. Some of them rose to very high positions at court: in addition to the eunuch naval commander Zheng He already encountered in Chapter 1, the Vietnamese eunuch Nguyễn An, known by his Chinese name Ruan An (1381–1453), served as architect of the Beijing palace complex. But they were not the only foreigners employed in the palace: the imperial Ming court was cosmopolitan, with Muslim astronomers and mathematicians from western Asia employed during much of the dynasty's first century. The Mongol ruler, Qubilai Khan (r. 1264–1294), had earlier established a Muslim Institute of Astronomy (*Hui hui sitian jian*) to capitalize on Iranian and other Muslim cultures' expertise, and this continued with minor changes in the early Ming, with the Astrological Institute (*Tai shi jian*)[33] being responsible for calendar-making, astrology, time-keeping and divination. The first Ming emperor commissioned

FIG. 61

Celestial globe with stand and ring

This Iranian globe, of a type that might have been used by Muslim astronomers and mathematicians from western Asia at the Ming court, depicts approximately sixty stars with inlaid silver points. Zodiacal names are engraved, while stars and constellations are identified in *kufic* script. Near the South Pole an inscription states that the placement of the stars was determined by calculations made in AH 834 (AD 1430–31), in accordance with the *Book of Fixed Stars* (*Kitāb sūwar al-kawākib al-thābita*) of al-Sufi. Such globes were used to teach calculations in observatories, such as that built in Samarqand in 1428 by the Timurid prince Ulugh Beg (c. 1394–1449).

Brass, engraved with silver inlays
Dated 1430/1
h 27 cm, diam. 10.5 cm
British Museum, London 1896,0323.1

Chinese translations of western Asian texts on astronomy, and included Arabic and Persian books from the Yuan imperial library in his own.[34] The Bureau for Translation (*Siyi guan*) was a permanent fixture at the imperial court, where multi-language texts circulated and permanent stele were erected, carved in different languages.

The imperial guard also engaged many non-Chinese soldiers and spies (see Chapter 3, p. 126).[35] Some high-ranking Tibetan priests at court provided advice for the emperors on military, civil and religious matters (fig. 209). Other visiting priests were also consulted and given lavish gifts (see Chapter 5, pp. 232–3). A monk from Bengal was invited to the Yongle emperor's court to teach people to chant the untranslatable '*Oṃ maṇi padme hūṃ*', a Buddhist incantation which, when recited, was believed to spread divine goodness. The Chinese official Li Jiding, who was a Reader-in-Waiting of the Hanlin Academy, sceptically remarked on observing the Bengal monk, 'If he has supernatural powers, then he should be well versed in Chinese! Why does he wait for a translator and [only] then comprehends [Chinese]? In fact the "*Oṃ maṇi padme hūṃ*" that he utters actually means, "I have cheated you". The people do not understand this.'[36]

At court lowly kitchen staff prepared and cooked daily meals, as well as food for rituals and state banquets for the emperor and his vast household, served by eunuchs and palace women. Cooks held a hereditary position, just as soldiers and most artisans did. Chefs specializing in different regional cuisines were brought to the capital. An edict issued by the Xuande emperor in 1435 made provision for 5,000 kitchen servants to be employed to supply the imperial table and state banquets.[37] Another smaller group of cooks was engaged to make food for religious and commemorative services. Eunuchs were in charge of procurement, including the storing of ice for refrigeration by cutting blocks of it from frozen rivers and ponds in the winter, which they then packed in clean straw and buried.[38]

PALACE FURNISHINGS

Our ability to imagine the courts of the early Ming and their decorative schemes comes not through surviving texts, but instead through excavated materials, and surviving objects and paintings. Ming courts were vibrant and colourful places, not just in their architecture or costumes, but also in their furniture and utensils.

The Yongle emperor's father, the Ming founder Zhu Yuanzhang, gathered together craftsmen and artists to construct a new imperial palace and centre of government in Nanjing. Similarly, the Yongle and Xuande emperors recruited a new generation of craftsmen and artists to construct and furnish the imperial palace in Beijing. There were few technological inventions in the Hongwu era.[39] However, the Yongle and Xuande emperors established a new visual vocabulary for courtly material, which was adopted by all later Ming emperors, and which was revived and referred to by Qing emperors to the end of the imperial era in 1911. The eighteenth-century Kangxi (1662–1722), Yongzheng (1723–1735) and Qianlong (1736–1795) emperors all consciously looked back to the early fifteenth century as inspiration for ceramics, lacquer wares and sculpture, sometimes commissioning direct imitations.[40]

Eunuch-run agencies supplied the imperial and regional courts with staff but

Anonymous, 'The true countenance of Lord Yao Guangxiao, [imperially] titled Junior Preceptor, [posthumously] ennobled as Duke of Rongguo [named] Gongjing' (Chifeng Rongguo Gongjing gong zeng shaoshi Yao gong Guangxiao zhenrong 敕封荣國恭靖公贈少師姚公廣孝真容)

FIG. 62 OPPOSITE

THIS IS the only surviving portrait of Yao Guangxiao (1335–1418), known by his monastic name Daoyan. The high-quality, anonymous court painting was produced as an image for a shrine dedicated to this remarkable man. He was a Buddhist monk from a family of doctors in Suzhou, Jiangsu, who became the Yongle emperor's chief mentor, and arguably his most trusted counsellor on both civil and military matters. From 1407 he also tutored the future Xuande emperor. Here he is depicted in the patchwork robes of a Buddhist monk and holds a fly whisk, a standard monk's implement.

Daoyan met the future Yongle emperor in Nanjing in 1382 at the state funeral of his mother: Yongle's father, the Ming founder, had sent a Buddhist monk to accompany each of his sons back to their regional palaces after the funeral. Later, after the Yongle emperor had seized power, Daoyan supervised the publication of a number of politically important works that legitimized the Yongle emperor's seizure of power. These included the Great Canon of the Yongle Reign (Yongle da dian) (1405–8), a compilation of all approved written texts, as well as the Veritable Record of Ming Taizu (Ming Taizu shilu) – an official historical account of the first Ming emperor's reign, which included important revisions to remove references to the Jianwen reign of Yongle's nephew (it was written in 1402 and revised in 1418). Daoyan also wrote Records of Obeying Heaven to Suppress Trouble (Fengtian jingnan ji) in 1403, a justification of the civil war, and The Genealogy of the Imperial Family (Tian huang yu tie) in 1403, which again was revised to support Yongle's position as legitimate ruler.

Daoyan studied broadly and his knowledge included an understanding of Chan Buddhism, Confucian classics, poetry, painting and historical writings, as well as Daoist skills such as divination, fortune-telling and physiognomy. This was complemented by an understanding of military science. Daoyan played a major role in the civil war by training soldiers and promoting his personal favourites for leadership roles within the army. He was given two palace ladies and an official residence, but although he dressed in the red robes, jade belt and gauze hat of a serving official for some court audiences, he mostly wore his Buddhist robes and stayed in his monastery in Beijing.

Japanese monks regarded Daoyan as a model monk and after visiting various Chinese monasteries often asked him to contribute a preface or postscript to their literary collections before returning to Japan. However, some later figures found Daoyan's dual role of political advisor and spiritual man difficult to comprehend. An inscription on the portrait written by Zibo Zhenke suggests dissatisfaction with this juggling of two different roles:

A monk's robe but serving as an official, [this is like] flies dotting an ice-pure face. To go against what is constant on behalf of the Dao, how broad are the waves of compassion? Whether one understands or blames this gentleman, the stars have their fixed pattern. Why! He obtained [Master] Wuchu's transmission of the orthodox line, [But] illumination and darkness never mixed with one another. Inscribed at Yiyin Hall, Jiafu Monastery at Mt Tantuo, four days after wangri [usually the fifteenth day of the month] in the tenth lunar month during winter of the year renchen of the Wanli reign [1592]. Later scholar monk Zhenke.

[Translated by Marsha Haufler]

染衣而官，蠅點冰顏。以道反常，慈波奚寬。知公罪公，星有定盤。咦！接得 無初傳正脈，從來明暗不相參。萬曆壬辰冬十月望後四日題於潭柘山嘉福寺一音堂。後學釋真可。

The inscription on the right by Recluse Xinyuan reads:

An official in monk's clothing; a face without shame. There is neither Dao nor constancy [chang]; the sea of Dharma is itself vast. Understand me or blame me, I have no fixed pattern. Ha-ha! Try to see the peak emerging from the white clouds; Let the bright moon act as it will, [the two are] unrelated. Xinyuan jushi of Jiangyou eulogized in response in the autumn of xinchou [1601?].

官爾緇衣，無腼爾顏。非道非常，法海自寬。知我罪我，我無定盤。呵呵，試看白雲閑出岫，任他明月不相關。辛丑秋江右心源居士和贊。

Hanging scroll, ink and colours on silk
c. 1403–18
Beijing
Image: h 184.5 cm, w 120.2 cm; with mount: h 357 cm, w 166 cm
The Palace Museum, Beijing. Once kept in the Tanzhe Monastery in the Western Hills near Beijing, it later entered the Qing-dynasty (1644–1911) imperial collection.

also with certain types of object made exclusively for the court. Departments supplying such goods included the Directorate of Imperial Accoutrements (*Yuyong jian*), Craft Institute (*Wensi yuan*), Work Project Office (*Yingshan suo*), Directorate of Astronomy (*Qiutian jian*), Royal Household Department of Sweetmeats and Delicacies (*Tian shi fang*) and the Silver Workshop (*Yinzuoju*). Some subdivisions of these bureaux were located within the palace, such as the cloisonné enamel, gold and silver workshops, and the Orchard Factory (*Guoyuan chang*). Other manufacturers were located in far-flung places, such as the imperial porcelain factory at Jingdezhen in Jiangxi and the textile-weaving centres south of the Yangtze River.

TEXTILES

Imperial textile production centres were located in the Yangtze Delta cities of Suzhou, Wuxi, Huzhou and Songjiang in Jiangsu province and Hangzhou in Zhejiang province. There was also a silk workshop in Beijing, which wove satins and tabbies for imperial use, and a workshop in the northeast corner of the palace compound, which made religious offering and presentation silks.[41] The scale of these workshops was impressive. The Nanjing weaving and dyeing bureau had 300 looms and 3,000 workers, with an additional workshop for ceremonial robes that had 40 looms and 1,200 staff.[42] Courts also needed soft furnishings and items to bestow as gifts (fig. 63). Exquisite quality embroideries were in addition made for court temples, including devotional images, monastic robes and temple hangings.

Thick, tightly woven wool carpets were imported from the 'Western Barbarian Regions' (*Xi fan*, meaning regions, such as Hormuz in the Persian Gulf), with never-fading red and green colours. These are also described by Ma Huan, author of an account of the Ming maritime expeditions, as 'clipped velvet blankets from the West'.[43] Other foreign textiles were imported, such as a tightly woven woollen fabric called *Sa hai la*, as thick as a blanket, made on a loom up to a metre wide. Cheaper versions were produced in Bengal and Gansu (China) on narrower looms.[44] Fluffy, velvet-like fabrics suitable for bed coverlets and clothes were imported from the south and west, and also brought from Yunnan. Sadly, textiles of this period survive in only tiny quantities.

CLOISONNÉ ENAMEL WARE

The early Ming writer Cao Zhao (fl. 1387–1399) opined in *The Essential Criteria of Antiquities* (*Gegu yaolun*), first published in 1388, that 'ware from the Devil's Country' made of copper and decorated in five colours, was 'appropriate for use in a woman's apartment, and would be quite out of place in a scholar's studio …'.[45] This has often been taken as evidence that the manufacture of Chinese cloisonné enamelled wares already existed in the Hongwu or even Yuan period. However, the words used suggest that they were imported goods. No single object or archaeological evidence, and no illustration in a book or painting, has been discovered to date to support convincingly the idea of fourteenth-century Chinese cloisonné.[46]

Other evidence, including surviving pieces with reign marks, points to Chinese cloisonné being a courtly invention of the early fifteenth century made exclusively

FIG. 63
Silk brocade

This silk is woven with a complicated geometric and floral design relating to western Asian metalwork and carpets, and to patterns painted on ornamental Chinese ceilings. The colour combinations are also found on early fifteenth-century lacquers. The complicated weave and large size of loom needed to produce such a silk, together with its high quality and the lavish use of gold thread, indicates that it was made under court orders. Very few silk brocades of this type survive. They were possibly woven as presentation goods between courts. In this instance, the silk may have been presented to a Tibetan dignitary. Known as lampas weave textiles, they may have been made as throne covers: similar coverings can be seen on the dais of seated *luohan* figures and in the portraits of high-ranking Tibetan priests. Textiles such as this were also presented to the Ashikaga court (1336–1573) in Japan and part of a similar textile that is now in a private collection was owned by Tokugawa Ieyasu (1546–1616).

Brocade silk and gold
Yongle period, 1403–1424
China
h (incl. tassels) 295 cm; max. w 193 cm
Private Collection

FIG. 64
Cloisonné jar and cover

Ming emperors ordered brightly coloured objects like this jar and cover to decorate the vast halls of their palaces. According to two inscriptions under the rim on either side, the jar was made under eunuch supervision in the Directorate of Imperial Accoutrements (*Yuyongjian*) for the Xuande emperor (1426–1435). The jar is decorated with magnificent dragons, which were symbolic of the emperor. Only one other cloissoné jar of this type survives, but the form is found in imperial porcelains made at Jingdezhen. Cloisonné manufacture demanded a sophisticated understanding of the different melting points of a range of coloured glasses. After the metal body was made, these liquid glasses were filled into cells (cloisons) formed by metal wires to create the final design.

Metal with cloisonné enamels
Xuande mark and period, 1426–1435
Beijing
h 62 cm, w 55.9 cm
British Museum, London 1957,0501.1

FIG. 65

Gold ewer with semi-precious stones

This gold vessel is incised with five-clawed dragons and festooned in semi-precious stones in raised settings. The supply of gold and precious gems was controlled by the imperial court in the early Ming period, so although we do not know which tomb this came from we can assume it was made for a member of the imperial family. The five-clawed dragon is also a common imperial emblem. However, decorating gold vessels with colourful precious stones has a long history in China and was particularly fashionable in the Tang dynasty (618–906).

Gold with engraved design; semi-precious stones
Xuande period, 1426–1435
Nanjing or Beijing
h 21.7 cm, w 20.8 cm
Philadelphia Museum of Art, purchased with the John T. Morris Fund,
1950 (1950-118-1)

FIG. 66

Gold basin with semi-precious stones

Like the ewer above, this gold basin is incised with the imperial emblem of the five-clawed dragon.

Gold with engraved design; semi-precious stones
Xuande period, 1426–1435
Nanjing or Beijing
h 7.1 cm, diam. 25.9 cm
Philadelphia Museum of Art, purchased with museum funds
1950 (1950-74.1)

FIG. 67

Gold basin

In 2001 archaeologists excavated this solid gold basin from the joint tomb of Zhu Zhanji, Prince Zhuang of Liang, and his wife, the Lady Wei. The prince may have washed himself using water in this very basin, which perhaps originally fitted into a wooden or lacquered wood stand. Such stands are found in miniature in the tomb of Zhu Tan, Prince Huang of Lu, in Shandong (see fig. 92). Similar gold basins were produced for the court over a long period and are found in imperial tombs, such as the later Ming tomb, *Ding Ling*, outside Beijing, which belonged to the Wanli emperor (1573–1620). Goldsmiths made the basin by hammering the metal into shape. Gold supply was controlled by the court and gold vessels are mostly found in the tombs of the nobility or their closest supporters.

Gold
c. 1424–41
Nanjing
h 7.5 cm, diam. 41 cm
Hubei Provincial Museum, excavated from the tomb of Zhu Zhanji, Prince Zhuang of Liang, and of Lady Wei at Zhongxiang, Hubei province

FIG. 68

Porcelain stem cup with hidden dragon design on a copper-red ground

Considerable quantities of underglaze red wares dating to the later part of the Yongle era have been found at Jingdezhen. They are most frequently decorated with the dragon-and-cloud motif. The surviving forms with this pattern are restricted to bowls, dishes, stem cups and small ewers. From the Yongle era onwards, the dragon was adopted as an imperial symbol. The dragon's most important function was to be in command of the waters – including rain and the water supply – literally having the power to destroy whole populations through flooding or drought. The dragons have cobalt-blue eyes; inside the cup is a secret design of incised dragons, which can only be seen when raised to the light.

Porcelain with incised decoration and underglaze copper-red
Yongle period, 1403–1424
Jingdezhen, Jiangxi province
h 9.0 cm, d 15.0 cm
British Museum, London 1968,0423.2

for palace and court temple use (fig. 64).[47] Decorative schemes were derived from a limited and tightly controlled courtly repertoire and palette, perhaps supplied through pattern books and supplied by supervisors. Later on in the Ming and Qing a much wider variety of styles was adopted. In his 1456 update of Cao Zhao's text Wang Zuo wrote: 'Nowadays some men from Yunnan in the capital make wine cups [in that technique] which is commonly known as inlay work from the "Devil's lands"(*Guiguo qian*). The pieces produced for the Imperial Palace are delicate, sparkling and lovely!'[48] This may refer to cloisonné, but as cloisonné may dazzle but could not be said to sparkle it is more likely that it refers to gold vessels (which do glisten) with inlaid jewels (figs 65 and 66). Cloisonné objects produced for the palace shared their shapes and decorative schemes with some porcelains made at Jingdezhen in Jiangxi province. Their colour scheme may also be found among imperial, silk book covers.[49]

PORCELAIN

While the scale of palace cloisonné production was very limited, that at Jingdezhen was unprecedented. The Ministry of Works controlled production for courts at Jingdezhen in the early fifteenth century, and by 1402 there were twelve kilns under imperial supervision. These factories divided labour tasks to increase efficiency – preparing the clay, forming the objects, decorating, firing, finishing, packing and distributing them. Enormous piles of sherds have been unearthed at the imperial kiln sites at Jingdezhen from the Yongle, Xuande and even Zhengtong eras, testifying to a far larger scale of production than in the Yuan dynasty.[50] This supports the much quoted textual evidence of orders for porcelain, including in 1433 an order for 443,500 porcelains with

FIG. 69

Stem bowl with dragons

By the Xuande reign, when this stem bowl was made, porcelain production was impressive in both scale and organization. Potters incorporated all the latest porcelain technology when making this stem bowl. It also included a dragon pattern inside that is only visible when held to the light.

Porcelain with incised decoration and underglaze cobalt-blue and copper-red
Xuande mark and period, 1426–1435
Jingdezhen, Jiangxi province
h 10.5 cm, diam. 15.2 cm
Sir Percival David Collection, PDF A626

FIG. 70

Porcelain stem cup, gold cover and silver stand

This covered porcelain stem cup and stand would have been a gift from the emperor. Such imperial gifts ensured a certain consistency in the appearance of the furnishings in regional courts. The cup, which has a design of an underglaze blue five-clawed dragon flying through the clouds and chasing a flaming pearl, was buried with Prince Zhuang of Liang. It is an extremely important piece, having as it does both a gold cover and a silver stand. Before its discovery, such sets were only known in early fifteenth-century paintings. The gold

cover is decorated with the same design of dragons pursuing flaming pearls, both incised on the rim and in relief. It has an inscription on the underside rim: 'This gold cover for a stem-cup [*zhong* 鍾] was made in the second year of Zhengtong era [1437] in the [Eunuch-supervised] Palace Office [*Chengfeng si*]. It weighs four liang and nine qian' (承奉司正統二年造金鍾蓋四兩九錢. There are ten *qian* in one *liang*, which is usually translated as ounces. The silver stand has survived burial less well, but is also ornamented with dragons.

Stem cup: porcelain with underglaze cobalt-blue decoration; stand: silver; cover: gold
Stem cup: 1426–35; silver stand c. 1426–35; gold cover: dated 1437
Stem cup: Jingdezhen, Jiangxi province; gold cover: Beijing; silver stand: probably Beijing
Overall h 19.3 cm
Hubei Provincial Museum, excavated from the tomb of Zhu Zhanji, Prince Zhuang of Liang, and of Lady Wei at Zhongxiang, Hubei province

FIG. 71

**Group of blue-and-white
wine vessels**

Regional porcelain production was
supervised by staff sent from the central
court. In contrast with the relatively freely
painted motifs of the preceding Yuan
dynasty, blue-and-white designs of the
Yongle era follow court painting styles
more closely and are standardized. Potters
at Jingdezhen working at the imperial
kilns made a series of technical advances
in the Yongle era. They enhanced the
combination of body materials, using a clay
with a higher aluminium content so that
they could produce finer porcelains, which
could withstand a higher-temperature
firing. Kiln workers also improved their
preparation of the imported cobalt and
local glaze materials. These technical
advances resulted in lighter, whiter,
glossier glazes than in the Yuan period.
Skilled porcelain decorators created
painterly motifs, using varied strengths of
blue pigment and washes to imitate the
shading of court painting styles found in
small-format paintings such as fans or
album leaves.

Porcelain with underglaze cobalt-blue
Yongle period, 1403–1424
Jingdezhen, Jiangxi province
bottle: h 33.5 cm; moon flask: h 30.8 cm;
meiping: h 33.2 cm
Sir Percival David Collection, PDF A614 (bottle);
PDF A612 (moon flask); British Museum,
London 1972,0621.1 (*meiping*)

dragon and phoenix designs, as recorded in the Collected Statutes of the Great
Ming (*Da Ming hui dian*) published in 1509.

Early fifteenth-century imperial ceramics were expensive to produce and
consumed extensive resources – vast quantities of timber were used to fuel the high-
temperature kilns and hundreds of labourers were required to prepare the clay and
glaze to form, decorate, fire and transport the vessels. Certain vessels were fired in
individual saggars (firing boxes), which could only be used once before they vitrified,
no longer allowing the vital air to circulate as part of the firing process.

Chemical analysis has shown that both the body and glaze of Yongle-era
imperial porcelains are different from earlier wares and mark an outstanding
technological achievement.[51] This highlights the Yongle era as a 'second founding'
of the Ming dynasty. Potters developed new recipes for the clay bodies so that the
porcelain could be made thinner, and new glazes so that the white porcelain would
appear purer and shinier than ever before. Very little was invented in ceramic
technology after the Yongle era until the eighteenth century, and many of the colour
combinations associated with polychrome decoration of the sixteenth century were
in fact already in use in the early fifteenth.

The metal cobalt is central to the production of blue-and-white porcelain.
Chemical analysis proves that cobalt used in the imperial kilns of the Yongle, Xuande
and Zhengtong reigns was imported from Iran and gives a stronger blue colour than
local Chinese cobalt, although local cobalt was sometimes mixed in. It could also
be manipulated to shade decoration on porcelain and thus to re-create motifs from
court paintings (fig. 71). Between 1400 and 1450 the imperial courts commissioned
a far wider range of shapes, from tiny bird feeders (fig. 142) or cricket cages of the
Xuande era to the largest vats ever discovered at Jingdezhen made in the Zhengtong
reign.[52] Archaeologists found pieces of huge broken vats in a channel full of sherds
outside the west wall of the Ming imperial porcelain factory. When whole, one vat
would have measured 88.8 cm in diameter and 75 cm in height.[53] At least twenty
similar vats on this impressive scale have been reconstructed.

The imperial court began ordering porcelain objects made in innovative
colour schemes (red and green, yellow and red, green and white), using new shapes.
Orders for porcelain were court-directed, with much more central control than
during the Yuan dynasty, yet there is some continuity with Yuan crafts. During the
Yongle and Xuande eras, through most of the material culture we see an improvement
in the quality of production standards, an increased conformity of design of goods
made for the courts, and great developments in technologies of production. There
were more patterns, forms and colour combinations but decoration conformed to
designs supplied by the court, possibly through printed models. This can be seen
particularly in the designs for cups with stems (figs 68–70). Despite their fragility,
considerable numbers of porcelain eating and drinking vessels survive, some from
tombs and some from continuous preservation above ground, as well as a smaller
number of the gold and silver vessels on which they were modelled.

Regional court tombs reveal some imperial-quality ceramics, which are likely to have been presented by the emperor and made to imperial order at Jingdezhen. However, other products of Jingdezhen found in the regional tombs do not measure up to the levels of quality demanded by the supervisors to supply the emperor in the period 1403–35. The three covered *meiping* vases with underglaze blue patterns of flowers and foliage in the tomb of Prince Zhuang of Liang and his wife Lady Wei were most likely supplied later in the period 1436–41 when top-quality wares were not available. Inferior-quality porcelains are known from several dated tombs of people outside the imperial clan.[54]

Outward-looking policies in the period 1400–50 brought trade and diplomatic contacts with courts across Eurasia. This interaction may have stimulated a desire to include some new 'foreign' shapes and designs using traditional Chinese materials. It is difficult to gauge how much the Mongol court left behind when they retreated from Beijing, but the distinctive blue-and-white porcelains in the form of Egyptian, Syrian

FIG. 72

Blue-and-white porcelain ewer

Ewers like this were made in the imperial porcelain factory at Jingdezhen in the Yongle era. Ewers with varying decoration, but of the same form, were excavated in the Yongle strata at Dongmentou, Zhushan, in 1994. Although made in the imperial factory for court use in China, ewers of this type were also exported, probably as diplomatic gifts. Two examples are in the collection of the Ardebil Shrine, Iran. The form is taken from contemporary early Ming gold examples. We know from the diary of an artist who was part of a Timurid embassy to the court of the Yongle emperor that the emperor enjoyed 'Yellow Wine' (*Huang jiu*). Other wines included clear rice wine and grape wine.

Porcelain with underglaze blue decoration
Yongle period, 1403–1424
Jingdezhen, Jiangxi province
h 29.2 cm, w (from spout to handle) 24.1 cm
British Museum, London, donated by Sir Augustus Wollaston Franks in 1876, Franks.151

FIG. 73

Gold ewer

This gold ewer is inscribed on the bottom with its date, place of manufacture and weight: 'Made by the Jewellery Service during the first month of the first year of the Hongxi reign [1425], 85 per cent pure gold, [weighing] 23 *liang*. The cover, spout and chain are all welded on the outside [with gold weighing] one *fen*.' (銀作局洪熙元年正月內成造捌成伍色金貳拾參兩蓋嘴攀索全外焊壹分). The Jewellery Service was responsible for producing imperial precious metal works within the palace in Nanjing. This vessel may have been used as a decanter for pouring wine, as a fifteenth-century painting showing imperial wine vessels on a table includes a similar gold decanter resting on a gold saucer.

Gold
Dated 1425
Nanjing
h 26.2 cm, w 15.2; cm, weight 868 g
Hubei Provincial Museum, excavated from the tomb of Zhu Zhanji, Prince Zhuang of Liang, and of Lady Wei at Zhongxiang, Hubei province

FIG. 74

Gold flask incised with dragons among clouds

This is the largest early Ming gold flask to survive today. Many gold vessels were perhaps melted down by later generations, as their forms fell out of fashion, or possibly buried in tombs that have not yet been discovered. The style of engraving on this flask is very similar to that on a bottle in the Capital Museum, Beijing, which has a phoenix design and is dated 1434. Gold workers at the imperial court incised this flask with an imperial dragon pattern. The modelling of the vessel, particularly the cover and method of fitting it, relates closely to the ewers in Prince Zhuang of Liang's tomb dated 1424. The shape of the flask ultimately derives from Middle Eastern metalwork and was also reproduced in porcelain, but no porcelain covers for such flasks of this period survive, if they were ever made.

Gold, incised
c. 1420–35
Nanjing or Beijing
h 29 cm, w 21.7 cm, d 8.9 cm
Smithsonian American Art Museum, Washington
DC LTS1985.1.295.1

FIG. 75

Silver ewer

Archaeologists excavated this silver ewer at the tomb of Zhu Zhanji, Prince Zhuang of Liang and his wife Lady Wei. In the early Ming more than 50 per cent of silver was mined in Yunnan. Although silver was less tightly controlled by the imperial court, the form of this vessel, which is replicated in gold in the same tomb, suggests that it, too, was a product of the *Yinzuoju* (Jewellery Service). Unlike gold, which never changes, silver tarnishes quickly; originally this ewer would have been bright and shiny.

Silver
c. 1425
Nanjing or Beijing
h 21.6 cm, diam. 7.6 cm
Hubei Provincial Museum, excavated from the tomb of Zhu Zhanji, Prince Zhuang of Liang, and of Lady Wei at Zhongxiang, Hubei province

and Central Asian metalwork and glass, which were commissioned by the Yongle and Xuande emperors, may have been based on objects already in China when the Yongle emperor was building his palace (fig. 77). In the same way that paintings from the Yuan imperial art collection (see Chapter 4, p.166) and Yuan imperial books were absorbed into the Ming court libraries, and important pieces of Yuan porcelain were placed in the tombs of high Ming officials, it is probable that Yuan court glass and metalwork were kept in the imperial collections. This would help to explain why the glass and metalwork models for the blue-and-white porcelain copies were earlier in date (see pp. 94–5).

Porcelains of the finest quality flowed into the imperial and regional courts from far away Jiangxi, but the town of Jingdezhen was not the only imperially patronized kiln site. Other regions supplied the courts with ceramics. Lavender and sky-blue glazed flower pots for cultivating colourful bulbs and small bushes were ordered from the northern province of Henan (fig. 84). These 'official Jun' wares have been found only in a Beijing palace context, where many remained throughout the later Ming and Qing dynasties.

FIG. 76

Flask inspired by a Middle Eastern shape

Both the Yongle (1403–1424) and Xuande (1426–1435) emperors sponsored important maritime trade and diplomatic missions to the Middle East. The form of this flask was not originally Chinese but inspired by a Middle Eastern shape, possibly that of an enamelled glass vessel. During both emperors' reigns, flasks in this large, heavy, bulbous form, but with variations in the decoration, were made at the imperial kilns at Zhushan in Jingdezhen. Archaeologists unearthed a flask similar to this one, with white dragons with incised details on blue waves, in 1994 at Dongmentou, Zhushan, Jingdezhen, from the Yongle strata. The imperial household either used such flasks as wine decanters or, more likely, because of their weight, as interior ornaments. They also traded them or gave them as gifts, as evidenced by similar flasks found in the Topkapi Palace in Turkey and in the Ardabil Shrine in Iran.

Porcelain with underglaze blue decoration
Yongle period, 1403–1424
Jingdezhen, Jiangxi province
h 44.6 cm
Sir Percival David Collection, PDF 662

FIG. 77

Four gourd-shaped flasks

An innovation of the Yongle era (1403–1424), these flasks were made for a period of just thirty years before falling out of fashion. They are crafted in a Chinese auspicious gourd form with side handles, but with Middle Eastern kaleidoscopic patterns derived from textiles, glass or metalwork, painted in shades of cobalt-blue, on the front and back. Yongle examples have no reign mark but the later examples from the Xuande reign (1426–1435) do. Porcelain was mass-produced for court use, using specific high-quality clays and raw materials reserved for imperial production. In the Yuan era (1279–1368), this mass production gave rise to hundreds of objects in the same form, but with differences in each individual decorative design: no two pieces are exactly the same. By contrast, the Yongle and Xuande manufacture was far more standardized, with only tiny variations in the finished product, suggesting a far greater control of the factories by the court. Patterns on these vessels were copied from designs sent by officials of the *Gong bu* ('Ministry of Works').

Porcelain with underglaze cobalt-blue decoration
Yongle and Xuande periods, 1403–1435
Jingdezhen, Jiangxi province
h c. 25.7–33 cm
(opposite) Victoria and Albert Museum, London V&A 554-1878;
(below) Sir Percival David Collection, PDF 674; British Museum,
London, bequeathed by Mrs Walter Sedgwick, 1968,0422.29;
Sir Percival David Collection, PDF 600

FIG. 78
Blue-and-white Chinese porcelain stand and Egyptian brass stand

The form and decoration of this porcelain stand for a tray or bowl was modelled after a silver-inlaid brass stand such as the one pictured here, made in Mamluk Egypt around 1300–50 and inscribed with the name and titles of the sultan Muhammad ibn Qalaun (r. 1293–1341). The fact that the porcelain stand is so much smaller may suggest that the design was copied from a drawing rather than from the original metalwork. However, the consistency of decoration and accurate placement of the roundels indicate that the designer knew the original metal stand well. Very often the inscriptions on such Chinese stands are illegible, written presumably by a porcelain decorator who was unable to read the original Arabic inscription that he was copying, and commissioned by an emperor for whom legibility was a secondary concern to aesthetics.

Sherds of blue-and-white stands of this type, with brighter cobalt-blue decoration, were unearthed at Dong, Zhushan in 1993. One of these has a Xuande imperial reign mark. We know that many of the designs for porcelains of Middle Eastern form or decoration were introduced in the Yongle era and that this practice continued into the Xuande.

Porcelain stand with underglaze cobalt-blue decoration
Yongle period, 1403–1424
Jingdezhen, Jiangxi province
h 17.0 cm, diam. 17.2 cm
British Museum, London, Brooke Sewell Bequest, 1966,1215.1

Brass stand inlaid with gold and silver
1300–50
Egypt
h 24.5 cm, diam. 23 cm
British Museum, London 1897.0510.1

FIG. 79
Blue-and-white Chinese porcelain candlestick and Iranian brass candlestick

Relatively large numbers of Chinese blue-and-white porcelain copies of Middle Eastern inlaid brass metalwork survive. As we do not find them in large quantities in the Middle East and Central Asia, we must suppose that they were ordered from the imperial factory at Jingdezhen to ornament the imperial palace. Sometimes their function was adopted in China, as is the case with this vessel that is called a candlestick in the Middle East, but fitted with a metal frame for supporting stick incense in China.

Porcelain candlestick with underglaze cobalt-blue
Yongle period, 1403–1424
Jingdezhen, Jiangxi province
h 29.8 cm, diam. 21.8 cm
Shanghai Museum

Brass candlestick
1300–50
West Iran
h 23.7 cm, max w 21.2 cm
Metropolitan Museum of Art, New York. Edward C. Moore Collection. Bequest of Edward C Moore, 1891 (91.1.580)

FIG. 80
Porcelain and brass basins

Similar shapes were created in both the Yongle and Xuande eras, during the periods of court patronage of the voyages to the Middle East and east African coast. These expeditions were designed to spread the influence of the Ming court and to exchange tribute goods. Perhaps the extension of trading networks created a fashion for these shapes at court, though the vessels themselves may well have been left behind by the Mongol Yuan rulers and known by the Yongle emperor since he was first sent to Beijing as a prince.

Porcelain basin with underglaze cobalt-blue decoration
Yongle period, 1403–1424
Jingdezhen, Jiangxi province
h 12.2 cm, diam. 26.5 cm
Private Collection

Brass basin engraved and inlaid with silver and black compound
c. 1321–63
Egypt orSyria
h 21.6 cm, diam. 46.5 cm
Metropolitan Museum of Art, New York. Bequest of Edward C. Moore, 1891 (91.1.589)

FIG. 81

Chinese porcelain pen box and Egyptian or Syrian brass pen box

This Chinese pen box adopts the Middle Eastern form externally, while inside it is decorated with the traditional Chinese motif of the 'Three Friends of Winter': plum blossom, bamboo and pine. More rounded forms of these boxes continued to be made in inlaid metalwork in Central Asia in the early fifteenth century. The blue-and-white porcelain versions of Middle Eastern metalwork forms were made for the Yongle emperor's court.

Porcelain pen box with underglaze cobalt-blue decoration
Yongle period, 1403–1424
Jingdezhen, Jiangxi province
h 7.2 cm, w 32 cm, d 7.8 cm
Sir Percival David Collection, PDF A629

Inlaid brass pen box
1300–50
Egypt or Syria
l 30.7 cm
British Museum, London, bequeathed by William Burges, 1881,0802.20

FIG. 82

Chinese porcelain tankard and Central Asian jade tankard

The shape of this porcelain vessel is modelled after a form found in Near Eastern metalwork and jade. The ridging around the neck suggests that the porcelain is imitating a tankard made from sheet metal, possibly silver, in which the shape would be strengthened by such a thickened section around the neck. Such jade tankards, possibly also imitating earlier metalwork, are known to have belonged to the Timurid ruler Ulugh Beg (r. 1394–1449).

Porcelain tankard with underglaze cobalt-blue decoration
1403–24
Jingdezhen, Jiangxi province
h 14 cm, w 14.2 cm
British Museum, London, donated by E.B. Havell, 1950,0403.1

Jade tankard
1400–1500
Central Asia
h 10 cm, d 9.6 cm
British Museum, London, bequeathed by Oscar Charles Raphael, 1945,1017.257

FIG. 83

Chinese porcelain flask and Syrian glass flask

This high-quality Chinese porcelain flask is dated to the Yongle era by comparison with a similar example that was excavated in 1994 from one of the Yongle strata at Dongmentou, Zhushan, Jingdezhen. The form is an adaptation of a much earlier foreign vessel. Leather bags or 'pilgrim bottles' inspired ceramic replicas in the Eastern Han (25–220) and Tang (618–906) periods. Such forms were also fashioned in glass in the Middle East and the shape was additionally made in low-fired ceramics in Syria.

Lychee trees are evergreen and in spring bear tiny flowers (visible here), followed shortly after by the lumpy red-skinned fruits. Wine made from lychee fruit was drunk in southern China in the Ming period. As this flask was made to present and contain wine, it is possible that it held lychee wine.

Porcelain with underglaze cobalt-blue decoration
Yongle period, 1403–1424
Jingdezhen, Jiangxi province
h 25 cm, w 22 cm, d 12 cm
British Museum, London, bequeathed by Henry J Oppenheim, 1947,0712.325

Polychrome enamel painted glass
1300–50
Syria
h 23 cm, w 23 cm, d 16.2 cm
British Museum, London, bequeathed by Felix Slade, 1869,0120.3

They were not exported or buried in tombs. Their method of manufacture in two-part moulds, which sandwiched the clay between them, and the composition of their glazes, were innovations of this period, although the kilns themselves had made purple and blue wares for hundreds of years previously.[55] These purple flower pots are included in a scroll painting, which depicts the emperor enjoying the four seasons within the imperial palace (fig. 85).

Watery-green serving dishes were brought to the imperial court from the Longquan kilns in Zhejiang province (fig. 86) about 800 miles away. The early Ming imperial court had a significant impact on production at Longquan, where court-designed shapes and patterns were made using finer quality materials than those employed for exported wares, such as those seen in the Turiang (*c.* 1370–1400) or Longquan shipwrecks (*c.* 1424–1440), both of which sank in Malaysian waters, carrying cargoes of typical early Ming Longquan export wares.[56] Patterns were shared between the cloisonné makers and lacquer workers serving the imperial court, and potters at Jingdezhen and Longquan. Production significantly declined at Longquan after imperial patronage was withdrawn in the mid-fifteenth century and transferred exclusively to Jingdezhen.[57] Copies of Longquan stonewares were then made in porcelain at Jingdezhen and in stoneware at other southern Chinese and Southeast Asian kilns. Earlier celadons from Korea similar to Longquan wares were also collected at court in the early Ming. Those with blue-green glazes were highly regarded but those with inlay in slip were not so valuable.[58]

FIG. 84

Group of flower pots

The Yongle and Xuande emperors commissioned these flower pots, which were fired in Henan, to furnish the new palace in Beijing. Manufacturers added incised numbers 1 to 10 to the bases before glazing and firing, perhaps reflecting their sizes, with 1 being the largest and 10 the smallest. This helped to match draining basins to flower pots. The flower pots were made using double moulds – a new technology developed at the Henan kilns in the early fifteenth century. In common with imperial red-glazed porcelains of the early fifteenth century, these stoneware flower pots have a glaze that uses oxidized bronze as a copper source.

This type of flower pot has not been excavated from any tomb context in China and they are not found in archaeological contexts beyond China's borders. However, many survive with eighteenth-century inscriptions describing which part of the imperial palace they were used in. This suggests that they were made especially for the palace and remained there for several hundred years as part of the interior gardens.

Stoneware with blue, purple and green glazes
c. 1403–35
Juntai, Yuxian, Henan province
Max. h 17.4 cm
Sir Percival David Collection, PDF A11 and A49;
and British Museum, London, bequeathed by
Brenda Seligman, 1973,0726.237

FIG. 85 OVERLEAF

Anonymous, detail from 'Amusements in the Four Seasons' (*Siji shangwan tu* 四季賞玩圖)

In this autumnal scene the emperor is admiring chrysanthemums in the gardens of the imperial palace. In the foreground are plants growing in Jun flower pots.

Handscroll, ink and colours on silk
c. 1426–84
h 35 cm, w 780 cm
Private Collection

FIG. 86
Stoneware serving dish incised with peonies

Longquan in Zhejiang province was the third of the official state-controlled kilns in the early fifteenth century, together with Juntai in Henan and Jingdezhen in Jiangxi; all three kilns produced ceramics for official court orders. The decorative designs employed at Longquan and Jingdezhen during this period are remarkably similar, suggesting that the Yuan-era tradition of copying designs from sample books provided by the central court persisted, but was even more tightly controlled. Similar designs of peonies, buds and leaves were used for lacquer wares produced at court and blue-and-white porcelain. After the mid-fifteenth century, the court withdrew its patronage from the Longquan kilns and consequently the quality of the product made there declined. Such large dishes were very hard to fire without warping in the kiln and few survive today.

Stoneware with celadon glaze
Yongle period, 1403–1424
Longquan area, Zhejiang province
h 10 cm, diam. 63.5 cm
British Museum, London, bequeathed by Basil Gray,
1989,1016.1

FIG. 87
Carved red lacquer tray

Early Ming lacquer employs fine sculptural forms, often cut down to the wooded core of the object to add greater depth to the image. We can deduce from the Taipei and Beijing Palace Museum collections, and from the records of gifts made to the Ashikaga court of Japan by the Ming court between 1403 and 1424, that carved red lacquer was more popular than *qiangjin* (gold-decorated) or black lacquer for vessels made for court orders. Often the combination of flowering plants portrayed is botanically impossible, symbolizing imperial control over the seasons and geography of China.

Scholars have suggested that because carved lacquer takes such a long time to produce, some of the Yongle-marked pieces may have been made earlier, in the Hongwu reign (1368–1398). Unmarked Hongwu pieces may have been taken from storage and augmented with the Yongle reign name, incised with a fine tool and then sometimes filled in with gold. Very few pieces of this large size survive from the Yongle era.

Carved red lacquer on wood core
Yongle (1403–1424) and Xuande (1426–1435) marks,
probably made in the Hongwu period, 1368–1398
h 6.2 cm, diam. 54.3 cm
Ashmolean Museum, Oxford, purchased from
the Beurdeley Collection, 1981, EA1981.9

LACQUER

Lacquer ware is not unlike modern plastic in that it is light, durable and clean. Lacquer furniture in particular appears to have been more resistant to foreign influence. For a period of only about twenty years ending in 1436, the Orchard Factory (*Guoyuan chang*) was set up to the northwest of the palace in Beijing, in the area today called Lingjing hutong.[59] It was headed by Zhang Degang and Bao Liang from Jiaxing in Zhejiang province, and made use of lacquer workers from Yunnan and Sichuan.[60] In the palace workshop luxury imperial lacquer wares were exclusively produced, using lacquer sap specially transported to Beijing from southern China, since the tree cannot grow in northern China's climate.

Carved red lacquer was extremely labour intensive and time-consuming to produce. The sap was filtered and heat-treated, then applied with a brush in layers on to a wooden core. Each layer of varnish took up to twenty-four hours to dry and needed to be polished before the next layer could be applied. Each piece took perhaps a year to make, with some of the palace items having up to one hundred layers of lacquer. Red lacquer is coloured with cinnabar, a common ore of the mineral mercury. While red lacquer with gilded decoration appears to have been used for utilitarian containers, Buddhist sūtra covers (fig. 200), furniture and even swings (fig. 88), carved red lacquer was kept for palace use or for court-to-court diplomatic gifts (fig. 201). Pieces from the Hongwu reign were even rebranded using the Yongle or Xuande mark and either used or gifted.

FIG. 88

Detail of princesses playing on a gilded lacquer swing from anonymous, 'Amusements in the Four Seasons' (*Siji shangwan tu* 四季賞玩圖)

Unlike the official imperial portraits that were meant to be seen by the imperial family, this genre of painting of amusements within the imperial palace was produced in multiple versions and circulated among elite officials from the Xuande reign onwards. Images of little girls are very rarely seen.

Handscroll, ink and colours on silk
c. 1426–84
h 35 cm, w 780 cm
Private Collection

FIG. 89

Box with figures in a landscape

Paintings of the early Ming depict this type of large lacquer box being carried by eunuchs, containing food for imperial picnics. They were also used to present gifts of food.

Carved red lacquer on wood core
Yongle mark and period, 1403–1424
Probably *Guoyuan chang* (Orchard Lacquer Factory), Beijing
h 15.5 cm, diam. 37 cm
British Museum, London 1939,0621.1

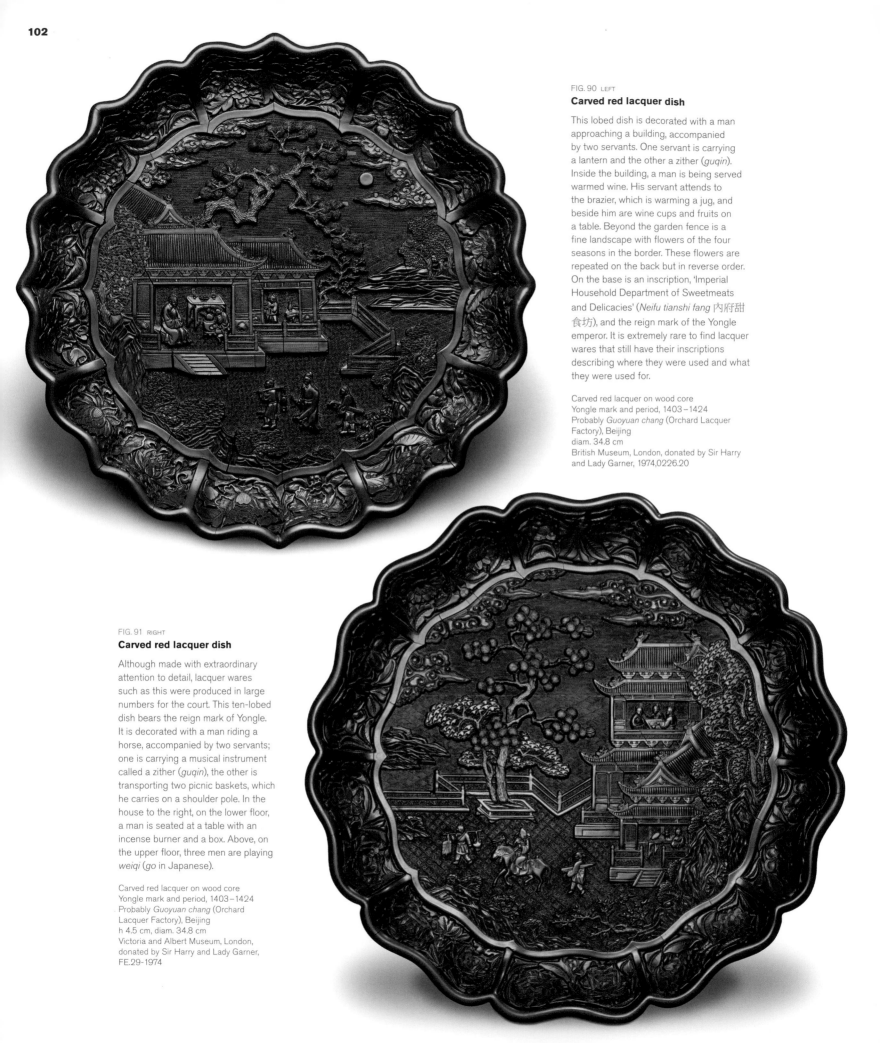

FIG. 90 LEFT

Carved red lacquer dish

This lobed dish is decorated with a man approaching a building, accompanied by two servants. One servant is carrying a lantern and the other a zither (*guqin*). Inside the building, a man is being served warmed wine. His servant attends to the brazier, which is warming a jug, and beside him are wine cups and fruits on a table. Beyond the garden fence is a fine landscape with flowers of the four seasons in the border. These flowers are repeated on the back but in reverse order. On the base is an inscription, 'Imperial Household Department of Sweetmeats and Delicacies' (*Neifu tianshi fang* 內府甜食坊), and the reign mark of the Yongle emperor. It is extremely rare to find lacquer wares that still have their inscriptions describing where they were used and what they were used for.

Carved red lacquer on wood core
Yongle mark and period, 1403–1424
Probably *Guoyuan chang* (Orchard Lacquer Factory), Beijing
diam. 34.8 cm
British Museum, London, donated by Sir Harry and Lady Garner, 1974,0226.20

FIG. 91 RIGHT

Carved red lacquer dish

Although made with extraordinary attention to detail, lacquer wares such as this were produced in large numbers for the court. This ten-lobed dish bears the reign mark of Yongle. It is decorated with a man riding a horse, accompanied by two servants; one is carrying a musical instrument called a zither (*guqin*), the other is transporting two picnic baskets, which he carries on a shoulder pole. In the house to the right, on the lower floor, a man is seated at a table with an incense burner and a box. Above, on the upper floor, three men are playing *weiqi* (*go* in Japanese).

Carved red lacquer on wood core
Yongle mark and period, 1403–1424
Probably *Guoyuan chang* (Orchard Lacquer Factory), Beijing
h 4.5 cm, diam. 34.8 cm
Victoria and Albert Museum, London, donated by Sir Harry and Lady Garner, FE.29-1974

FURNITURE

Most early Ming court furniture was portable and could even be set up outdoors (figs 94 and 97). The court was frequently on the move on expeditions to the new capital in Beijing, or on campaigns against Mongol leaders. One of the most remarkable archaeological discoveries from this period is the furniture excavated from the Prince of Lu's tomb in Shandong. This encompasses wooden tables inlaid with coloured stone tops (fig. 96), as well as a group of miniature model furniture, including a bed with pillows and mattress, wash stands with towels, and storage boxes (fig. 92). This furniture gives a good idea of how the prince slept, ate and bathed.

These models hint at the luxuriousness of the real materials, and finds in other regional tombs firmly prove it, such as the gold wash basin from the tomb of Prince Zhuang of Liang (fig. 67) or jewel-covered pillow ends from an unknown prince's tomb (fig. 98). Soft furnishings from this period have, on the whole, not survived China's climate, but we can reconstruct their appearance through paintings and some rare examples (fig. 63).

FIG. 92
Group of model tomb furniture

This selection of model furniture comes from the tomb of Zhu Tan (1370–1389), Prince of Lu. Model furniture, made to scale, is an extremely rare find in the early Ming fourteenth and fifteenth centuries; it is more common in later Ming tombs of the sixteenth and seventeenth centuries. From these models we can reconstruct an image of the prince's sleeping quarters, his utensils for personal ablutions and dining space equipment. The details of the bed are executed perfectly, such as the rolled bamboo mat for summertime coolness, the soft silk pillow and the thick padded silk mattress. Practical equipment included this wash basin set on a stand and a towel rack with original white fine-cotton towel. The chest has bronze fittings, and traces of its painted lacquer and gold decoration remain. The tomb also included different varieties of wooden tables and chairs, as well as storehouses for grain and poultry, and woven baskets for storage.

Wood, silk, cotton, bronze, bamboo, lacquer and gilding
c. 1380–89
Shandong
Bed frame: h 34 cm, w 19.5cm, l 33.8 cm
Towel rail: h 23 cm, w of bar 15.5 cm, l of towel 55 cm
Wash basin: diam. of mouth 9.7 cm, diam. of base 8.3 cm, h 4.5 m; stand: h 12.4 cm, w 10.8 cm
Chest: l 14.2 cm, w 8.8 cm, h 7.8 cm; stand: l 18.7 cm, w 10.2 cm, h 10.4 cm
Shandong Museum, excavated from the tomb of Zhu Tan, Prince Huang of Lu at Yanzhou, Shandong province

FIG. 93
Low table

The original red lacquer from the top surface has become worn through use. The red lacquer surface of the legs and frame is decorated with fine etched lines filled with gold leaf or powdered gold to reveal a pattern of scrolling lotus and foliage. Supporting struts on both of the long sides were painted white, then pink, before being gilded. Portable tables such as this appear in both Chinese and Middle Eastern paintings of the period. Producing this kind of decorated lacquer was cheaper and less time-consuming than carved lacquer wares, which could take up to a year to make.

Wood with red lacquer and gilding
c. 1400–50
China
h 28.3 cm, w 94 cm, d 41.2 cm
Victoria and Albert Museum, London,
purchased with the assistance of The Art Fund,
V&A FE.1913-1993

FIG. 94
Portable chest of drawers

This wooden cabinet is decorated in coloured lacquers with imperial motifs of dragons and phoenixes, even on the gilded-bronze lock at the top. The extraordinarily rich colour palette used to decorate this unique piece is reminiscent of that used to dye the silk threads woven into early fifteenth-century imperial textiles. The front panel can be removed to reveal four small drawers at the top, three medium-sized drawers below, two in the next layer and one large drawer at the bottom. The chest of drawers has been made portable by the addition of carrying handles either side. The early Ming court was regularly on the move, whether between the cities of Beijing and Nanjing, or following the emperor as he made military advances against the Mongols in the north.

Incised multi-coloured lacquer and gold on wood core
Xuande period, 1426–1435
Beijing
h 48 cm, w 56.5 cm, d 42 cm
Victoria and Albert Museum, London,
FE.7-1973

FIG. 95

Box with gold dragon design

Zhu Tan was buried with this *qiangjin* (gold-decorated) lacquer box, which was made to contain a jade tablet (*hu*), an emblem of imperial authority. From studying excavated and heirloom examples, and paintings and murals, we know that *qiangjin* lacquer was mostly used for furniture and containers. This method of decorating lacquer with incised lines filled with gold powder or gold leaf was first used in the thirteenth century, as evidenced by a group of vessels excavated in Wujin, Jiangsu province. The technique was used to ornament a range of different court boxes for family records, religious documents, jade tallies and gifts. Similar boxes were included in other princely burials, such as that of the Crown Prince of Shu.

Red lacquer, incised and gilded on wood core
c. 1370–89
South China
h 7.2 cm, w 36.2 cm, d 10.9 cm
Shandong Museum, excavated from the tomb of Zhu Tan,
Prince Huang of Lu at Yanzhou, Shandong province

FIG. 96

Table with stone top

Four tables of this type were excavated from the tomb of Zhu Tan, Prince Huang of Lu. They were positioned in the front chamber of the tomb and covered with some of the prince's treasures. Consequently, when the tomb flooded these precious objects were saved. These tables demonstrated the cosmopolitan tastes at provincial courts. Local Shandong stone is inlaid at the top, but the lacquer for the wood was imported from southern China. Six-hundred-year-old full-size tables are unknown in any other tomb found to date in China.

Lacquered wood with stone top
c. 1389
China
h 94 cm, w 110 cm, d 71.5 cm
Shandong Museum, excavated from the tomb of Zhu Tan, Prince Huang of Lu at Yanzhou, Shandong province

Table with drawers

FIG. 97

LACQUER is the sap or resin collected from the trunk of the Chinese lacquer tree (*Toxicodendron vernicifluum*, or formerly *rhus verniciflua*). The raw sap is toxic and contact with it can cause extreme dermatitis. The sap is filtered and heat-treated, then applied with a brush in layers on to a wooden core covered with textile. Red lacquer is coloured with cinnabar, a common ore of the mineral mercury. Each layer of varnish took up to twenty-four hours to dry. A carved red lacquer object such as this has up to one hundred layers of lacquer. After carving, the edges of the design were polished using a powder possibly of bone, horn or clay.

This carved red lacquer table was created for the imperial palace in the reign of the Xuande emperor. On the top, within a lobed panel, has been carved a five-clawed dragon ascending and a phoenix descending on a ground of lotuses with ornamental rocks at the bottom. The dragon symbolizes the emperor and the phoenix the empress. Within the four corners, simpler phoenixes are depicted, with an outer band of dragons and phoenixes all against a ground of lotuses. The three drawer-fronts are decorated with a rising dragon and descending phoenix against a ground of lotuses and foliage. The legs are carved with peonies, chrysanthemum and prunus, completing the flowers of the four seasons. The underside of the table is lacquered black, while the drawers are lacquered red inside and black outside. It bears an incised six-character Xuande mark with traces of gold leaf and lacquer.

As part of the early Ming tax system, about five thousand lacquer workers from southern China went to court for four years at a time to work in the imperial lacquer workshops, where this table was made. It is the world's only surviving piece of lacquer furniture made in the *Guoyuan chang* (Orchard Factory), the imperial lacquer factory in Beijing. This workshop was established with Zhang Degang as its head. He was a native of Xitang, Jiaxing, Zhejiang province. Another man from Jiaxing, Bao Liang, also worked for the Xuande court in the Beijing lacquer factory.

Carved red lacquer on wooden core; gilded-bronze
drawer pulls and escutcheons
Xuande mark and period, 1426–1435
Beijing
h 79.2 cm, w 119.5 cm, d 84.5 cm
Victoria and Albert Museum, London, FE.6:1 to 4-1973

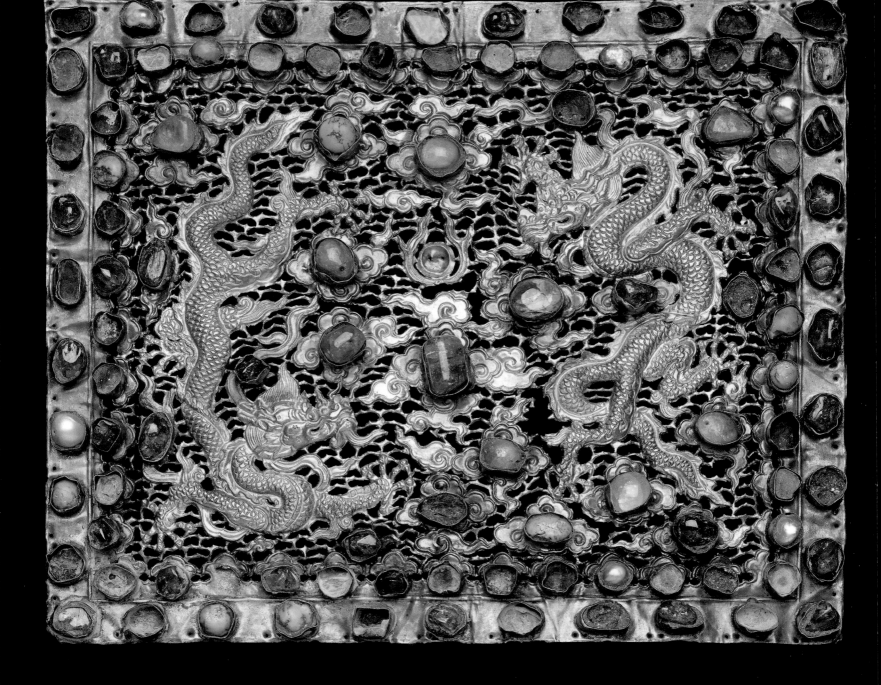

FIG. 98

Pair of gold pillow ends inlaid with semi-precious stones

These pillow ends are decorated with two gold dragons and a flaming pearl among clouds. Both plaques are pierced around the edge for attaching to a textile pillow. They are worked in relief with chased detail and openwork, and are inlaid with semi-precious stones. The gems were imported from south Asia. Many jewels, hairpins and belts, decorated in this style of setting jewels into gold, were excavated from the Hubei tomb of Prince Zhuang of Liang (1411–1441) and from other princely tombs, such as that of Prince Huang of Lu (1370–1389). As the use of these

materials was restricted through sumptuary laws, it is likely that this pillow was made for a member of the early Ming imperial family.

Gold, rubies, turquoise and other precious and semi-precious stones
Xuande period, 1426–1435
Beijing or Nanjing
h 14.47 cm, w 18 cm each
British Museum, London 1949,1213.1 and 2

FIG. 99
Gold ladle

Workers in the imperial Jewellery Service made this gold ladle and added its twenty-character inscription, which reads: 'Made by the Jewellery Service during the first month of the first year of the Hongxi reign [1424], from 85 per cent pure gold, [weighing] two *liang*, five *qian*' (銀作局洪熙元年正月內造捌成伍色金兩伍錢). The ladle was excavated at the tomb of Prince Zhuang of Liang outside Zhongxiang in Hubei province, and was found alongside a strainer and a pair of chopsticks on a silver tray. The Hongxi emperor was Prince Zhuang of Liang's father, and the prince gained his official title in 1424.

Gold
Dated 1424
Nanjing
l 26 cm, weight 94.2 g
Hubei Provincial Museum, excavated from the tomb of Zhu Zhanji, Prince Zhuang of Liang, and of Lady Wei at Zhongxiang, Hubei province

FIG. 100
A pair of gold chopsticks

Chopsticks have been the traditional Chinese eating implement for over two thousand years. Longer chopsticks are used in cooking for mixing and stirring. Two pairs of chopsticks were excavated at the joint tomb of Prince Zhuang of Liang and Lady Wei, his wife. They are inscribed with the name of the office where they were made, the date and their weight. One pair is inscribed: 'Made by the Jewellery Service during the first month of the first year of the Hongxi reign [1425], from 85 per cent pure gold, [weighing] one *liang*, two *qian* and five *fen*' (銀作局洪熙元年正月內造捌成伍色金壹兩貳錢伍分). The other is inscribed: 'Remade by the Jewellery Service during the tenth month of the twenty-second year of the Yongle reign period [1424], from 80 per cent pure gold, [weighing] one *liang*, five *qian*, seven *fen*, and five *li*' (銀作局永樂貳拾貳年拾月內改造捌成色金壹兩伍錢柒分伍厘).

Gold
1425
Nanjing
l 24.7 cm, w 0.5 cm, weight 92.4 g
l 24 cm, w 0.5 cm, weight 117.2 g
Hubei Provincial Museum, excavated from the tomb of Zhu Zhanji, Prince Zhuang of Liang, and of Lady Wei at Zhongxiang, Hubei province

EATING AND DRINKING

Entertaining guests with good food and drink is an important part of Chinese culture. Ghiyath al-Din described in his diary the hospitality extended to the Timurid embassy on 24 August 1420. At the first city within China proper, in a meadow, 'they made platforms, set up canopies, placed seats and chairs and arranged foodstuffs, goose, roast fowl, cooked viands and all types of fruit, both dried and fresh on china platters; and there they gave a banquet that would have been difficult to hold in a great city'.[61] The number of visitors and their servants was recorded, and they were given provisions, including sheep, flour and barley. Banquets were accompanied by lively musical and theatrical performances. Two days later, a high-ranking official entertained the embassy again:

> Singers and musicians played on psalteries [stringed instruments], viols, flutes, cymbals, tambours, castanets and drums. Beautiful boys made up like girls with rouge and powder rubbed on their faces and pearls in their ears performed…. The players had made animal masks out of papier mâché and fastened them over their heads in such a manner that their faces, ears and necks could not be seen at all [and they danced in the Chinese fashion].

Ghiyath al-Din goes on to explain how 'moon-faced, tulip-cheeked boys' passed around 'wine, hazelnuts, jujubes, walnuts, chestnuts, citrons, pickled garlic and onions with slices of melon and watermelon'. Another boy danced in a giant stork's costume.[62]

Much of the ephemeral equipment for these banquets, such as the costumes and musical instruments, does not survive, and representations of the actors and entertainers are extremely rare. By piecing together snippets of written texts, and gleaning information from surviving paintings and depictions of people eating and drinking on lacquer and porcelain wares, we can build a picture of some of the foods and drinks that were consumed. From the Timurid embassy's description of an

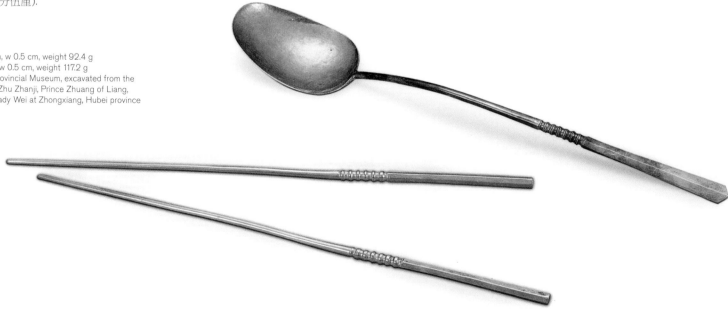

imperial banquet, we know that the Yongle emperor liked to drink yellow wine made from grain or rice (*huang jiu*) and that a variety of meats was served in a single meal, including lamb, goose and chicken, all eaten with chopsticks and served with ladles (figs 99 and 100). Recipes were recorded for historical and contemporary regional dishes, an example being the bean dishes included in the encyclopaedic *Great Canon of the Yongle Reign* (*Yongle da dian*) completed in 1408 (figs 136–7). In the Xuande period 51,850 wine containers were ordered annually from Junzhou in Henan and Cizhou in Hebei, and stored in special warehouses before shipment to the capital.[63]

CONCLUSION – COURTLY DECORATIVE SCHEMES

In the early fifteenth century Ming emperors approved and selected distinctive decorative schemes, establishing a visual vocabulary for Chinese palaces, costumes and furnishings. Court objects are identified by the quality of the materials and craftsmanship used to produce them, but also by their ornament. Early Ming emperors also favoured an intense use of bright colours as building materials and as decorative objects. In the early 1400s the courts defined and standardized imperial motifs, including particular representations of dragons and specific designs of phoenixes, which then came to represent the emperor and empress until the end of the imperial era in 1911.

FIG. 101

Two rectangular porcelain floor tiles

Commissioned for a grand court building or temple, these porcelain tiles were made at Jingdezhen in the imperial kilns, as evidenced by the remains of such tiles that have been excavated there. Some scholars have suggested they were made for the Timurid ruler Ulugh Beg (1394–1449), whose capital lay in Samarqand, now in Uzbekistan. Others have proposed they were made to be part of the Great Monastery of Filial Gratitude (Da Baoensi) in Nanjing. Building materials were made in expensive porcelain even in the Hongwu era, as evidenced by some white roof tiles with underglaze red patterns of phoenixes and dragons excavated in the Nanjing palace area. In the Yongle era thousands of white porcelain bricks were fired for the construction of the Da Baoen Monastery.

Porcelain with underglaze cobalt-blue decoration
Xuande period, 1426–1435
Jingdezhen, Jiangxi province
l 23 cm, w 23 cm, d 3.5 cm
British Museum, London 1993,1027.1 and 2

3

WU
THE ARTS OF WAR

David Robinson

*We will, on the occasion of hunting, personally
visit the passes and order them to military readiness.
You will ready the men and mounts in preparation.*

EDICT OF THE XUANDE EMPEROR, 1428[1]

FIG. 102
Bronze gun

Soldiers in the Yongle emperor's Mongolian campaigns used this type of gun, mounted in a wooden trough and angled by placing wood to raise it under the tip. The world's earliest extant bronze guns were made in the Yuan dynasty (1271–1368). The first Mongolian campaign was launched in 1410 by the Yongle emperor in retaliation for the execution of a Chinese envoy sent to the Eastern Mongol Khan Bunyashiri the previous year and for the subsequent defeat of General Jiu Fu.

The Chinese inscription on the gun gives its serial number and date of manufacture. The inscription reads: 'Made on … day of the ninth month of the seventh year of the Yongle reign [1410]' Wuyu number 4344 (永樂柒年玖月 … 日造 …武宇肆千叁佰肆拾肆號). In March 1410, after careful preparations including amassing sufficient artillery, the Yongle emperor personally led an army of 300,000 men from Beijing into Mongolia via Xuanfu and Xinghe, and up the Kerulen River. According to *Ming shi*, the standard dynastic history of the Ming (1736), in the battle of 1410 the Ming army were armed with guns. The Yongle emperor led his troops into battle on five campaigns against the Mongolian armies (1410, 1414, 1422, 1423 and 1424) and died on his last campaign in 1424. Royal Artillery Museum records suggest that this gun was found centuries later in Mongolia, perhaps having been abandoned on the battlefield of the first Yongle campaign in Mongolia.

Bronze
Dated 1410
Beijing
l 60 cm
Royal Artillery Museum, London
2/261

INTRODUCTION

The early decades of the fifteenth century are sometimes remembered as the Ming dynasty's military acme, a glorious moment between the bloody convulsions of the late fourteenth century and the trials experienced by the Ming dynasty in the sixteenth and seventeenth centuries . The Yongle emperor's bold campaigns into the steppe, the military occupation of Đại Việt (modern northern Vietnam), and massive naval armadas along the main trade routes of Southeast and south Asia seem proof of vaulting ambitions, enormous resources and global engagement. In recent decades, the Ming's military exploits of the early fifteenth century have been seen as both a lost opportunity that opened the doors to European expansion in Asia, and a harbinger of how a newly confident China might use its economic and military resources on the world stage. Less explored but equally vital, however, is the significance of this period for understanding the place of the military in China and the place of China in the emerging early modern world.

This chapter explores three themes: the celebrated campaigns of the early fifteenth century; Ming military institutions, particularly their role in integrating recent immigrants and conducting foreign relations; and finally martial spectacles at imperial and princely courts in the capital and the provinces. It shows that the arts and institutions of war played an integral role in both the Ming's domestic order and in its interactions with neighbouring polities and peoples.

MILITARY CAMPAIGNS

Integral to most states, coercive force played a vital role in all early modern empires across the world, and the Ming dynasty was no exception. Its central focus was

domestic order and, in the name of Heaven's will and the people's interests, the early Ming state waged nearly constant warfare against domestic challengers – from small, poorly organized bands to large-scale, well-armed rebel armies, from farmers outraged at local officials' corruption to imperial family members attempting to usurp the throne. The Yongle emperor (r. 1403–1424), in particular, directed his military forces outward. These campaigns have frequently been understood as a product of his status as a usurper; having seized the throne in a bloody civil war, it is said, the Yongle emperor felt compelled to prove his legitimacy through massive military campaigns. Without discounting such an explanation, a look at wider developments in Eurasia yields additional insights into his behaviour.

The collapse of the Mongol empire created by Chinggis Khan (*c.* 1162–1227) was the most significant development of the fourteenth-century world, and its consequences continued to unfold in the early fifteenth century. Successor states to the Mongol empire, including Muscovite Rus, the early Ottoman polity, the Timurid dynasty, Mogulistan (in present-day Uzbekistan and western China), Joseon Korea and Ming China, all operated in its shadow. The Yongle emperor's campaigns on the Mongolian steppe, his occupation of Đại Việt and his extravagant armadas all grew from the Mongol age, when military prowess was an indispensible qualification for a ruler, and a strong interest in foreign conquest and trade were considered vital for dynastic vigour. Thus, to see the Yongle emperor's grand campaigns as an effort to win contemporary praise and legitimacy really only makes sense if we keep in mind that he operated in a Mongolian-inflected world, where standards of rulership and strategic vision prevalent during the Mongol age continued well into the fifteenth century.

The Yongle emperor was not, however, the first Ming emperor to wage war against the Mongols. His father and founder of the dynasty, the Hongwu emperor (r. 1368–1398), had driven the Mongol court out of the city of Daidu (present-day Beijing) in 1368, and for the next several years his leading generals harried the beleaguered Mongol Yuan emperor Toghun Temür (d. 1370). However, military fortunes shifted when in 1372 Yuan commanders lured Ming armies deep on to the steppe. There, low on food, suffering from frigid temperatures and often lost, Chinese forces suffered steep losses. Later the same year, another Yuan commander, Naghachu (d. 1388), launched a devastating strike against a critical Ming grain depot in Liaodong (in the modern northeastern province of Liaoning), stopping the Ming advance into

FIG. 103

Bronze gun

The early Ming army regarded this portable gun as a revolutionary weapon. It consisted of a front chamber, a chamber for the powder and the stock, originally mounted in a wooden frame. The land battles of the early Ming leaders were arguably some of the largest in human history. Such guns were made in great quantities: 100,000 guns were produced in 1436, for example. Gunpowder was invented in China and guns developed there long before they were manufactured in Europe. This gun was excavated at Juyongguan near Beijing. Although this weapon is sophisticated, the logistical demands of fighting steppe armies meant that firearms could not replace mounted cavalry.

Bronze
1403–24
Excavated at Juyongguan, Beijing
l 43.5 cm
Capital Museum, Beijing

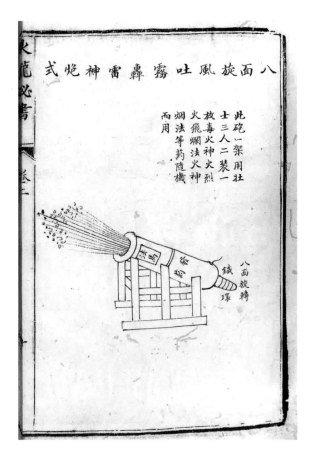

FIG. 104

Detail from 'Fire Dragon Manual' (*Huolong jing* 火龍經)

First published in 1412, this woodblock-printed book combined contemporary late fourteenth- and early fifteenth-century military knowledge with historical material. Illustrations show gunpowder, firearms and other weapons, as well as the men that used them.

Printed ink on paper
1821–50 edition
h 20.6 cm, w 13.5 cm
UCLA Library Special Collections

this strategic region.² In the wake of these military defeats, the Ming and Yuan courts settled into an uneasy (and on the Ming's part unacknowledged) rivalry for power and recognition in eastern Eurasia that played out in tumultuous relations with neighbouring states. One of these was the Goryeo dynasty (918–1392) in Korea, which over the course of two decades accepted investiture (usually signalling an exclusive relationship of suzerainty) from both the Yuan and Ming at least twice. Through a combination of military pressure, economic incentives and diplomatic efforts to win over key Mongol commanders, the Hongwu emperor eventually won the war against the Yuan court, which had been substantially weakened by intensifying conflict among steppe nobles.

However, the legacy of the Mongol empire survived through at least the first century of the Ming period, in the form of political institutions, patterns of international relations, expectations about rulership, and memories of a rich and powerful empire that spanned Eurasia. People and polities that claimed direct descent from the Mongol empire, most especially those of the Chinggisid lineage (the descendants of Chinggis Khan), also formed a critical element of the living Mongol legacy across Eurasia during the late fourteenth and early fifteenth centuries.

Viewed in the light of Chinese history, the Yongle emperor's decision to lead five imperial campaigns in person was remarkable. His father, the Hongwu emperor, had earned his spurs as a military commander during the 1350s and 1360s, but as ruler did not lead armies in the field. In fact, no reigning Chinese emperor in four centuries had ventured on to the battlefield. In contrast, Mongol rulers such as Chinggis, Möngke (1209–1259) and Qubilai (1215–1294) had routinely led their men in battle.

The Yongle emperor built Beijing on the ruins of Qubilai's prize and capital, Daidu. From there he tried to shape events on the steppe, where by the early fifteenth century several contending polities had emerged. The most important of these were the Oirats (or Western Mongols), the Eastern Mongols and the tribal grouping known as the Three Guards (or the Uriyangqad), all of whom were tied in different ways to the Chinggisids and/or the Yuan court, and all of whom entered into alliances with the Ming court at one time or another.³

Any attempt to reduce the Yongle emperor's five campaigns (1410, 1414, 1422, 1423, 1424) to 'the Ming against the Mongols' misses their essence. At no point was he trying to destroy all steppe powers. Rather, he was attempting to cultivate clients, forge alliances (of convenience, to be sure), and selectively strike against individual steppe leaders whom he considered threats to Ming interests. *Account of the Northern Campaign* (*Bei zheng ji*), the memoir of one senior official (Yang Rong, 1371–1440) who accompanied the Yongle emperor to the steppe in 1424, reveals his ruler taking pains to isolate individual Mongol leaders from their followers. 'We are lord of the realm', the emperor announced at one point, 'The people of China and the barbarians are all my children. How could I discriminate one from another?' He offered generous gifts and appointment to official posts for any who joined him in good faith. They would be allowed to select good lands and live in peace, he promised.⁴ Given that three of the five commanders heading his vanguard forces were in fact Mongolians who had joined the Ming forces, this was not empty talk.

The Yongle emperor's first and last campaigns to the steppe were directed against Arugtai (d. 1434), a powerful figure who had murdered his khan, engineered the enthronement of another and then, in 1409, crushed a Ming army that had been sent against him. At one point, having suffered a devastating loss to a steppe rival, Arugtai had sought refuge and support from the Yongle emperor, who, seeing an opportunity to counter the growing strength of another group of Mongols to the west (the Oirats), had been happy to oblige. In time and with Ming military assistance, Arugtai regained his power on the steppe and showed less deference to the Ming court. As his army marched northward into the steppe, Yongle cast Arugtai as an ingrate who had betrayed the emperor's trust and generosity, a fact that everyone, including his Mongolian audience, knew. Arugtai 'attacks Our border regions and harms Our people without end', he observed, 'Who is at fault here?'[5] Rhetoric was not the only arrow in the Yongle emperor's quiver; he also drew on the massive economic and logistic resources of the Ming state. In the 1422 campaign, for instance, he mobilized some 235,000 men, nearly 118,000 carts of supplies and 340,000 heads of livestock.[6]

The Mongolian diaspora spread members of Chinggisid family lineages throughout Inner Eurasia. It ensured that developments among the Oirats, the Eastern Mongols and the Uriyangqad were linked not just to the Ming but also Moghulistan (the eastern successor state of the Chaghatayid dynasty based in Uzbekistan and western China) and smaller states in Inner Eurasia. For instance, the Oirat leader Esen (r. 1438–1455) pushed back Moghulistan rulers to the west, conquered the Uriyangqad Three Guards and Jurchens to the east (located in today's Inner Mongolia and the northeast provinces of Liaoning, Jilin and Heilongjiang), and then inflicted a devastating defeat on the Ming to the south in 1449, capturing the Zhengtong emperor (1436–1449) at Tumu Fort (fig. 106) and throwing his court into confusion.[7] Thus, the Ming's engagement with the Mongol legacy tied it to wider developments that extended far beyond just those peoples and polities immediately contiguous to Chinese territory.

The Yongle emperor did not try to hide either his keen interest in the memory of the Mongol empire or his fear that contemporary steppe leaders might attempt to exploit its powerful legacy. While on campaign on the steppe in 1410, he informed civilian ministers in his entourage where Mongol emperors had hunted and camped, and what they had said there. He destroyed stone steles commissioned by the Yuan, explicitly stating that he did not wish contemporary steppe leaders to claim sovereignty over the territory on the basis of historical claims. To demonstrate his dominance over the steppe, the emperor renamed more than a dozen prominent Mongolian mountains and lakes as he moved through the region on campaign. As a permanent reminder of his power and sovereignty, in one township the Yongle emperor ordered that the following be inscribed on a stone marker:

FIG. 106

The Tumu Fort (*Tumu bao* 土木堡)

This photograph shows part of the original fortress walls on the left and a modern reconstruction of the wall on the right. The fortress is 20 kilometres outside modern Tumu and the interior of the fortress is home to a village. This was the site of a frontier conflict between the Oirat Mongols and the Ming imperial armies, which led to the capture of the Zhengtong emperor on 1 September 1449.

FIG. 109

**Glazed earthenware tomb figures
of two generals**

The Ming army included at least one million professional soldiers who received a state wage. These figures were part of a model army, buried with Zhu Yuelian, the Crown Prince of Shu (1388–1409). The military figures wear body armour and helmets, and are fully equipped with bows and arrows. They would originally have wielded long spears. Other weapons at their disposal would have included firearms, gunpowder and rockets. Princes of the early Ming had their own personal guard and troops, as one of their major roles was to defend the borders and rivers of the empire against outside invasion and to represent the emperor's military strength across China. At the beginning of the period 1400–50, each prince commanded between 3,000 and 15,000 men.

These earthenware tomb models were mass produced using moulds and then hand-finished before being painted, glazed and fired in large batches in kilns. Later they were painted with gold, red and black details to make them look more life-like. They were intended to re-create the serried ranks of trained military fighters who would defend the Crown Prince of Shu in the afterlife and demonstrate his status as part of the imperial clan.

Earthenware with multi-coloured lead-fluxed
glazes and gilded details
c. 1400–9
Sichuan
h 51–81 cm
Sichuan Museum, excavated from the
tomb of Zhu Yuelian, Crown Prince of Shu,
Fenghuangshan, Sichuan province

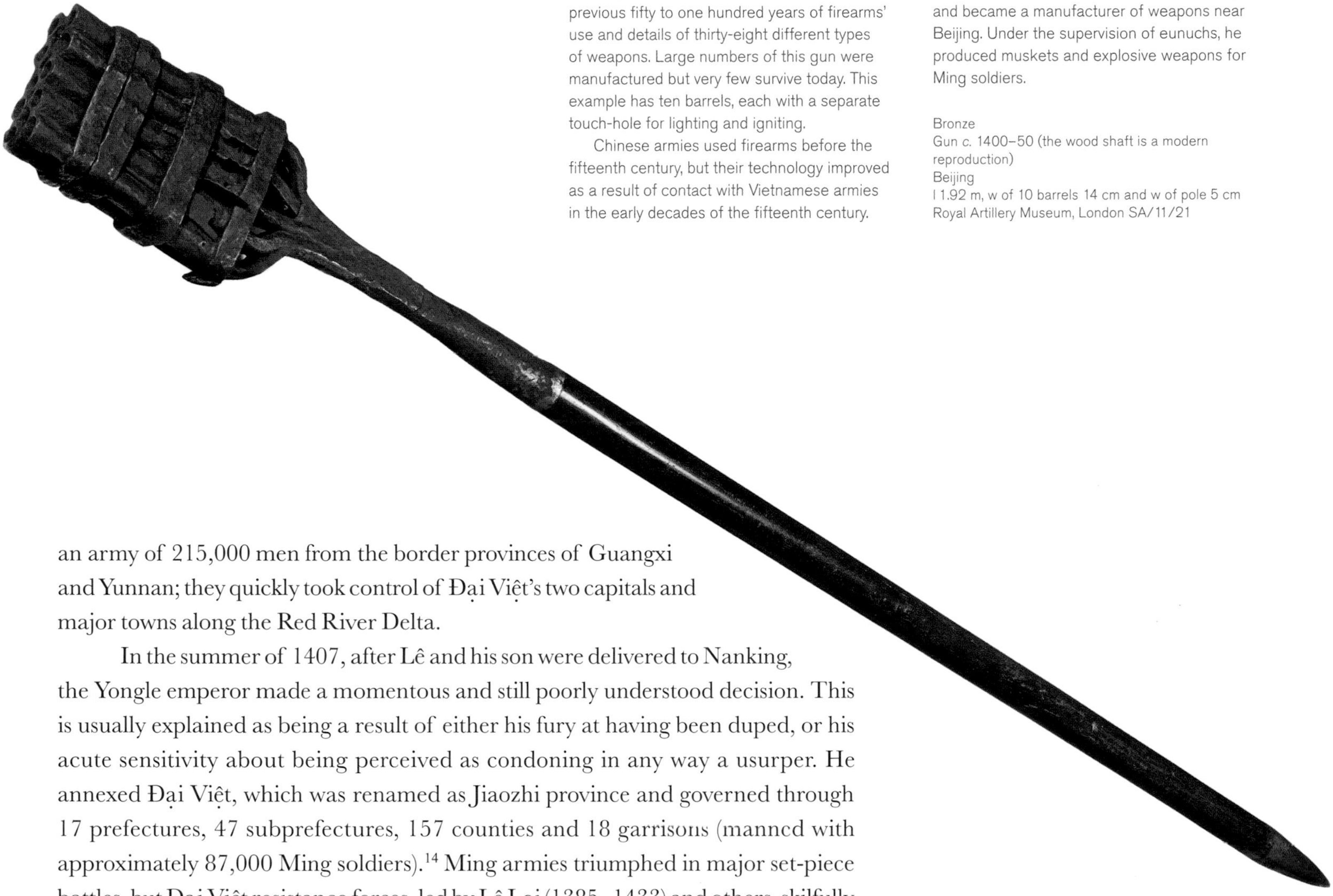

FIG. 110
Bronze ten-barrelled gun

The Yongle emperor trained his army in firearms at a specialist camp in Beijing. Multi-barrelled weapons made an early appearance in Chinese arsenals. This gun is illustrated in the *Artillery Manual* (*Huolong shenqi zhenfa*), first published in 1412, which contains information on the previous fifty to one hundred years of firearms' use and details of thirty-eight different types of weapons. Large numbers of this gun were manufactured but very few survive today. This example has ten barrels, each with a separate touch-hole for lighting and igniting.

Chinese armies used firearms before the fifteenth century, but their technology improved as a result of contact with Vietnamese armies in the early decades of the fifteenth century.

In 1407 Chinese generals captured the Vietnamese leader Hô Quý Ly, his sons and other family members, and took them as prisoners to Nanjing. His eldest son Hô Hán Thuong (also called Hô Nguyen Trung and Le Tr'ung, 1374–1446), was a Vietnamese firearms expert and became a manufacturer of weapons near Beijing. Under the supervision of eunuchs, he produced muskets and explosive weapons for Ming soldiers.

Bronze
Gun *c.* 1400–50 (the wood shaft is a modern reproduction)
Beijing
l 1.92 m, w of 10 barrels 14 cm and w of pole 5 cm
Royal Artillery Museum, London SA/11/21

an army of 215,000 men from the border provinces of Guangxi and Yunnan; they quickly took control of Đại Việt's two capitals and major towns along the Red River Delta.

In the summer of 1407, after Lê and his son were delivered to Nanking, the Yongle emperor made a momentous and still poorly understood decision. This is usually explained as being a result of either his fury at having been duped, or his acute sensitivity about being perceived as condoning in any way a usurper. He annexed Đại Việt, which was renamed as Jiaozhi province and governed through 17 prefectures, 47 subprefectures, 157 counties and 18 garrisons (manned with approximately 87,000 Ming soldiers).[14] Ming armies triumphed in major set-piece battles, but Đại Việt resistance forces, led by Lê Lợi (1385–1433) and others, skilfully exploited local resentment against the occupation and Ming extractions to conduct a gruelling guerilla war. This undermined Ming administrative capacity in Jiaozhi and eventually wore away imperial commitment to its newest province. Within two years of taking the throne, the Xuande emperor (r. 1426–1435) withdrew Ming personnel and abolished Jiaozhi province.[15]

The Xuande and Zhengtong emperors first scaled back and then abandoned the large-scale campaigns on the steppe, wide-ranging armadas and the annexation of Đại Việt. Explanations for these reversals abound: they were expensive in terms of treasure and blood; they distracted from more critical concerns closer to home; they created opportunities for military officers and eunuchs to win influence with the emperor; and they did nothing to improve either dynastic security or coffers.

Shifting our attention to the long-term consequences of these expansive policies, China's deep engagement in Asia is noteworthy. In the following decades and centuries the Chinese diaspora would gain momentum, as Ming subjects settled on the steppe and in much of Southeast Asia. This spreading network of people, skills and capital, however, grew without the Ming state's support. Indeed, the diaspora developed in the face of dynastic regulations that sought to sharply restrict private trade and migration, demonstrating that such laws were enforced with uneven vigour and efficacy. Additionally, the early fifteenth-century campaigns, whether on the steppe, in Đại Việt, or through the Southeast and south Asian seas, were not just military but also economic and demographic phenomena. They forced large-scale and intensive contact among not just generals and their soldiers, but also porters, cooks, senior officials, minor functionaries, local farming families, fishermen, merchants and accompanying family members. Ming forces brought an infusion of advanced firearms, including both guns (figs 102, 103, 110) and cannon, while Chinese forces quickly adopted Vietnamese military technology, such as the wooden wad and an improved igniting device.[16]

During the Ming occupation thousands of Vietnamese travelled to Nanjing. The personal and socioeconomic networks that grew from such interactions have only recently begun to be examined. How exactly did these state-driven campaigns contribute to the largely private Chinese diaspora that would exercise such a lasting influence on Southeast Asia and beyond? For the time being, it is enough to note that the Ming throne's shift away from large-scale steppe campaigns, the spectacular armadas and the abolition of its Đại Việt province are not the same thing as Chinese withdrawal from the world.

FIG. 111

Present-day celebrations held to commemorate the Vietnamese victory over the Ming army. Lam Kinh 2005

INSTITUTIONS

The sheer scale and pervasive nature of Ming military institutions can sometimes obscure their importance; they are hidden in plain view. A set of interlocking institutions exercised an enormous impact on social control, taxation, land tenure, farming, settlement patterns, administrative records, law codes and education, thus profoundly shaping the world in which individuals and families pursued their interests. Before turning to their role in the incorporation of immigrants and the conduct of foreign relations, a brief description of the Ming's central military institutions is useful.

To restore social stability, enhance state control and revive agrarian production, the early Ming dynasty leaned heavily on hereditary military households. This institution had antecedents in previous Chinese dynasties, but had achieved unprecedented importance under the Yuan Mongol state. Military households drew men from several major sources: those who had fought in the Hongwu emperor's rebel armies; those who had been captured or had surrendered from rival rebel armies; and those from the dynastic armies of the defeated Yuan dynasty. These were supplemented with convicts and forcible recruitment among local civilian populations. Hereditary military households were responsible for supplying one able-bodied male for military service and one or more men who would contribute financial support to the active service soldier generation after generation.

Although garrisons units were often housed together in forts or in neighbourhoods in walled cities, many also lived interspersed among the general civilian population. To limit direct costs to the state, the dynasty distributed plots of land to military households, the size of which varied according to region and fertility, on which garrisons would grow sufficient food to support themselves. During the early Ming, agricultural colonies, staffed by members of hereditary military households, opened up previously uncultivated lands. The state also designated land for pasturages for horses used for hauling supply wagons or for cavalry units. Military household registration tracked births and deaths, changes in domiciles, occupations, and tax and corvée responsibilities to both local and dynastic authorities.[17]

Garrison manpower was also regularly used as labour for the construction and maintenance of the transportation infrastructure, delivering tax grain to the capital, and on occasion even refurbishing Buddhist temples. Thus, the Ming dynasty used hereditary military families and garrisons to organize and regulate a large segment of the total population (as high as 30 to 40 per cent in places like the capital and even higher in some border regions) and direct its labour towards agricultural production, in addition to their duties as soldiers, whether located in the capital, provincial seats of government, or along the dynastic frontiers.

The state also used military institutions to incorporate immigrants from the north into the polity. During its first century the Ming dynasty actively recruited Mongolian and Jurchen men and their families with offers of housing, land, titles, positions in the imperial army and the opportunity for further advancement through service to the state, usually meaning military campaigns. Early Ming rulers and their ministers spent much time criticizing the corrupting influences of the Yuan dynasty,

stressing the importance of reviving pure Chinese customs, and chastising Mongol and Jurchen leaders who failed to cooperate with Ming policies. Yet the Ming state nonetheless valued Mongol and Jurchen personnel for their martial prowess (especially their skill in mounted archery; fig. 112), and their knowledge of steppe politics, languages and geography. Every Mongol or Jurchen recruited to Ming service reduced the pool of manpower and stock of political legitimacy available to potential steppe rivals. When they joined the Ming, Mongol and Jurchen nobles often came with large families and even larger groups of subordinate populations that could easily number in the hundreds. The Ming state registered these new immigrants into hereditary military households, most commonly in elite capital units and northern border garrisons, but also in hinterland units, where some descendants survived until the very end of the Ming dynasty in 1644 and beyond.[18]

During the reigns of the Yongle, Xuande and Zhengtong emperors, Mongols and Jurchens served in the upper echelons of the Ming military, including in senior positions within the capital high command. Mongol commanders also accompanied the Yongle emperor on his steppe campaigns and the Xuande emperor on his northern border patrols. Less exalted Mongols served under the Yongle, Xuande and Zhengtong emperors, providing detailed information about sources of water on the steppe, good grazing lands for horses, and counsel about how the Ming might best exploit divisions among leading Mongolian nobles on the steppe.

This intimate contact between Mongol warriors and Chinese emperors worried some Ming officials. During one hunting expedition the Xuande emperor was accompanied by several hundred Mongol officers, including Esen-Tügel, who in 1423, having pledged his loyalty to the Yongle emperor, had received a Chinese name (Jin Zhong) and an aristocratic title, 'Loyal and Valorous Prince'. The Xuande emperor's ministers suggested that he was putting his life at risk by embarking on this trip, although they let the emperor draw his own conclusions as to whether the greater peril was a riding accident or the Mongols' treachery.

Despite such worries and periodic efforts to render the Mongols less threatening by dispersing their communities to China's deep south, in general the surrendered Mongols served the Ming dynasty with loyalty and distinction. In many ways, the incorporation of Mongols and Jurchens into the Ming polity resembles the integrative function of the military in other places and other times (such as the Roman or British empires or Muscovite Rus), where 'martial races' might on occasion be viewed with suspicion as potential fifth columns or as uncivilized, but could nonetheless win recognition and material benefits from the state.

Border garrisons were another military institution important for interactions with neighbouring states and people. Although their primary responsibility was the defence of dynastic territory, they often also oversaw border control. Controlling a region at the intersection of Chinese, Korean, Jurchen and Mongol lands, the Liaodong Regional Military Commission and its twenty-five garrisons served as the linchpin of Ming imperial order in northeast Asia, functioning as the administrative, economic and cultural point of first contact with neighbouring peoples and polities, just as the Shaanxi Regional Military Commission did in the empire's northwestern corner. As noted above, during the reigns of the Yongle and Xuande emperors, the central court regularly offered resettlement packages for Jurchens who requested to relocate to Liaodong.[19] For instance, in 1408 the Ming court granted the request of one group to live in the Three Tümens Garrison, ordering that local authorities provide the group with 'cash, clothing, saddles and horses' as well as 'lodgings, sundry utensils, firewood for cooking, rice, oxen and sheep'. These émigrés were registered in military garrisons, where they received posts that reflected their relative importance in Mongolian or Jurchen society.

Some border garrisons were deeply involved in frontier trade, supervising state-managed fairs, where Jurchens and Mongols traded horses for a variety of Chinese manufactured goods.[20] Some such Jurchens were from the so-called 'loose rein' garrisons, 'loose rein' referring to peoples and polities outside effective Ming military or administrative control that might nonetheless be influenced through the bestowal of gifts and titles, periodic and regulated admittance to Ming territory, and occasional military or relief assistance.

The Liaodong Regional Military Commission also handled the reception of Jurchen, Mongolian and Korean envoys, validating their credentials, processing their paperwork, reporting the size, composition and objectives of envoy missions to the court, and gathering intelligence. Garrison personnel, often first- or second-generation immigrants themselves, not only provided interpretation and translation assistance but also often acted as cultural brokers, guiding newly arrived Mongols and Jurchens through the administrative processes of securing positions within the imperial military system, housing and initial packages of land, livestock and seed, household registration and more.[21]

Military personnel from border garrisons frequently exploited their physical proximity to the frontier, as well as their power as imperial officers and soldiers, to engage in illicit economic activities. Garrison officers along the northern border led hunting parties beyond Ming territory, a violation of imperial law. Such activities imperilled the physical safety of soldiers and, perhaps even more importantly, risked the possibility of a border clash with steppe groups that jealously guarded rich hunting grounds. Some northeastern officers ordered their men to cut lumber, gather the valuable ginseng root and conduct trade for precious sable furs beyond the border, again risking clashes with Jurchen groups and undermining the state's efforts to monopolize trade. Similarly, garrison personnel along the southeastern coast formed an integral element of an illicit maritime trade network that connected China to east and Southeast Asia. Whether along the northern border or the southeastern coast, military garrison personnel drew on their access to institutional resources and social networks, gained through their dual status as dynastic agents and local insiders, to pursue individual, family and community interests. Although such activities might run counter to court directives, they again illustrate the importance of military institutions and personnel for China's relations with neighbouring polities and peoples.

Turning our attention back from the borders to the capital, one final influential Ming military institution must be noted, the Brocade Uniform Guard (*Jinyiwei*). It began as an office in charge of imperial regalia, was reorganized as a bodyguard and was finally reconstituted into the most influential of the thirty-three imperial guards, all of which fell outside regular military hierarchy. It performed functions related to the personal needs of the emperor and his family, from the selection of girls from the capital for the imperial harem and the management of wet nurses for the imperial palace, to being a convenient administrative vehicle for supporting men whom the emperor found useful (including painters). But the Brocade Uniform Guard is perhaps most famous (or infamous) for running the dynasty's security and intelligence units, gathering information, interrogating commoners and officials suspected of crimes against the state (which routinely involved torture), and operating prisons such as the notorious Eastern Depot.

The Brocade Uniform Guard also protected the emperor's safety and enhanced the majesty of court events through its imposing physical presence. Dressed in their distinctive brocade uniforms, wearing brilliantly polished armour, and hefting halberds, members of the guard stood to attention to the west of the imperial throne and ascended the emperor's dais from the west.[22] One unit, the Commandants, all wore Mongolian-style silk robes and often served as the emperor's outriders when he left the palace. Another major unit within the guard, the Three Thousands Garrison, originated from Mongol riders who had pledged their allegiance to the throne early in the dynasty.

Despite the Brocade Uniform Guard's scale and visibility, its operations were opaque to outsiders. The civil bureaucracy seldom knew how many men served in the guard at any given time, nor were even senior officials privy to its promotion process, budget or internal administration. The guard was intended as an emblem and instrument of the emperor's power, quite pointedly not subject to bureaucratic oversight. Privileged access to the throne conferred great influence, which periodically tempted commanding officers of the guard, usually through political alliances with elite palace eunuchs, to overstep their authority. However, the Brocade Uniform Guard, the Eastern Depot and affiliated palace eunuchs were usually acting on the emperor's orders when they gathered intelligence on suspected 'traitors', encouraged confessions through torture, and inflicted horrible and humiliating punishments on those found guilty.

FIG. 113
Anonymous, 'Portrait of General Yang Hong'
(*Yingguo Wuxianggong Yang Hong xiang* 穎國武襄公楊洪像)

Yang Hong (1381–1451) was an important military commander in the early Ming period. He was posted by the court to take charge of the Xuanfu garrison along the Great Wall, northwest of Beijing, on Ming China's most sensitive frontier. This commemorative portrait of him is inscribed by Yu Qian (1398–1457), Minister of War. Yu Qian was beheaded for high treason in 1457, as the restored Zhengtong emperor blamed him for the installation of the Jingtai emperor while he had been captured by the Oirat Mongol leader. In 1466 Yu Qian was pardoned and his former titles were restored. Yu Qian's inscription on the painting describes Yang Hong as possessing 'intestinal fortitude of iron and stone'. He is further praised for wielding his sword and halberd 'like the sparkling rays of the stars'.

Yang is dressed in the red robes of a civil official. The hat, with its long side flaps and flat top, is unusual. On either side of his belt tinkling jade pendants are suspended (of the type seen in fig. 52). The clean-shaven figures at the back of the painting are dressed in a style of clothing that had its origins in Mongolian gowns but had grown popular among Chinese populations during the Yuan period, and continued to be fashionable in some quarters well into the Ming period. One of the figures wears a single earring, a popular nomad fashion. A portrait such as this one was used by descendants of the sitter for ancestor worship. The arrangement of the figures echoes contemporary Ming and earlier representations of deities.

Hanging scroll, ink and colours on silk, with red underdrawing
Anonymous, inscription by Yu Qian (1398–1457) dated 1451, and later inscription by Xu Yongzhong dated 1558
Beijing
Image: h 220.8 cm, w 127.5 cm
Arthur M. Sackler Gallery, Smithsonian Institution, Washington. Purchase Smithsonian Collections Acquisition Program and partial gift of Richard G. Pritzlaff, S1991.77

FIG. 114

**Hu Cong (胡聰) (fl. 1426–1456),
'Two steeds under the shade of a
willow tree' (*Liuyin shuangjun tu*
柳蔭雙駿圖)**

Equestrian art was very popular in the
early Ming period at court, whether
showing hunting, polo-playing or portraits
of military horses. Horses were vital for
the Ming army as mounted archers were
probably more important than firearms
at this period.

The horses depicted here are from
the imperial stables. They are tethered
in an imperial park rather than in the
countryside; the wall can be seen about
a third of the way up on the right. A hilly
park like this was built on the northern
outskirts of Beijing by the Yongle emperor
to house his collection of exotic animals
and birds. According to the inscription, it
was 'painted by the court artist Hu Cong
from the Eastern Gao [Rugao, Jiangsu]
who served at the Hall of Military Valour'
(直武英殿東皋胡聰寫). The Xuande
emperor had a personal involvement
in the appointment of court artists. He
interviewed potential candidates for
appointment in the Hall of Benevolence
and Wisdom (*Renzhi dian*) and the Hall
of Military Valour (*Wuying dian*).

Hanging scroll, colour on silk
c. 1426–56
Beijing
Image: h 101.2 cm, w 50.5 cm; with mount:
h 240 cm, w 82 cm
The Palace Museum, Beijing

MARTIAL SPECTACLES

Like many courts around the globe, the Ming dynasty conducted lavish spectacles that demonstrated military prowess, whether it was skill in riding, mounted archery or coordinated action directed towards killing game.[23] Martial spectacles were embedded in traditions of military display and ritual that included dances and music, the presentation of war prisoners to the throne, ceremonies for conferring command on military generals, sacrifices to battle flags, prayers for victory in war, and pre- and post-campaign reports at the ancestral shrine. In the palace and on the road Ming emperors were conspicuously protected by the imperial guard, which provided both security and an imposing sense of grandeur for any occasion (fig. 115).

Martial spectacles advertised rulers' ability to mount extravagant events beyond the means of potential competitors, from enemies abroad, ambitious military men at home and disaffected local leaders (both religious and secular) to scheming court ministers and resentful imperial clansmen. To celebrate these displays, the throne held banquets for favoured participants and distributed silver ingots, silver medallions and textiles to others. Displaying treasure and manpower was costly, but far cheaper than suppressing rebellions or palace coups. The spectacles were both grand entertainment and reminders that military force remained a central pillar of the dynasty.

Horsemanship and skill in mounted archery loomed large in martial spectacles, because throughout inner Eurasia and its periphery the mounted archer remained the premier military weapon during much of the medieval and early modern periods. Steppe powers had access to large numbers of high-quality horses and men who had grown up riding and shooting. Polities in west, south and east Asia, such as Muscovite Russia, the Mughals in India or the Ming, used their superior economic resources to secure horses from the steppe to supplement domestically bred mounts, which were generally of lesser quality and quantity (figs 114 and 119).[24] Thus, while today we might assume that high-tech firearms were the gold standard for military reviews and that horses were more for show, polities surrounding the steppe knew through painful experience that the reality of war was quite different. The importance of firearms certainly grew as they improved, but the mounted archer was essential for most of inner Eurasia in the fifteenth century.

FIG. 115
Stone figure of a general from the 'spirit way', Beijing, c. 1424–50

FIG. 119
Anonymous, 'Tethered horses under a tree' (*Shuyin shuangjun tu* 樹蔭雙駿圖)

Horses were essential to success in battle, particularly in the steppe lands along China's northern frontier. The Yongle emperor dreamed of a god, riding a white horse, just before he won a great military victory at Yashili. Each imperial and princely court maintained fine stables of horses for war and hunting. Government pasturages were founded in the Beijing and Shanxi areas, but large horses did not breed successfully in China because of the climate and lack of pasture, so many were traded in exchange for other commodities or given as tribute. To compensate for the Ming army's weakness in cavalry warfare, they also welcomed trained Mongol soldiers who were willing to fight for the Ming court in exchange for livestock, land, homes, furnishings, food and clothing. Often these men were commanded by other Mongols and were stationed in northern China along the frontier.

Hanging scroll, ink and colours on silk
c. 1400–50
Probably Beijing
h 57 cm, w 47.5 cm
British Museum, London 1910,0212,0.452

FIG. 120 OPPOSITE
Anonymous, 'The Xuande emperor hunting' (*Xuanzong shelie tu* 宣宗射獵圖)

Here the Xuande emperor is shown with the dark complexion and beard also seen in his official court portrait. He has a quiver of arrows and is hunting in open fields, rather than being presented in Chinese costume in a palace interior. He holds a deer in his hands and looks back at another deer that is escaping. Beneath the saddle, his grazing horse is covered with a tiger pelt. This painting is almost certainly a fragment from a much larger work and would not have been in the hanging scroll format. The fact that the emperor has his back to us and is dismounted from a horse that is neither pure white nor completely dark is unusual. However, the costume is the same as that worn by the Xuande emperor hunting in a monumental painting by Shang Xi in the Palace Museum, Beijing.

Early Ming emperors strove to incorporate the Mongol world into their courts. We can see this demonstrated through the role of hunting at court and the emphasis on military skills, as well as in the adoption of some forms of Mongol dress, such as the felt hat and riding tunic with tight-fitting sleeves worn by the emperor in this painting.

Hanging scroll, ink and colour on silk
Xuande period, 1426–1435
Beijing
Image: h 29.5 cm, w 34.6 cm;
with mount: h 215 cm, w 72 cm
The Palace Museum, Beijing

Martial spectacles showcased the ruler's discernment of men and their abilities; he judged their skill in riding and shooting, and rewarded bravery and prowess in the hunt (figs 120 and 124). Rulers made manifest their generosity with lavish entertainment for their subjects and bountiful rewards to participants. Control, discernment and munificence were essential elements of rulership in most places and times. Ming emperors were considered wise to the extent that they recognized and cultivated talented scholars by offering trust, office and rewards. Martial spectacles make clear a fact that literati would pass over quietly – that such rewards had an equally vital place in the military realm.

Hunting formed an important element of the Yongle and Xuande emperors' identity as rulers.[25] They maintained large hunting parks and encouraged their civil

صید رها کرده از قضا باز در طلب
صیدی برفت و در جنگ نا هیلی صید شد

FIG. 121
'Baysunghur watches a hunt'
(illustration in an anthology
of prose and poetry)

Ink and colours on paper
Herat, 1427
h 19.8 cm, w 11.8 cm
Florence, I Tatti (Harvard University
Center for Renaissance Studies)

officials to compose commemorative accounts of hunting outings. They also commissioned portraits of themselves hunting with bow and arrow, often on horseback and usually dressed in short riding tunics and felt hats that had been popular during the Mongol period (see p. 139). The hunts represented wealth, power and prestige for the ruler, his hunters and those invited to join the chase. Ming emperors would have immediately recognized the dynamics of the royal hunt held by Timurid (fig. 121), Ottoman and, later, Mughal rulers. They were all part of a common Eurasian court culture. These shared practices were made possible by, and simultaneously facilitated, gift exchanges of horses, hunting raptors, dogs (fig. 122) and their trainers or grooms.

During the long progresses between his two capitals, Beijing and Nanjing, the Yongle emperor hunted. In one poem the senior court minister Hu Guang (1370–1418) expressed his thanks to the emperor for granting him a portion of venison from the imperial bag taken just south of Beijing.[26] He also vividly recalled

FIG. 122
Zhu Zhanji (朱瞻基) (1399–1435), 'Two Salukis' (*Shuangquan tu* 雙犬圖)

These hunting dogs were not a native Chinese breed, but imported from the Middle East. They traditionally chased deer, foxes and hares, running at great speed and hunting by sight. The Xuande emperor enjoyed hunting with his elite troops and high-ranking courtiers.

Album leaf, ink and colours on paper
Dated 1427
Beijing
h 26.2 cm, w 34.6 cm
Arthur M. Sackler Museum, Harvard Art Museums, Gift of Charles A. Coolidge, 1931.20

FIG. 123
Anonymous, 'White gyrfalcon'

This painting of a hunting bird, executed in a Ming court workshop, was exported to Iran, where it was included in an album of paintings from diverse sources.

Album leaf, opaque pigment and gold on silk
1400–1500
h 44.8 cm, w 26 cm
Topkapi Palace Museum, Istanbul

how a pack of hunting hounds had chased down an enraged tiger in the mountains near Teng County in Shandong province.[27] Another of his poems described how the emperor used the soldiers of his army to conduct a vast encirclement hunt. Among their ranks were 'Purple-bearded Mongols who fed black leopards'.[28] These Mongols, who comprised a part of the imperial hunting staff, were specialists with knowledge of hunting cats such as the 'black leopards' and, one assumes, raptors such as the gyrfalcon (fig. 123). On the road, the Yongle emperor's court sometimes also included exotic animals such as lions and giraffes.[29]

Hunting provided the Yongle emperor with knowledge of local conditions in his empire and beyond. He understood the impoverished circumstances of farming families from encirclement hunts held when he was the Prince of Yan.[30] He learned steppe geography from these expeditions, pointing out specific sites where he had hunted in the past.[31] He took advantage of his trips to remind his civil officials that he commanded the direct, experiential knowledge of distant lands that they lacked, observing at one point, 'Not until you arrive at that point [Mount Bayan] will you understand the scenery beyond the pass. When you study, you only see things on paper.'

Like so many other rulers in Eurasia, the Yongle and Xuande emperors used the hunt to prepare for war. En route to the northern border in 1422, the Yongle emperor explained to his officials, 'It is not that I am inordinately fond of the hunt. [I] observed that the soldiers accompanying me on campaign have nothing but the hunt for riding their horses and brandishing their arms, for stimulating military affairs, and for bolstering morale.'[32] On the same campaign, the emperor also conducted more straightforward military drills and reviews to keep his men sharp.[33] Days later, he viewed his troops at archery practice. When one soldier hit the target three times in three tries, the emperor rewarded him with an ox, a sheep, one hundred cash and two silver bowls, because 'with generous rewards people are motivated'.[34] In late September 1428 the Xuande emperor explained to his senior commanders, 'Each year, when autumn arrives and the horses are fat, the barbarian slaves [a derogatory term for the Mongols] are bound to harass the borders. Recently border defences have not been vigilant … Now, the agricultural busy season is almost over. We will on the occasion of hunting personally visit the passes and order them to military readiness.'[35] That both the Yongle and Xuande emperors felt obliged to justify the royal hunt suggests that some officials remained sceptical, whether out of concerns for security, costs or needless distraction.

Finally, the hunt provided an opportunity for the emperor to cultivate relations with his military commanders. On the way back from a short campaign against the Mongols on the northern border in 1421, the Yongle emperor viewed several hunts by his generals, allowing him to spend time with his commanders in a less formal setting that showcased their skills in riding, shooting and command.[36] The ruler's attendance was a form of imperial favour that was less easily granted once he returned to the daily routines of administration in the capital.

Ming emperors commissioned portraits of themselves as hunters in the field, but most are attributed to the patronage of the Xuande emperor. The provenance of some imperial portraits is less certain: an anonymous hanging scroll, for instance, in ink and colours on silk, depicts five hunters galloping on horses in pursuit of winged prey (fig. 124).[37] Each rider is equipped with a bow in its case slung along his left leg and a quiver full of arrows (each one distinct) on the right side. The central figure, noticeably larger than his companions, rides a chestnut-coloured horse. In all these finely executed portraits the Chinese emperor wears a Mongolian-style cap and Mongolian riding tunic with narrow sleeves, sits on or stands near richly caparisoned horses, and is engaged in a hunt or outing with many riders. This face of Ming rulership is often ignored, but in light of the ritual, cultural and political importance

FIG. 124

Anonymous, 'Hunting by a lake'
(***Hupan shelie tu*** 湖畔射獵圖)

Hunting was an essential part of court culture in Europe
and Asia at this time, to maintain military fitness and to
promote mutual trust between the ruler and his officers.
This painting shows the Xuande emperor hunting in
the open countryside with members of his court. He
is the largest figure in the group but each of the other
riders has an individual portrait-style face. The location
is probably the imperial hunting ground south of the
Forbidden City known as the Southern Ponds (*Nanhai zi*).

The idea of an imperial hunting portrait derives from
the Mongol tradition of portraying khans hunting or on
horseback. To maintain their military skills, such as good
horsemanship, early fifteenth-century emperors often
travelled great distances to hunt. Although the Xuande
emperor is perhaps better known as an aesthete than a
soldier, he crushed the rebellion of his uncle, the Prince
of Han, in 1426 using military strategy he had learned
from his grandfather. He also defeated an incursion of
northern nomads in 1428, personally killing three men
as he led his own troops. Physical fitness and strength
were essential attributes of Chinese emperors at this
time. Campaigns in the steppe were not designed to
wipe out all the Mongols but to deal with individual
Mongol leaders who were threatening the security of
the Ming empire. The Yongle, Xuande and Zhengtong
emperors all employed Mongol and Jurchen officials
who had been incorporated into the Ming military.

Ink and colour on silk
c. 1426–35
Beijing
Image: h 107 cm, w 123.5 cm;
with mount: h 208 cm, w 142 cm
The Palace Museum, Beijing

FIG. 125

Anonymous, 'Emperor Xuanzong on horseback' (*Ming Xuanzong mashang tu* 明宣宗馬上圖)

Hunting portraits were popular in the early Ming. Here the Xuande emperor (Xuanzong) is depicted galloping on horseback with a quiver full of arrows. As well as the reins, he is holding a white falcon tightly in his arms, ready to release it to fly to its prey. He has startled a flock of wild geese. The painting is inscribed 'Emperor Xuanzong's Amusements' and may originally have been part of a larger work. The Xuande emperor regularly hunted with his elite troops and led them into battle.

Hanging scroll, ink and colours on silk
1426–35
Beijing
h 68.1 cm, w 84.1 cm
National Palace Museum, Taipei

of clothing, the celebration of the royal hunt in poetry by leading court ministers, and the widely acknowledged role of the military in dynastic fortunes, hunting portraits (fig. 125), alongside those portraits depicting the emperor as a seated sage, were clearly intended as claims about authority and rulership.

Imperial princes at their provincial courts also conducted hunts, which may have begun when the Hongwu emperor stipulated that his sons were to organize annual hunting expeditions as military training.[38] Perhaps the most famous princely hunt occurred in 1404, when the Prince of Zhou (Zhu Su, 1361–1425) happened across 'an exotic beast' (a *zouyu*) during a hunt at Junzhou, located in present-day central Henan province. The prince, who was the Yongle emperor's younger brother and frequently rumoured to harbour plans of treason, presented the strange animal to the new emperor as an auspicious sign of the emperor's virtue and Heaven's approval.[39] With the body of a tiger and the head of a lion, the *zouyu* was believed to be a compassionate being that would not eat the flesh of living animals, and appeared only when a just and benevolent ruler was on the throne (fig. 126). More than two dozen officials at the central court then composed congratulatory poems to celebrate the event. Court painters commemorated the auspicious moment by rendering the *zouyu*'s likeness on silk in a decorative style, suggesting that it may have been intended for display within the palace complex.

Fig. 126
Anonymous, 'Picture of the zouyu' (*Mingren neifu zouyu tu* 明人內府騶虞圖)

This painting commemorates the discovery and presentation in 1404 of an auspicious white animal called a *zouyu* to the Yongle emperor by his brother, the Prince Su of Zhou (1361–1425). The appearance of the *zouyu* was interpreted as a sign of Heaven's approval of the reigning emperor. After the civil war, the prince was anxious to demonstrate his loyalty.

Handscroll, ink and colours on silk
c. 1404–5
Nanjing
h 51.9 cm, w 125 cm
National Palace Museum, Taipei

Iron helmet with gold patterns

FIG. 130 OPPOSITE

COMPARED to furnishings and paintings, very few items relating to martial culture are found in addition to the few that were preserved through burial. This partly reflects the gradual change in society over the Ming period (1368–1644) from one in which martial prowess and skills were ranked most highly to one in which civil virtues were valued above military skill. It may also be that materials used to make weapons such as iron are more difficult to preserve.

The form and construction of this head armour is influenced by the manufacture of Mongolian helmets, but the patterns in gold relate to early fifteenth-century Chinese imperial porcelain, textile and lacquer designs. This integration of 'foreign' technology with Chinese taste in ornament is typical of a court object of the early fifteenth century. The helmet is made of iron and to decorate it gold leaf was added, fused to the iron and engraved with further details. This technique, known as damascening, is rarely seen on armour but is often used for religious ritual equipment such as the ritual sceptre (see fig. 202).

At the front of the helmet is a seated Buddha placed within a flaming mandorla (halo). At the back are two horizontally placed confronting dragons fighting over a flaming pearl. On either side are four-clawed dragons standing on their hind legs, with stylized lotus flowers and scrolling lotus blooms. There are also smaller ornaments of clouds and auspicious symbols from a set known as the 'Seven Gems'. The helmet is constructed of two halves that are riveted together, with an iron strap along the seam and a finial with a round knob at the centre. There are fourteen holes along the rim for the attachment of further armour to protect the cheeks and nape of the neck.

A comparable helmet damascened with a similar design in silver, in a private collection, had three fragments of paper printed with a Tibetan text rolled up inside the short plume tube of the helmet's finial. This presumably acted as a protective talisman, together with the image of the Buddha, in battle. Such talismans were also integrated into Mongol culture.

Iron and damascened in gold
c. 1400–50
Nanjing, Beijing or Tibet
h 19 cm
Metropolitan Museum of Art, New York, Purchase,
Arthur Ochs Sulzberger Gift, 2005 (2005.270)

Sword and scabbard

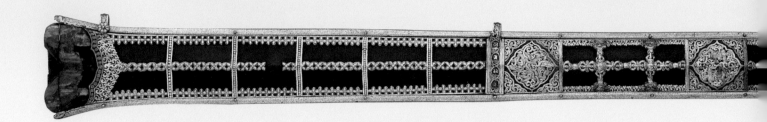

FIG. 131

THIS IRON SWORD and its scabbard is one of the most beautiful and technically intricate weapons to survive from the early Ming period. Commissioned by the Yongle emperor, it was made in China either for presentation to a Tibetan ruler – such as one of the Phagmodrupa, who were the predominant power in central Tibet from 1358 to 1434 – or for the Yongle emperor himself. At the centre of the scabbard is a Sanskrit inscription, which has been interpreted as meaning: *'khadgaratna or ral gri rin po che'* in Tibetan ('Precious Sword'). Precious Sword is the last of the Seven Jewels of Royal Power (the others being Precious Wheel, Precious Jewel, Precious Queen, Precious Minister, Precious Elephant and Precious Horse) – symbolic attributes of monarchy.

Swords were not only weapons but indicated, by their quality and craftsmanship, both the rank and power of the owner. This fine sword is decorated with gold, silver and semi-precious stones. The sword guard is in the form of a three-dimensional monster mask with flame-like mane and jewelled eyes. While its jaws appear to bite

down over the top of the scabbard, its body is suggested by a spine that leads to the pommel. In turn, the pommel is decorated on the front with a dragon and on the other side with another Tibetan-style creature. The sides of the pommel are decorated with the Eight Auspicious Symbols commonly used as a Chinese motif. The blade itself is double-edged. The scabbard is shrouded by a damascened iron frame made up of lines of *vajras* (thunderbolts) and set with panels of cavorting, sinewy dragons. The chape at the bottom is filled with scrollwork. The sword would have been suspended from the waist using the two loops on the righthand side of the scabbard. One of the guardian figures from a set of paintings in the British Museum, originally from a monastery in Shigatse, clasps an almost identical sword, suggesting that this Chinese sword was modelled on a Tibetan prototype.

Iron, gold, silver, wood, leather and semi-precious stones
Yongle period, *c.* 1420
Beijing
Overall l 90.3 cm, l of blade 76.2 cm
Royal Armouries Museum, Leeds (XXVIS.295)

4

WEN
THE ARTS OF PEACE

Craig Clunas

Water pours in a stream down the stairs
The pots beneath the stove still not inundated;
Quickly, I run to save my books from my desk.
If only I could be like my eastern and western neighbours:
Calmly sleeping, not a thing to worry about.

YANG SHIQI (1365–1444), 'NIGHT RAIN: A WALL COLLAPSES – SENT TO MY NEIGHBOURS'[1]

In Ming China the imperial court was a place where the written language, and the manipulation of that language, mattered to a high degree, and where skills in using language were both highly rewarded *and* potentially highly dangerous. The ideal of the early Ming emperors lay in the phrase '*wen wu shuang quan*', 'complete in the arts of both peace and of war'. If *wu*, military force, the arts of war (as discussed in Chapter 3), was one central aspect of Ming imperial power, then equally crucial were the more peaceful arts of *wen*, 'culture', as embodied above all in the written language.

Later historians recorded a brutally shocking (if almost certainly apocryphal) event where force and writing came together in the summer of 1402. This was the supposed confrontation between the triumphant Prince of Yan, Zhu Di (1360–1424), victorious after a three-year war with his nephew the Jianwen emperor, and Lian Zining (d. 1402), counsellor of the defeated monarch. Lian's verbal defiance of his new lord, soon to be the Yongle emperor, led to him being silenced by having his tongue ripped out. To demonstrate his mastery of the classical tradition of history and politics, Zhu Di asserted that he was no usurper, comparing himself instead to the ancient Duke of Zhou, who had come to the aid of, and served as regent for, the infant King Cheng at the dawn of recorded history. In a particularly gruesome gesture, Lian Zining is supposed to have reached into his tortured mouth and written in his own blood, 'Where *is* King Cheng?'[2] Defiance brought only violent ends for Lian Zining and other more senior officials like him such as Fang Xiaoru (1357–1402), but also for all members of their extended families, slaughtered in large numbers; even ownership of their writings could earn a death sentence.[3]

Both the emperor and his defiant servant were using history to support their stand, history as part of what the sage Confucius called '*si wen*', 'this culture of ours'. But Lian Zining was also using *wen* in its narrower sense of 'text', of writing. The control of both was of great importance to the rulers of the early Ming, who strove to make their version of events the only acceptable one for the entire literate population of the empire, in a context where the scholarly elite was always a potential source of resistance. Writing played a part in the lives of ordinary people too, even for that majority who could not read at all, or at least could not read well enough to have full access to the huge archive of China's written culture. The forty-seven written contracts (fig. 134) for the sale of land that we have from the years 1403–49 (the Yongle, Hongxi, Xuande and Zhengtong reigns) – only a tiny fragment of what must

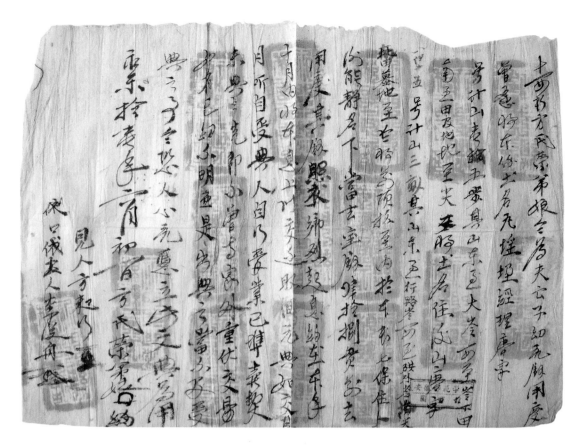

FIG. 134
Contract for the sale of land

The body of land contracts that survives
from Huizhou is a major source for
Chinese social and economic history,
as well as demonstrating the role that
written documents played in the lives
of ordinary people.

Ink and red seals on paper
Dated 1413
Huizhou prefecture, Anhui province
h 26.7 cm, w 36.8 cm
Anhui Normal University Library

FIG. 135
**Printed placard of regulations on
the circulation of paper money**

With its large characters nearly
7 cm high, this public proclamation is
a rare survival from the many texts,
announcements and advertisements
that once filled the streets of early
Ming cities.

Woodblock-printed, ink and red seals
on paper
Dated 1422
h 94.5 cm, l 276 cm
Shanxi Museum

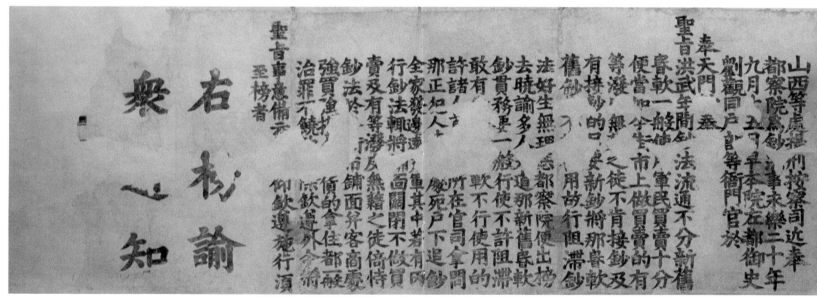

have been a huge number of such documents – are a testimony to the presence of
the written word as a part of the lives of quite humble people.[4] The very rare survival
of a huge printed placard (fig. 135) from the year 1422, bearing regulations written
in characters almost 7 centimetres high relating to the circulation of paper money
(itself a printed artefact bearing writing and pictures), shows that the streets of early
Ming cities carried messages that were visible, if not always fully comprehensible, to
the many.

Great Canon of the Yongle Reign
(*Yongle da dian* 永樂大典)

FIG. 137

ALTHOUGH often referred to as an encyclopaedia, the *Great Canon of the Yongle Reign* (*Yongle da dian*) is instead a compilation of complete texts, rather than extracts, or specially written entries. As such, it is the largest and most comprehensive example of a class of literature that in Chinese is called *leishu* (類書), which literally means 'classified writings'. It was commissioned by the Yongle emperor and replaced earlier versions such as the *Great Collection of Written Documents* (*Wenxian da cheng*),

compiled from 1401 to 1404, with which the emperor was not satisfied.

His chief advisor, the monk Daoyan (1335–1418), supervised its production, making use of 2,169 scholarly compilers from the Hanlin Academy and National University, who began in 1405 and completed their selection by 1408. By commissioning this project, the Yongle emperor was promoting himself as a sage Confucian ruler preserving ancient texts. He took total control of the written historical record, removing any texts he disapproved of. It was produced as a handwritten manuscript and scholars strove to use a style of handwriting that was coherent across the series of volumes, so they adopted Shen Du's court clerical style of handwriting.

As well as an entire Yuan-dynasty (1279–1368) compilation of texts, *Great Canon for Governing the World* (*Jing shi da dian*), the *Yongle da dian* included writings on religions, philosophy, science and many different forms of literature, including plays and poetry. There is even a section on the Yuan-dynasty postal system. The original *Yongle da dian* was made in Nanjing and then moved to Beijing in 1427.

In 1557 it was nearly destroyed by a palace fire so the Jiajing emperor ordered a manuscript copy to be made. No part of the original 1408 version survives. By the eighteenth century, when the Qianlong emperor (r. 1736–1795) had the set checked, many volumes were missing. Out of 22,877 volumes in 11,095 books, today just 700 volumes survive, all dating to the late Jiajing to Longqing era (1562–1572).

Ink on paper, silk cover
This edition, Jiajing to Longqing periods, 1562–1572
Beijing
Book closed: h 50.5 cm, w 30 cm; book open:
h 50.5 cm, w 60 cm; book text with inner printed
border only: h 35.5 cm, w 23.5 cm
British Library, London OR 11543, 11758

FIG. 141

White porcelain bowl with Yongle reign mark

The Yongle emperor (1403–1424) introduced the use of reign marks at the imperial porcelain kilns at Jingdezhen. These marks were only applied to specific types of ceramics: white and red stem cups and bowls, and some underglaze blue cups. The seal script reign mark followed the archaic script style of the court calligrapher Shen Du (1357–1434), 'Made in the Yongle reign' (*Yongle nian zhi* 永樂年製). This ancient writing style evoked a historical continuity with the remote past, as it was a script used on oracle bones and bronzes of the Shang dynasty (*c.*1500–1050 BC). Creating the idea of continuity with the past – and thus establishing his legitimacy to rule – was a major preoccupation of the Yongle emperor. Chinese archaeologists have shown that these delicately potted, bodiless bowls were fired at the imperial kilns between 1403 and 1412, under close imperial supervision.

Porcelain with incised and *anhua* (hidden) decoration
Yongle mark and period, *c.* 1403–12
Jingdezhen, Jiangxi province
h 6.6 cm
British Museum, London, donated by Sir Augustus Wollaston Franks in 1876, Franks.1

was Zhu Youdun (1379–1439), Prince Xian of Zhou, a nephew of the Yongle emperor and a prolific artist as well as a playwright and the owner of the 'Eastern Library' collection. Projects such as his 1417 engraving of the single most esteemed piece of Chinese calligraphy, the 'Orchid Pavilion Preface' of Wang Xizhi (303–361), most famous of all ancient calligraphers, showed the princes in their role of spreading the *wen*, the 'culture' of the dynasty throughout the vast space of the Ming empire. Many princely households, such as that of the Princes of Jin at Taiyuan, Shanxi province, collected extensive holdings of works of art from earlier dynasties (fig. 139), as did great aristocratic houses such as that of the descendants of Mu Ying (1345–1392), companion-in-arms of the Ming founder and conqueror of Yunnan.

As well as curating the cultural legacy of the past, in its most valued form of calligraphy and text, the early Ming imperial court sought to establish a standard form of calligraphy for use in a wide variety of written and printed contexts. This script form, known as the *taige ti*, or 'eminent court official style',[15] is closely associated with calligraphers who were members of the Shen family, from Huating near modern Shanghai.[16] Shen Du (1357–1434), who had served in the retinues of several imperial princes requiring documents whose elegance and poise matched their status, was talent-spotted by Zhu Di very shortly after the conquest of Nanjing in 1402, and soon became the emperor's favourite calligrapher. His portrait (fig. 144) shows him in the red robes, jewelled belt and stiffened horsehair hat of an imperial official. An even more personal survival, the stone used for grinding the ink that was central to his art (fig. 145), bears evidence of his service in the Hanlin Academy, the body of officials who served closest to the person of the emperor. Shen Du's younger brother, Shen Can (1379–1453), as well as his son, Shen Zao (active late fifteenth century), continued to be favoured by later emperors. Their style, based on that of the great Yuan calligrapher Zhao Mengfu (1254–1322), can be seen not only in works written

by themselves (fig. 143), but also in the writing of anonymous court scribes, such as those responsible for an edict from the first year of the Xuande emperor's reign (fig. 146).[17] In fact, the 'eminent court official style' of the Chinese written and printed script, first systematized in the early Ming, spread far beyond the confines of the palace and the imperial government apparatus, to become familiar to very large numbers of viewers. It appeared on books and placards, on the paper currency (fig. 243) and on the copper coinage that even the most humble may have handled (fig. 237). Coins marked '*Yongle tong bao*', 'Circulating treasure of the Yongle era', began to be produced in the new capital of Beijing from about 1410, and circulated in time in considerable quantities beyond the confines of the Ming empire, carrying not only the imperial name but also the imperial script in which it was written to a wide audience.[18]

Objects too could carry that name far and wide. The early fifteenth century is the first epoch in Chinese history when the reign mark, 'Made in the Yongle reign' (fig. 141) or 'Made in the Xuande reign of the Great Ming' (fig. 142), began systematically to be applied to objects in a whole range of media, from porcelain to lacquer, metalwork to textiles. From the Xuande reign it was in the 'eminent court official style' of calligraphy that these marks were inscribed, creating the authority for this script form, which has led to it becoming one of the most widely used fonts of the digital era for written Chinese, under the broad name of *Ming ti*, 'Ming style'.

Calligraphy and printing were also crucial in communication with the wider world, as Chinese elites could confidently communicate with those elsewhere in east Asia in the widely understood written form of classical Chinese, secure in the knowledge that they would be able to write back (fig. 147). Texts such as the Confucian classics (figs 148 and 150) and guides to writing classical Chinese poetry (fig. 149) were printed in Japan and Korea, testimony to a shared literary culture across the region.

FIG. 142

Bird feeder in the form of two joined peaches

Although the reign mark was introduced in the Yongle era for certain types of porcelain, textiles, bronzes and lacquer, its use was more widespread in the Xuande era. This bird feeder has a six-character Xuande reign mark, 'Made in the Xuande reign of the Great Ming' (大明宣德年製 *Da Ming Xuande nian zhi*). The style of script may be based on the regular handwriting style of the court calligrapher Shen Du (1357–1434), or possibly even on the Xuande emperor's own handwriting. He would have been trained to write using Shen Du's style, which was so popular with his grandfather, the Yongle emperor. From the Xuande era, the reign mark is almost always written in a script chosen for its clear legibility.

The earliest blue-and-white porcelain bird feeders were made in the Yuan dynasty (1271–1368). Bird rearing was popular at the imperial court, and such feeders for water and hemp seeds (to make the birds sing more sweetly) have been unearthed at Jingdezhen in a variety of shapes, including other fruits such as pomegranates.

Porcelain with underglaze cobalt-blue
Xuande mark and period, 1426–1435
Jingdezhen, Jiangxi province
h 4.5 cm, w 11.5 cm
British Museum, London, bequeathed by Harry Oppenheim, 1947,0712.173

FIG. 143

Shen Zao (沈藻) (fl. c. 1426), 'Record of bamboo building at Huangzhou in regular script' (*Kaishu Huangzhou zhulou ji* 楷書黃州竹樓記) (composed by Wang Yucheng, 王禹偁 [954–1001])

Shen Zao came from Huating (modern-day Songjiang in Shanghai). He was the son of the famous calligrapher Shen Du (1357–1434), and was appointed to the Central Secretariat (*Zhongshu*) as a Drafter (*Sheren*) on account of his father, moving to the Ministry of Rites (*Li Bu*) as a Vice-Director (*Yuan Wailang*). This hanging scroll reproduces the text of 'Record of bamboo building at Huangzhou' by the Song-dynasty writer Wang Yucheng (954–1001). The calligraphy of this piece continues the Shen family's 'eminent court official style' (*taige ti*), but also has more antique overtones as it is based on the style of the Tang-dynasty calligrapher Yu Shinan (558–638). It reads:

The land of Huanggang has many bamboos. The large ones are like rafters. The bamboo workmen split them in half, remove their joints, and use them in place of ceramic tiles. Every house has them since they are cheap and easy to make. In the northwest corner of the small city within the larger one, the city walls are ruined, plants grow wild and the area is desolate. I used [the land there] to build two small storied-buildings that adjoin with Yuebolou (moon wave building). [From it] one can take in a view of the mountains from afar and look ahead to the waves on the river. It is quiet and expansive and impossible to describe in detail. In summer sudden rain is most suitable, as there will be sounds of waterfalls. In winter heavy snow is most suitable, as there will be sounds of jade shattering. This place is suited to playing the zither, as the tone of the zither comes out harmonious and flowing. It is suited to reciting poetry, as the rhymes come out supremely clear. It is suited to playing weiqi [a type of chess], as the tinkling sound of each piece will be pleasant to the ear. It is suited to playing a game of throwing arrows in a vessel, as the clang of the arrows will be melodious. All these [pleasures] are aided by the bamboo building.

In my leisure after official business is done, I would wear a Daoist robe, don a huayang [Daoist] hat, and carry a volume of Book of Changes in my hand. I would sit in meditation with the incense burning, and clear away all my worries in the world. Then beyond the rivers and mountains, I only see the sails of boats, birds on the beaches, mist and clouds, bamboos and trees. When I grow sober from the wine, and the tea and incense are finished, I bid farewell to the setting sun and welcome the clear moon. This is also one of the pleasures of living in exile.

That Qiyun (Even Cloud) [Building] and Luoxing (Falling Star) [Building], they are indeed tall! Jingan (Wooden Lattice) [Building] and Liqiao (Beautiful Tower) [Building] are indeed lavish! Yet they are only for storing prostitutes, concealing song and dance. These are not matters for poets and I will not partake in them. I have heard a bamboo craftsmen say, 'Bamboo roof tiles only last ten years. If you lay two layers, then they will last twenty years.' Alas, in the year yimo of the [Song-dynasty] Zhidao reign (995), from the position of Hanlin Academician I was exiled to Chuzhou. Then in bingshen (996) I was sent to Guangling, in dingyou (997) I was transferred back to the Secretariat. On New Year's eve of wushu (998) I was ordered to Ji'an, and in the third month of yihai (999) I arrived at the county. During these four years, I have moved constantly from place to place. I do not know where I will be next year. What worry do I have that the bamboo building will decay easily? In posterity there will be those of same mind as me who will continue to maintain it, so that this bamboo building will never decay.

Written by Shen Zao of Yunjian in autumn, on the first day of the eighth month of the first year of the reign of Xuande, the year bingwu [1426].

[Translated by Luk Yu-ping]

Hanging scroll, ink on paper
Dated 1426
Beijing
Image: h 81.5 cm, w 26 cm;
with mount: h 248 cm, w 55 cm
The Palace Museum, Beijing

FIG. 144
Anonymous, 'Portrait of Shen Du'
(*Shen Du xiang* 沈度像)

In the early Ming talented men entered government service either through passing the imperial examinations or by being recommended by those already in office. Only after about 1450 did holders of degrees dominate the Ming government. These men were all trained in the Confucian tradition through the study of classical texts on history, philosophy and morality. Shen Du (1357–1434) was a famous calligrapher who retired from office aged seventy-two. He is depicted here with one hand on his belt of office, standing beneath a pine tree in a garden setting with a crane. His calligraphy was praised by both the Yongle and Xuande emperors, and became adopted as a standard script for the Ming court. Shen Du's handwriting style is clear and well balanced. His calligraphic style is one of the sources of the Chinese font most popularly used on computers today.

Handscroll, ink and colour on paper
Anonymous, *c.* 1420–30
Probably Nanjing
Image: h 39.9 cm, w 95.9 cm;
with mount: h 42 cm, w 95.9 cm
Nanjing Museum

FIG. 145
Ink stone

The four 'treasures' required for fine handwriting are a writing brush, ink, ink stone and paper. Ink was produced by grinding an ink stick against an ink stone and adding a little water to the resulting powder. This ink stone belonged to Shen Du. Shen Du's archaic script was used as the basis for the Yongle emperor's seal script porcelain reign mark and his clerical script style was used as the basis of the Xuande emperor's reign mark.

The cavity at one end of this ink stone was ergonomically formed to allow a hand to be inserted. Its inscription records its ownership and date: 'Written by Shen Du of the Hanlin Academy in the autumn of the year yiwei of the Yongle reign [1415]' (*Yongle yiwei qiu hanlin Shen Du shi* 永樂乙未秋翰林沈度識). The Hanlin Academy was an academic institute, which performed both bureaucratic and literary tasks for the court.

Dark brown stone
Dated 1415
Anhui or Jiangxi province
h 2.2 cm, w 7.5 cm, l 13.2 cm
Shanghai Museum

Anonymous, 'Edict to civil and military officials Xia Yuanji and others' (*Chi yu wenwu qunchen Xia Yuanji deng* 勅諭文武群臣夏原吉等)

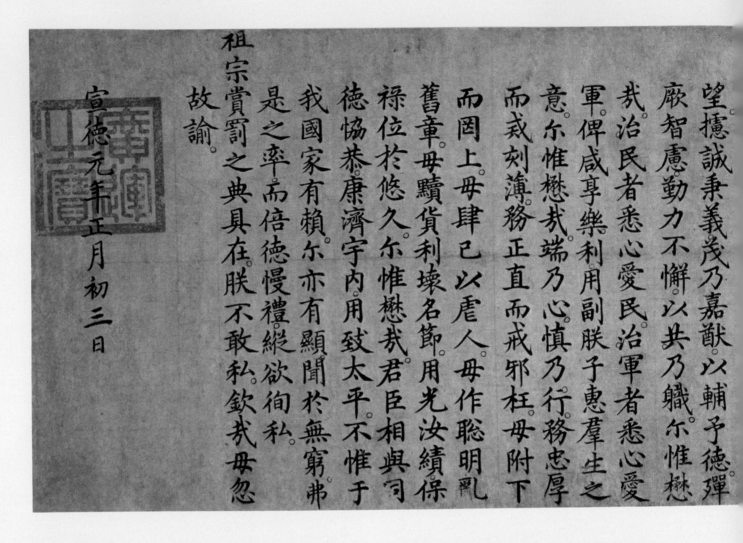

THIS IMPERIAL EDICT of the Xuande emperor (1426–1435) is in the hand of an anonymous court scribe, but the content still gives the reader an insight into the personality and preoccupations of the emperor. The form of calligraphy is known as 'eminent court official style' (*taige ti*), associated with court calligraphers such as Shen Du (1357–1434) and practised by members of the bureaucracy as well as by the emperor himself. Issued on the third day of the very first month of his reign (equivalent to 10 February 1426), it is addressed to Grand Secretary Xia Yuanji (1366–1430) and 'all civil and military officials', confirming them in office and exhorting them to 'love the people … love the troops'. It goes on to caution against factionalism and corruption, and reminds officials that 'the ancestral system of rewards and punishments is still in force'. This official document reads:

The emperor's edict to civil and military officials

For me as ruler of the state nothing is greater than serving the Heavens. To preserve present accomplishments nothing is more important than following the example of ancestors. For the way of officials nothing is more pressing than loyalty to the emperor and love for the people. I have inherited great achievements, granted to me by the Heavens and my ancestors. Day and night I pay my respects, exerting myself to contemplate principles, I do not dare to be idle and at peace. At the start of this year the imperial reign has changed, it is a renewal shared with all under the heavens. You civil and military officials were all chosen by my ancestors to serve. Those who remain with me must hope to assist me. Express sincerity and

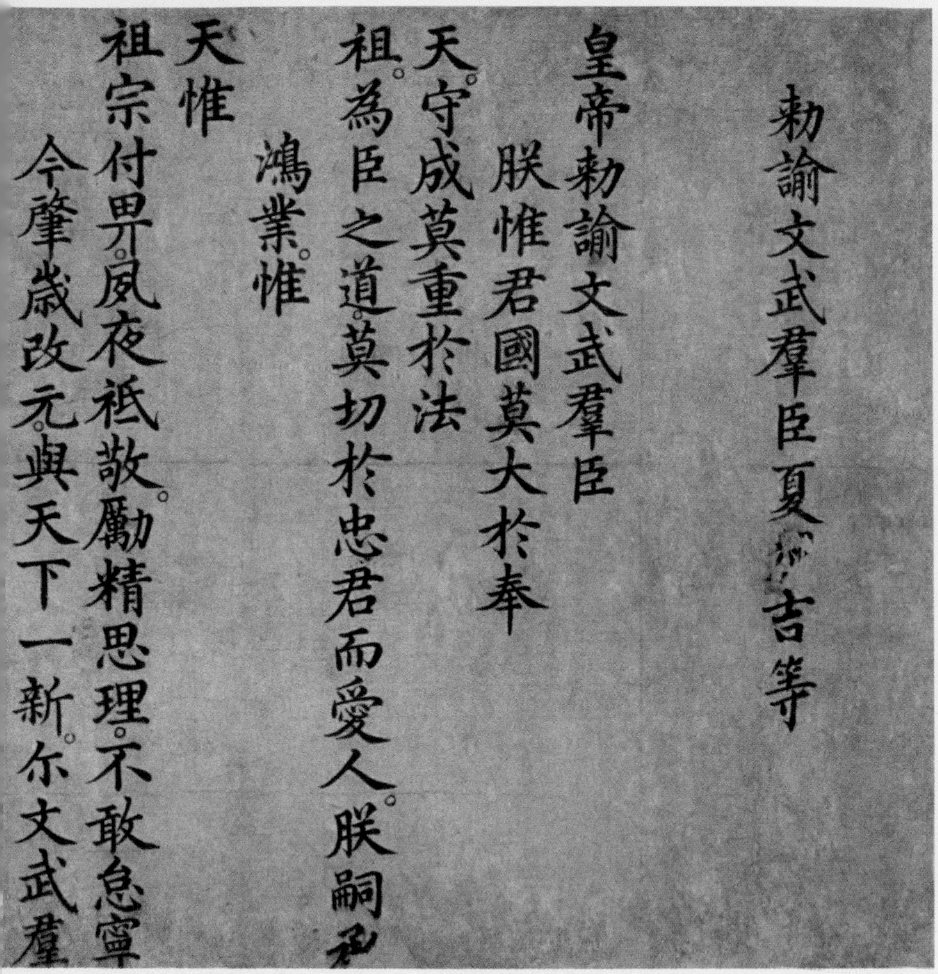
勅諭文武羣臣夏[illegible]吉等
皇帝勅諭文武羣臣
朕惟君國莫大於奉
天。守成莫重於法
祖。為臣之道。莫切於忠君而愛人。朕嗣
鴻業。惟
天惟
祖宗付畀夙夜祗敬。勵精思理。不敢怠寧
今肇歲改元。與天下一新。尔文武羣

FIG. 146
Ink on paper
Dated 1426
(Seal: 'Treasure of expanding fortune'
Guang yun zhi bao 廣運之寶)
Beijing
Image: h 39.3 cm, w 103 cm;
with mount: h 54.3 cm, w 150 cm
The Palace Museum, Beijing

bear righteousness, endeavour to give good advice on government, so to support virtue. Exercise utmost your wisdom and consideration, work hard persistently to serve your position. You are encouraged! Those who govern the people should love the people with all their hearts; those who govern the military should love the military with all their hearts. Use all enjoyments and gains to assist in my purpose of benefiting the lives of people. You are encouraged! Straighten your hearts, be cautious in your deeds; strive for sincerity and kindness, and abstain from being harsh and unfeeling; strive for an upright character and abstain from wickedness; do not parrot your subordinates and deceive your superiors; do not indulge in excess and harm others; do not try to be clever and disrupt the old order; do not taint yourself with profits, spoiling your reputation and character. Brighten your achievements, preserve your rank for longevity. You are encouraged! Ruler and officials together, with the same virtue working diligently in partnership, so that there is wellbeing and relief to all in the world, bringing about great peace. Not only will my state have you to rely on, you will also become illustrious and known beyond all limits. [However, if] in rashness [you] take this lightly, betray virtue and slacken in propriety, indulge in desires and practise favouritism, then the ancestral standards for reward and punishment are all here. I do not dare to practise favouritism. From the emperor himself! Do not neglect this. So it is proclaimed. In the third day of the first month of the first year of the Xuande reign [1426].

[Translated by Luk Yu-ping]

FIG. 149
Dictionary of Chinese Verse
(*Shūbun inryaku* 聚分韻略)

A Japanese monk called Shōsho once owned this book and left a handwritten note inside, dated 1431. Chinese poetry was fashionable in the early fifteenth century in Japan and this text in particular was popular with monks in the monasteries of the Gozan Mountains. It is a dictionary that helps Japanese authors compose Chinese-style verse using classical Chinese characters. Rhyme dictionaries were based on the Chinese *Wu* dialect of the Jiangnan area, and reflect a desire for orthodox and correct pronunciation of classical Chinese characters. The characters are grouped together by tone and rhyme in categories that challenge our modern systems of classification. The original compiler of this text was a Zen monk of Nanzenji (1278–1346). This is the earliest dated Japanese edition of this book to survive.

Woodblock-printed, ink on paper
Printed in 1412
Reigen'an, Tofukuji, Kyoto, Japan
Each page: h 26 cm, w 19.5 cm
British Library, London, acquired from Ernest Satow in 1884, OR 75. g. 20

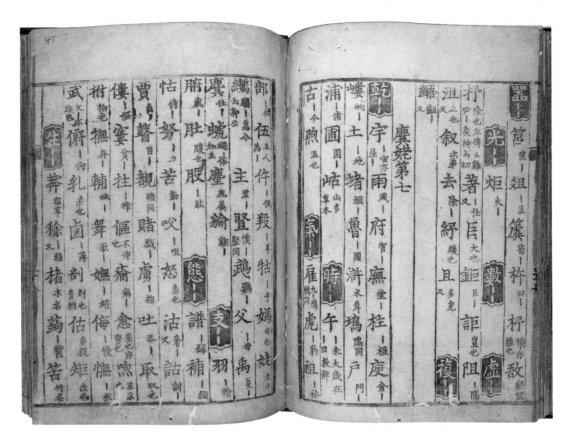

FIG. 150
The Analects of Confucius
(*Rongo* 論語)

This book publishes commentary on the text of the Confucian *Analects*, compiled by He Yan and other scholars of the third century AD. The *Analects* are the teachings of the philosopher Confucius, which form the basis of Confucian doctrine. This edition, published in Japan, demonstrates the popularity of Chinese philosophical ideas in Japanese society in the early fifteenth century: as well as goods and people, ideas moved freely between China and Japan at this time. This edition contains a few printing errors in the characters that were used. The book is open to show the title page.

Woodblock-printed, ink on paper
Printed *c.* 1390–1450
Kyoto, Japan
Each page: h 28.5 cm, w 21.5 cm
British Library, London, once owned by the eminent Japanese physician Tanba Motoyasu (1755–1810), acquired from Ernest Satow 22 September 1884, ORB 30/171

PICTURING CULTURE

Although it was the junior partner in the central cultural practice of 'calligraphy and painting' (*shu hua*), painting still played a major role in attempts to show the imperial and princely courts as centres of *wen*, of 'culture'. Courts held huge collections of earlier painting and became production centres for new painting. The choice of subject matter, as well as the style in which it was depicted, conveyed messages that were meaningful to those equipped to read them. Thus in 1416 Prince Xian of Zhou, based in the old Song-dynasty capital of Kaifeng, both created the 'Eastern Library' collection of model calligraphy and also painted an image of a historical character with rich contemporary relevance. This was an imaginary portrait of Zhuge Liang (181–234) (fig. 151), the half-mythical strategist and loyal advisor of the State of Shu during the heroic Three Kingdoms period (220–265). As a loyal servant to his lord, Zhuge Liang could embody the ideal relationship between the nephew–prince and his uncle, the Yongle emperor (both presumably very well aware that the latter had won the empire in a war with another nephew).

The image of the loyal genius likewise denotes trustworthy service in another painting of the early fifteenth century, created by the most artistically gifted of the early Ming emperors (indeed, by one of the most talented of all Chinese rulers with the brush), the Xuande emperor. The handscroll 'The Marquis of Wu takes his ease' (fig. 152), painted in 1428, uses another of Zhuge Liang's titles, 'Marquis of Wu', to indicate that the portly figure lying beneath bamboos is none other than the fabled thinker.[19] The Xuande emperor then gave this painting to a close courtier, as he gave away most of the works he produced. The recipient was Chen Xuan (1365–1433),[20] a senior military officer with a distinguished record, who had changed sides at a crucial point in the war of 1402 and been rewarded with the title Earl of Pingjiang. His most valued achievement in Ming service was his oversight of the essential system of transport of tax grain from the south to the new capital of Beijing. In 1411 he had

FIG. 151

Zhu Youdun (朱有燉) (1379–1439), 'Zhuge Liang reading' (*Zhuge dushu tu* 諸葛讀書圖)

Zhu Youdun (1379–1439), Prince Xian of Zhou, was the elder son of Zhu Su (1361–1425), Prince of Zhou. He was the Yongle emperor's nephew and a grandson of the founding Ming emperor. He wrote at least seventy books, including a manual for playing the lute, and at least twelve Northern Musical Dramas (*zaju*) and books of poetry. One *zaju* published in 1408, titled *Capture of a Zouyu during the Autumn Battle on Mt Shenhou*, commemorated his father's gift of a *zouyu*, a mythical tiger-like creature, to the Yongle emperor (see fig. 126).

Zhu Youdun, a gifted artist, painted this picture of Zhuge Liang (181–234), who was the counsellor of the righteous ruler of Shu in the Three Kingdoms period (220–265), as well as a central character in the then contemporary novel, *Romance of the Three Kingdoms*, attributed to Luo Guanzhong (*c.* 1315–1400). Zhuge Liang represented a paragon of loyalty

from the past. He was a native of Henan, where Zhu Youdun's princely palace was located. In some ways this painting can be seen as a self-portrait of Zhu Youdun, whose father was the Yongle emperor's last surviving brother. When this image was painted, relations with the emperor were tense: the Princes of Zhou had previously been banished by the Jianwen emperor to Yunnan. They were restored in 1402 when the Yongle emperor seized power but always feared a second term of banishment, or worse. This painting effectively portrays the message that Zhu Youdun was a loyal subject.

Hanging scroll, ink and colour on paper
Dated ninth month, fourteenth year of Yongle, equivalent to 1416
Image: h 134 cm, w 54.4 cm;
with mount: h 254 cm, w 74.4 cm
Capital Museum, Beijing

FIG. 152 ABOVE
**Zhu Zhanji (朱瞻基) (1399–1435),
'The Marquis of Wu takes his ease'
(*Wuhou gaowo tu* 武侯高臥圖)**

Depicting the ancient general and strategist Zhuge Liang (181–234), this picture was painted by the Xuande emperor as a gift for one of his own leading military men, Chen Xuan (1365–1433).

Handscroll, ink on paper
Dated 1428
Beijing
h 27.7 cm, w 40.5 cm
The Palace Museum, Beijing

FIG. 153 RIGHT
**Zhu Zhanji (朱瞻基) (1399–1435),
'Shouxing, Star God of Longevity'
(*Shouxing tu* 壽星圖)**

This painting of an auspicious deity by the most artistically talented of all Ming emperors is inscribed as a gift to the senior official Xia Yuanji (1366–1430), a trusted counsellor who had served the emperor's father, grandfather and great-grandfather. It may have been painted on the occasion of Xia's birthday, and is a major sign of imperial favour towards him.

Handscroll, ink and colours on silk
1426–30
Beijing
h 29.3 cm, w 35.6 cm
The Palace Museum, Beijing

FIG. 154
**Zhu Zhanji (朱瞻基) (1399–1435), 'Lotus pond
and pine tree' (*Lianpu songyin tu* 蓮蒲松蔭圖)**

The Xuande emperor painted this image of a lotus
leaf, seed pod and bird as a courtly gift, and wanted
it to seem as if he had dashed it off. Despite this
lightheartedness, his painting has a serious intent.
Instead of using his natural cursive handwriting style he
uses a standard court style of calligraphy to mark this
work as an official presentation. Imperial inscriptions
have a standard construction and, like the porcelain
and lacquer marks, typically include his reign name
Xuande (宣德). This one reads simply 'imperial brush'
(*yu bi* 御筆). Before the Xuande emperor no imperial
painting inscription included the reign name. With this

gift painting, he is showing the scholarly community
that, although an able military leader, he can also excel
in the civil arts of the Confucian educated world. The
painting is mounted with another painting of a pine tree
and some very fine later paper with gold dragons at
either end.

Handscroll, ink and colours on silk
1426–35
Beijing
Two images, each: h 31 cm, w 53.8 cm;
The Palace Museum, Beijing

taken command of the reopening of the Grand Canal, the vital waterway on which
the imperial economy rested down to the coming of the steamship in the nineteenth
century. He was thus an embodiment of the concept 'complete in the arts of both
peace and of war', and a worthy recipient of a highly personal gift in the emperor's
own hand.

In all, twelve paintings by the Xuande emperor survive today (figs 152–4).
They include works in what was a relatively new format, destined to become one of
the most widespread in all of Chinese painting, the folding fan. Fans dated 1426 (fig.
156) by the emperor are in fact the earliest surviving Chinese works in this form,
which was first developed in Japan or Korea, and originally seen as an exotic novelty;
perhaps it still had some of those connotations in the fifteenth century. But imperial
leisure had a serious purpose, in that it demonstrated to all the fact that the empire
was so well governed, the situation so peaceful, that the arts of peace, of *wen*, could
triumph over those of war, of *wu*.

FIG. 155 BELOW
**Li Zai (李在) (fl. 1426–1435),
'Landscape in the manner of Guo Xi'
(Shanshui tu 山水圖)**

Born in the southern province of Fujian, Li Zai was one of many artists who were drawn to the new northern capital of Beijing by the possibilities for patronage there. He worked for the imperial court as well as for other clients, and may have seen the Song-dynasty original of this composition in the imperial collections.

Hanging scroll, ink and colours on paper
1430s
h 83.3 cm, w 39 cm
Tokyo National Museum

FIG. 156 OPPOSITE
**Zhu Zhanji (朱瞻基) (1399–1435),
'Folding fan with figures in a
landscape' (Shanshui renwu shan
山水人物 扇)**

Folding fans had been introduced to China from Japan and Korea in the Song dynasty, but their use became more widespread in the early Ming. Here the Xuande emperor is demonstrating both his artistic skill and fashionable cosmopolitan tastes. He is regarded as one of the most gifted imperial painters in Chinese history, and a dozen paintings by him survive to this day. An imperial present of a fan implied 'imperial grace for the summer'. The Xuande emperor had a very personal style of government and mixed directly with his high-ranking civil and military officials. His inscriptions on such gifts are however quite standardized, noting that the gift was made by the emperor himself, giving the date and place where it was painted. The inscription on this fan reads: 'On a spring day of the second year of the Xuande reign [1426] painted by the imperial hand at the Hall of Military Valour' (宣德二年春日武英殿御筆). The seal reads: 'Treasure of the Hall of Military Valour' (Wuyingdian bao 武英殿寶).

Fan now mounted as a hanging scroll; ink and colours on paper
Dated 1426
Painted in Beijing
Each image: h 58.5 cm, w 151 cm;
with mount: h 284 cm, w 173 cm
The Palace Museum, Beijing

Much of the painting produced at the imperial court in the early Ming served a celebratory purpose, with its message of peace, prosperity and good governance. This was true of work by the emperor, but equally of that produced by the professional painters who served at court (fig. 155), often with nominal ranks in the imperial bodyguard (a way of paying their salaries, but also emphasizing the intertwining of the arts of peace and war). Bian Wenjin's exact dates are unknown, but his earliest dated painting was completed in 1394, and his last in 1428. He was a native of Fujian in the coastal south, who may well have made the transition from the imperial court in Nanjing to that in Beijing, until he was sacked by the Xuande emperor in 1426 for obscure reasons involving financial corruption.[21] He is famous above all for lavish images of birds, carrying auspicious meanings and replicating in their social interactions the gorgeous life of the imperial court (fig. 157). He also produced, after his dismissal, works such as 'Auspicious arrangement for the New Year' (1427), picturing plants of good omen in a massive archaic bronze vessel (fig. 158).

FIG. 157
**Bian Wenjin (邊文進)
(c. 1354–c. 1428), 'Birds, flowers
and trees of spring' (Chunqin
huamu tu 春禽花木圖)**

The dates of Bian Wenjin (also called
Bian Jingzhao) are unknown, but he
probably lived from about 1354 to
1428. His earliest dated extant work
was painted in 1394, so he began
his career at the Nanjing court of the
Hongwu emperor. He was originally
from Fujian. Bian Wenjin was a court
artist specializing in meticulously
realistic depictions of birds and plants
in the Southern Song court style. His
manner of painting these subjects
was greatly influential at court in the
early Ming. Bian may have painted this
picture early in his career when he was
working in the then capital, Nanjing.
Later he fell out of favour with the
Xuande emperor, was sacked in 1426
and charged with accepting bribes from
those men seeking court office, before
being put in prison in 1427. The birds
are regarded as both auspicious and as
a visual metaphor for the complex social
interactions of people at court.

Hanging scroll, ink and colour on silk
c. 1400–1
Painted in Nanjing
Image: h 141.3 cm, w 53.4 cm;
with mount: h 290 cm, w 96 cm
Shanghai Museum

Good omen, and praise of the good government that produced it, is the prevailing theme of much surviving early Ming court painting. A large painting by Ni Duan (active *c.* 1426–1435) shows the officers of an ancient emperor penetrating deep into the mountains to recruit a humble but worthy hermit to his service (fig. 159). The painting of a giraffe (figs 192 and 218), a present from the Sultan of Bengal that arrived at the imperial court in 1414, is not simply a record of an exotic beast from far-off lands; rather, it is a testimony to the favour bestowed on the dynasty and its emperor by the highest cosmic powers, commemorated by court artists along with a magical white deer and white elephant (fig. 232), and even the rarely seen phenomenon of the muddy Yellow River running clear. Multiple versions of the image were produced, probably to be given as gifts to courtiers; at least one of them bears the calligraphy of Shen Du, illustrating the close-knit circle of imperial artists.[22] Equally worthy of commemoration was the mythical *zouyu* (fig. 126) presented to the Yongle emperor in 1404 by his brother (a brother with whom he had a prickly relationship), Prince Su of Zhou (1361–1425), and celebrated in a play written by that prince's son Zhu Youdun (1379–1439) (fig. 151) in 1408.[23]

This was one of many celebratory plays (works that often stress the theme of *zhong*, 'loyalty') that were written by the prince, a key figure in the establishment of the court as the setter of standards in drama, as in so much else. The *zaju* (Northern Musical Drama) of the Yuan period is today seen as one of the glories of pre-modern Chinese literature, but the 'Yuan' drama that comes down to us today does so in the form of Ming court texts, as performed before the imperial family, and in a number of cases written by members of it.[24] Of the collections of this drama that we have today, only one is actually from the Yuan period, and most 'Yuan' drama is in fact early Ming in date, representing the taste of the Ming imperial court, rather than that of any more popular audience.[25]

The painting of the magical *zouyu*, as celebrated in these courtly shows, is anonymous, its artist too low in social status to have been deemed worthy of record, but men of higher standing also painted in the orbit of the imperial court. Wang Fu (1362–1416) was another figure with bureaucratic rank, and hence a gentleman not an artisan, whose brush was at the service of the imperial project. He was one of those who joined the personal staff of the Yongle emperor at the time of his victory, alongside the calligrapher Shen Du, with whom he is known to have been friendly. His most important project may have been the 'Eight Views of Beijing' (fig. 7), a long scroll painted after an imperial tour of inspection to the site of the new northern capital in Beijing in 1413. Suitably adorned with laudatory poems and inscriptions by leading officials, this scroll, which may have existed in multiple versions for distribution to key figures, signalled the imperial determination to site the capital in what had been his old powerbase when he was Prince of Yan; but it also signalled the acquiescence of key members of the elite in what was a politically tricky decision. Wang Fu might have painted in what has come to be known as the 'literati' style associated with non-courtly elites, but in the early Ming this was a style that, like so much else, was designed to serve an imperial purpose.

FIG. 158
Bian Wenjin (邊文進) **(fl. 1403–1435), 'Auspicious arrangement for the New Year'** (*Suichao tu* 歲朝圖)

This arrangement of pine branches, plum blossoms and other flowers in an ancient bronze vase carries the meaning of good wishes for the coming year. It was painted by one of the most prolific and successful artists employed directly by the imperial court, Bian Wenjin.

Hanging scroll, ink and colours on paper
Dated 1427
h 108 cm, w 46.1 cm
National Palace Museum, Taipei

FIG. 161

Xie Jin (謝縉) (1369–1415), 'Travelling early from Yunyang' (*Yunyang zao xing tu* 雲陽早行圖)

This scene, of an old man travelling on horseback as morning mists lift after a night of heavy rain, was painted in 1417 by Xie Jin. For an educated man such as Xie, painting would have formed part of the range of cultural activities at which he excelled. The style of this work is based specifically on that of the Yuan-dynasty painters Wu Zhen (1280–1354) and Wang Meng (c. 1308–1385), who were favoured by educated artists outside court circles. Xie lived and worked in the southern city of Suzhou, and this is in part in a regional style. He painted this work as a parting gift for his friend Sheng Yin, a doctor who served in the Imperial Academy of Medicine as a court physician. It carries inscriptions by a number of other friends of Sheng Yin, at least one of whom was also an imperial court doctor. The artist's inscription reads:

People of the past at the moment of dawn, do not sleep but listen to the morning rooster. With happiness brimming at one's brow, light wind breezes past the horse's hooves. Mt Kunling is far then near, the trees of Mou Garden are high then low. Expecting to return home in the evening, [when] with longing moonlight fills the streams. Doctor Qi Dong is about to return to Wu [present-day Suzhou area]. Kui Qiu [Xie Jin] paints the scroll 'Travelling early from Yunyang' and adds poetry as a gift to him. The day after wangri [normally the sixteenth day], on the tenth month of the year dingyou of the Yongle reign [1417].

[Translated by Luk Yu-ping]

故人明發處，不寐聽晨雞。喜色盈眉睫，輕風入馬蹄。昆陵山遠近，茂苑樹高低。料得還家夜，相思月滿溪。啟東醫學將還吳，葵丘謝縉為寫雲陽早行圖軸並詩以贈。時永樂丁酉歲十月既望也。

Qidong is the sobriquet or nickname of Cheng Yin (盛寅); Kuiqiu (葵丘) is the sobriquet of Xie Jin.

Hanging scroll, ink and colours on paper
Dated 1417
Nanjing
h 102.1 cm, w 47.5 cm; with mount: h 267 cm, w 78.5 cm
Shanghai Museum

group of senior officials given the rank of 'Grand Secretary' in 1421; four years later he was one of those confirmed in office by a surviving edict in the hand of the Hongxi emperor (fig. 27). In 1421 he was also appointed for the first time to serve as Chief Examiner for the highest of the three tiers of civil service examinations; success in these would give a man the coveted title of *jinshi*, 'Presented Scholar', almost guaranteeing a significant career in the imperial bureaucracy. In the Yongle, Hongxi, Xuande and Zhengtong reigns from 1402 to 1449, a total of 2,799 men succeeded in the sixteen sessions held.[27] The influence of the system went beyond Ming borders, and in 1442 a now-liberated Vietnam held its own examinations, though still using the commentaries on the Confucian classics approved by the Yongle emperor in 1415.[28] But the exam system over which Yang Shiqi presided in the early fifteenth

FIG. 162

Attributed to Sesshū Tōyō (雪舟等揚)
(1420-1506), 'Broken-ink landscape
painting' (*Haboku sansui zu* 破墨山
水図**)**

This is a very significant early work by
the great ink painter and Japanese monk
Sesshū Tōyō (1420–1506), produced some
time before he visited China between 1468
and 1469, perhaps in the 1440s to 1460s.
It demonstrates the attraction of Chinese
styles of ink painting for elites across east
Asia in the early Ming. His work is executed
in *haboku* ('broken ink') style, which employs
no outlines. It carries the seal of Tenshō
Shūbun (天章周文 1414–63), Sesshū's
teacher in painting, and shows his mastery
of the kind of landscape style, originating
in China, which was particularly valued in
Japan in his day. Through elite and monastic
exchanges, Chinese culture spread to
Japan. Later Sesshū travelled to Ming China
as a member of a group sponsored by the
Ōuchi family.

Hanging scroll, ink on paper
1440s–60s
Kyoto
h 63.5 cm, w 31.7 cm
British Museum, London, donated by Sir William
Gwynne-Evans, Bt in 1913, JP 352
(1913,0501,0.97)

FIG. 163
**Anonymous, 'Evening bell
from mist-shrouded temple'
(*Yeonsa manjong* 煙寺晚鐘)**

Early Ming paintings that echoed earlier
Song- and Yuan-dynasty styles were
collected and admired outside China.
Prince Anpyeong (Yi Yong) (1418–1453),
the third son of King Sejong of Korea
(r. 1418–1450), possessed a large
collection of classical Chinese painting
of the Song and Yuan dynasties, which
was inventoried in 1445. The Korean artist
An Gyeon (fl. *c.* 1440–1470) studied this
princely collection and based one of his
most important works 'Dream journey to
the Peach Blossom Land' on a landscape
by the Northern Song artist Guo Xi
(*c.* 1020–*c.* 1090).

This anonymous painting is clearly
in the style of An Gyeon and is part of
a set of eight hanging scrolls depicting
the landscapes of the Xiao and Xiang
Rivers in the modern-day province
of Hunan, which were celebrated in
classical Chinese literature. Joseon
court collections of classical Chinese
paintings even inspired the artwork of
many members of the Korean Joseon
royal family.

Hanging scoll, ink on silk
1440–1500
Korea
h 88.3 cm, w 45.1 cm
Metropolitan Museum of Art, New York,
purchase, Joseph Pulitzer Bequest, and Mr and
Mrs Frederick P. Rose and John B. Elliott Gifts,
1987 (1987.278)

Anonymous, after Xie Huan (謝環) (1377–1452),
'Elegant gathering in the Apricot Garden' (Xingyuan yaji tu 杏園雅集圖)

FIG. 164

THE HIGH OFFICIAL Yang Rong (1371–1440) is depicted in this painting hosting nine colleagues at a party in the garden of his home in the new northern capital of Beijjing, during an official holiday on 6 April 1437. Here the officials are painted in their court robes, the different colours and patterns signifying their ranks. Among the men depicted here are the Three Yang – Yang Shiqi (1365–1444) (wearing a blue robe), Yang Pu (1372–1446) (wearing a red robe) and Yang Rong (1371–1440) (also wearing a red robe) – who were part of the Yongle emperor's Grand Secretariat (*Neige*). These men went on to work for the Hongxi, Xuande and Zhengtong emperors as senior advisors. Their longevity in government demonstrates the relative stability of senior office in the early fifteenth century. Their power and influence increased further during the regency of the boy Zhengtong emperor after

1436, when power was shared between high officials and senior imperial women.

Another version of this painting exists in the Zhenjiang Museum in China, which may in fact be the model for this work. This version of the painting may have been executed by lesser court painters and distributed to participants in the event. Xie Huan (1377–1452), the painter of the original, came from a scholarly family in Yongjia, Zhejiang province, and was esteemed by the Three Yangs. He became a court painter under the Yongle emperor and was also awarded special ranks by the Xuande emperor. The variety of styles in which he worked, sometimes for the court and sometimes for private clients, gives an insight into the art market of early Ming Beijing. In the other surviving version of this painting, he is actually depicted in the scroll, placing himself at the event and thus indicating his status at court.

Handscroll, ink and colours on silk
Dated 1437
Beijing
h 37.5 cm, w 240.7 cm
Metropolitan Museum of Art, New York,
Purchase, the Dillon Fund Gift 1989
(1989.141.3)

dullness ever since'.[45] Poems that praise the Yongle emperor's decision to move the capital to Beijing (flagrantly defying the dynastic founder's instructions), or praise imperial prowess in the hunt (see Chapter 3, p. 114) or in patrolling the borders, all the eulogies on the rare and exotic animals in the imperial menagerie, and signs of Heaven's blessing on the imperial project, remain excluded from modern anthologies of Chinese literature. But these poems fulfilled a purpose and played a role for their authors and their audiences, binding the educated elite of the empire into a close alliance with the ruling house, and consolidating a network of power and authority that had remarkable stability and resilience.

THE APRICOT GARDEN: CALLIGRAPHY, PAINTING, ZITHER AND CHESS

That stability was tested in 1436, when the Xuande emperor died leaving only infant offspring. Zhu Qizhen (1427–1464) was only nine years old when he became emperor, and the activist style of rulership favoured by his father and great-grandfather was no longer an option. It was an alliance between the senior women of the imperial family and the official network headed by the 'Three Yang' that took control of the empire's fate. The female part of that power structure is almost invisible to us in surviving visual and material culture, and the explicit voices of empress dowagers and other senior women are similarly not clearly recorded in the written sources, though their powerful role is implied in the historical records of the time. But painting male elites was a different matter.

'Elegant gathering in the Apricot Garden', by Xie Huan (1377–1452) (fig. 164), was, when painted in 1437, a new instance of an age-old theme in Chinese painting – men of taste and discernment gathering together to enjoy conversation around the arts and culture. It shows a number of key figures of the new Zhengtong regime, including Grand Secretary Yang Shiqi, gathered in the Beijing garden of his colleague Yang Rong (1371–1440) and accompanied by Yang Pu (1372–1446), third and youngest of the 'Three Yang'. The painting was again probably produced in a format of multiples, allowing more than one participant their own copy of it. An inscription by the host, Yang Rong, carefully identifies all the participants by their names and titles: 'Junior Tutor to the Heir Apparent', 'Vice Supervisor of the Imperial Household', 'Hanlin Academy Reader-in-Waiting' and so on. Their robes, some with the woven badges of their ranks, confirm their varying status levels and tell us that, though they are engaged in cultural activities, these men are never 'off-duty'. Rather, their grasp on the realm is so safe and secure that they can afford to spend time on other things that matter. In this case it is the four gentlemanly pastimes: playing the zither-like *guqin*, playing the strategy game of chess, practising their own calligraphy and engaging in the connoisseurship of the art of painting. In Chinese these four activities are known as *qin qi shu hua* ('zither, chess, calligraphy, painting'), all a part of the broader category of *wen*, the cultural arts of peace.

These same activities appear on two massive porcelain jars of the Zhengtong period, where the practitioners of the four arts are elegant ladies (fig. 165). The actual apparatus needed to carry out these activities (the musical instrument, the chess set,

FIG. 165
Wine jar showing palace ladies engaged in cultural pursuits

Cultivated men and women were expected to take an interest in the arts of playing the zither (*guqin*), a stringed musical instrument of great complexity; playing chess (known by the Japanese name *go*), an important demonstration of the art of strategic thinking in which the object of the game was to place counters on a board and surround those of your opponent; writing fine Chinese calligraphy in the styles of past great masters; and appreciating and critiquing classical Chinese paintings. These acomplishments took years of application to perfect.

This large porcelain jar was made for storing wine, which was then decanted into smaller bottles and ewers for serving. It was produced at the imperial porcelain kilns at Jingdezhen and has four scenes painted in underglaze blue cobalt that are punctuated by banks of clouds. Groups of palace ladies are depicted engaged in the Four Arts, bejewelled and dressed in fine robes. See also p. 156.

Porcelain with underglaze cobalt-blue decoration
Xuande or Zhengtong period, 1426–1449
Jingdezhen, Jiangxi province
h 34.4 cm, diam. 22.1 cm
Shanghai Museum

FIG. 166
Zither

Prince Huang of Lu, Zhu Tan (1370–1389), was buried in Shandong with this ancient *guqin* (zither). It is inscribed 'Heavenly Winds and Ocean Waves' (*tian feng hai tao* 天風海濤), describing the sound that it makes. It is very difficult to play well: the accomplished playing of the zither was a marker of a man or woman's high-level education. Practising civilizing music was a demonstration of the Confucian value of self-cultivation, while encouraging the rejection of other musical forms. Court music developed through imperial and princely interaction with palace eunuchs, court officials and commoner musicians. The Hongwu emperor gave written operas and songs to the regional princes,

helping them to establish local centres of music. Some of the other regional princes, such as the Prince of Ning, Zhu Quan (1378–1448), who was also buried with a zither, compiled and published anthologies of music, brought master musicians together and hosted performances. Zhu Youdun, Prince Xian of Zhou (1379–1439), wrote thirty-two musical dramas.

Wood and black lacquer, jade
Made 609–916, buried in 1389
China
h 121 cm, w 19.5 cm
Shandong Museum, excavated from the tomb of Zhu Tan, Prince Huang of Lu at Yanzhou, Shandong province

FIG. 167
Wine jar showing men engaged in cultural pursuits

The designs for these men engaged in the arts of playing the zither, playing chess and admiring calligraphy and painting may relate closely to illustrations in an early fifteenth-century printed book *More Tales while Trimming the Lamp Wick* (*Xinkan Jian deng yu hua*), compiled by the princely counsellor Li Changqi (1376–1452) and completed in 1433. Whereas figures are quite rare on surviving blue-and-white porcelains of the Hongwu, Yongle and Xuande reigns, they became very popular by the mid-fifteenth century. This may suggest broader patronage of the kilns and a wider circulation of designs after the strict control of the Yongle and Xuande eras.

Porcelain with underglaze cobalt-blue decoration
Zhengtong period, 1436–1449
Jingdezhen, Jiangxi province
h 35.6 cm, diam. 39.4 cm
Victoria and Albert Museum, London, purchased in 1860, 6840-1860

the calligraphy brushes and the paintings) were laid in the tomb of at least one Ming prince, Zhu Tan, Prince of Lu (1370–1390) (figs 166 and 168). Thus the arts of peace were seen as the common property of prince *and* minister (who might be of much more lowly birth), as well as, at least in the imagination, of women of the highest class.

The painter Xie Huan, humblest participant in the 'Apricot Garden' gathering, is a figure who illustrates the close connections at this period between the culture of the imperial court and that of wider society. An officer in the Brocade Uniform Guard, most prestigious of the imperial bodyguards (see Chapter 3, p. 128), he not only produced work directly to imperial command, but also painted for individual officials and aristocrats who were well enough connected to be able to call on his services.[46] In the same year that he and his workshop (for we can assume he had assistants to produce the multiple versions required) painted 'Elegant gathering in the Apricot Garden' for Yang Rong, he also produced work for Yang Shiqi, a picture entitled 'Joy on a snowy night'.[47]

A much later anecdote found in Ming texts about the art of painting tells how Xie Huan maintained his dominance at court by ruining the promising career there of the rising star of painting Dai Jin (1388–1462), a man who came to Beijing to seek his fortune (he was there by 1428 at the latest) but who never made it on to the imperial payroll, working instead as a (very successful) professional artist on private commissions. Dai's work includes paintings completed for the many social occasions of official life, such as the scroll 'Saying farewell at Jintai' (fig. 169). He probably painted this in the last years of the Xuande reign to record the send-off given by friends and colleagues to the official Wei Jing, a protégé of Yang Shiqi (who seems to have had a hand in almost everything that happened in the capital). A court calligrapher called Cheng Nanyun supplied the title inscription, again illustrating the fluid nature of interactions between those theoretically inside and those theoretically outside the imperial government at this period.[48]

FIG. 168
Chess set

This chess set (called *weiqi* in Chinese, but often known by its Japanese name *go*) is from the tomb of Zhu Tan, Prince Huang of Lu (1370–1389). The excavated set includes 175 black counters, 181 white counters, two ceramic containers with lacquer coating for the counters, and a paper board to play on. It is a game of strategy and skill played by two people. The board has 19 × 19 lines, creating more squares than a Western chess board. The object of the game is to alternately place white and black counters on the intersecting lines, to occupy as much of the board with your counters as possible and to remove your opponent's counters by surrounding them. Play continues until one player declares he can make no more moves.

Ceramic, lacquer, paper and stone
Before 1389
Shandong
diam. of counters 1.8–2.3 cm
Shandong Museum, excavated from the tomb of Zhu Tan, Prince Huang of Lu at Yanzhou, Shandong province

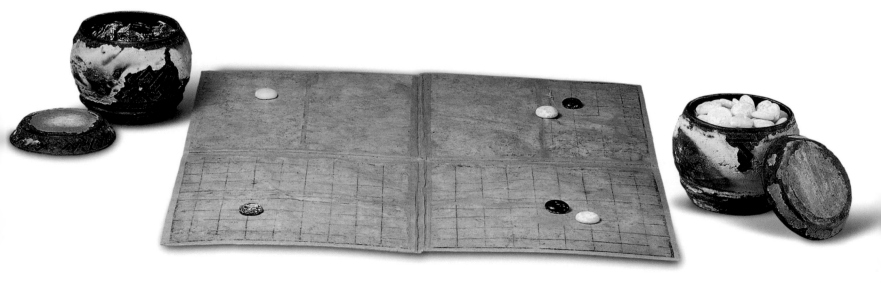

This fluidity is further underlined by the interaction between Dai Jin and Xia Chang (1388–1470), the artist of a great scroll depicting bamboos, the subject for which Xia was most famous (fig. 170). He is known to have painted a picture of this theme for Dai in Beijing in 1436, possibly in connection with the latter's departure back to the south, since paintings of bamboo were understood in the visual language of the court to be particularly appropriate parting gifts.[49] He and his brother Xia Bing, like the Shen brothers, owed their status at court under the Yongle and Xuande emperors primarily to their calligraphy, and were responsible for the giant characters that named the halls of the new imperial palace in Beijing.

THE LIMITS OF COURT CULTURE

Dai Jin's departure back to his native Hangzhou, where he continued his successful practice as a professional artist, reminds us that there was a Ming culture outside imperial and princely courts. This would assert itself more and more in the aftermath of the disastrous imperial foray into Mongol territory in 1449. The transmission of courtly styles of painting beyond the physical confines of the court is symbolized by the facts that the great literati painter of the southern city of Suzhou, Wen Zheng-ming (1470–1559), a dominant figure in the resolutely *non*-courtly culture of the mid-Ming period, was married to a granddaughter of Xia Chang, and that the earliest accounts of Wen's career see him as continuing the style of that master.[50]

FIG. 169

Dai Jin (戴進) (1388–1462), 'Saying farewell at Jintai'
(*Jintai songbie tu* 金臺送別圖)

Dai Jin lived in Nanjing in the early Yongle reign and
during Xuande's reign in the late 1420s moved to Beijing.
Although he did not work directly for the imperial court, he
was patronized by a number of senior officials and enjoyed
an extremely successful career. In Beijing he associated
with leading officials such as Huang Huai (1367–1449),
Yang Shiqi (1365–1444), Yang Rong (1371–1440) and Xia
Chang (c. 1388–1470), and they added inscriptions to his
paintings. He returned to Hangzhou but around the first year
of the Zhengtong emperor in 1436 went back to Beijing. He
retired in 1442, aged sixty, and moved back to Hangzhou.

This painting was made for Wei Jing (Yijia), a Secretariat
Drafter, who had served the Yongle and Xuande emperors,
as a farewell gift on his departure from Beijing, some time
in the last years of the Xuande reign (1426–1435). The
figures bidding farewell on the shore, together with the still
river, evoke an atmosphere of separation and sadness.
It is inscribed: 'Dai Jin of Qiantang respectfully painted this
for Mr Yijia of the Hanlin Academy' (錢塘戴進敬為翰林以
嘉先生寫). The artist's seals are 文進 (Wenjin) and 靜庵
(Jing'an).

Handscroll, ink on silk
c. 1430–5
Beijing
Image: h 27.8 cm, l 90.7 cm; with mount: h 29 cm, w 276 cm
Shanghai Museum

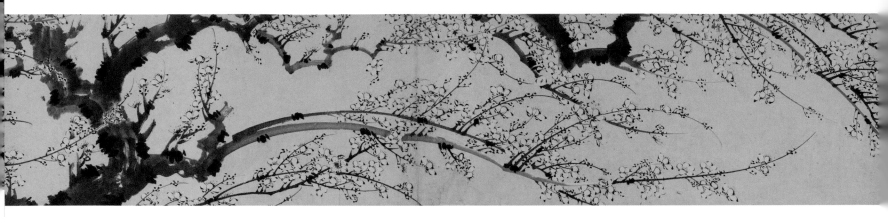

FIG. 171

Chen Lu (陳錄) (fl. 1436–1449), 'Plum blossoms and moon light' (*Meihua tu* 梅花圖)

Little information is available about Chen Lu, but we know that he specialized in painting pine trees, bamboo, orchids and particularly plum blossom. He came from Kuaiji, in Zhejiang province, and does not seem to have interacted to any degree with the imperial court, showing that cultural activity, even at the highest level, was not confined to that setting. This painting has been described as one of the most spectacular works made in the Ming dynasty of plum blossoms, a plant with particular associations of purity and moral goodness among the educated elite of the period.

Handscroll, ink and colour on paper
1436–49
Probably Zhejiang
h 32.4 cm, w 778.5 cm
Staatliche Museen zu Berlin, Museum für Asiatische Kunst

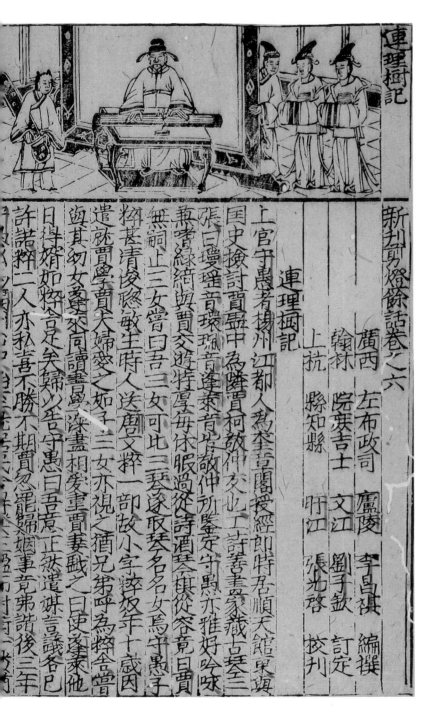

連理樹記

新刊剪燈餘話卷之六

廣西
左布政司
廬陵
李昌祺
編撰

翰林院
庶吉士
文江
劉子欽
訂定

上杭
縣知縣
明江
張光啓
校刊

FIG. 172

Li Changqi 李昌祺 (1376–1452), More Tales while Trimming the Lamp Wick (Xinkan Jian deng yu hua 新刊剪燈餘話)

This edition of a collection of tales authored by Li Changqi, an official at a princely court, was published in Jianyang, Fujian province, a centre of the Ming book trade.

Woodblock-printed, ink on paper
Dated 1433
Tenri Central Library

This marriage alliance (one in which the role of women as transmitters of cultural values was probably crucial, if little documented) points to a world in which the court did not set the standards for everything. And even in the first half of the fifteenth century itself, when court culture was so dominant and so prestigious, much escaped its surveillance and control. Those who wrote in scripts other than Chinese – whether the Muslim community of Beijing (fig. 176), the small but significant Jewish community of Kaifeng, or the readers of the inscriptions that were still being written in this period in a range of other Asian languages – escaped the standardizing norms set by court calligraphers such as Shen Du and Xia Chang.

Books were being printed privately for the use of scholars in styles that varied considerably from the lavish productions of court presses. The Yongle emperor might have once remarked to his councillor Xie Jin that it was hard for scholars to buy books, but there was more going on in the wider empire than he knew about: by 1426, for example, the Qiu family on remote Hainan Island had a library of several hundred volumes, and may not have been alone in doing so.[51] There were libraries in institutions too, this being one of the key functions of the Confucian schools that carried *wen* into the remote borderlands of the empire, to civilize the natives. By 1440 the ritual sacrifices made to the ancient heroes of *wen*, which were another function of those schools, were being pictured in privately published illustrated collections of ritual instructions.[52] They were part of a growing wave of *non*-imperial, *non*-courtly cultural output that was producing illustrated primers designed to spread the skills of literacy to the young (fig. 19); books about medicine, foreign lands and how magistrates ought to govern their territories; and plays and collections of short stories, such as the bestseller of early Ming fiction, *More Tales while Trimming the Lamp Wick* (*Xinkan jian deng yu hua*), published in 1433 (fig. 172) and banned by the government for its supposedly corrupting qualities in 1442.[53]

One of the earliest surviving Chinese cookbooks, *Yi Ya's Testament on Cuisine* (*Yi Ya yi yi*), was published some time in the early fifteenth century. It was written by a native of the great southern city of Suzhou, which was then only just beginning to emerge from the shadow of the imperial disfavour that it had suffered under the Ming founder. This book testifies to the fact that whatever the standard spoken language of officialdom might be, it would be the cooking of *Jiangnan*, 'South of the Yangtze', and not that of imperial northern Beijing, which would set the standards for fine dining in the centuries to come.[54] 'Culture', *wen*, was in the end about more than just writing.

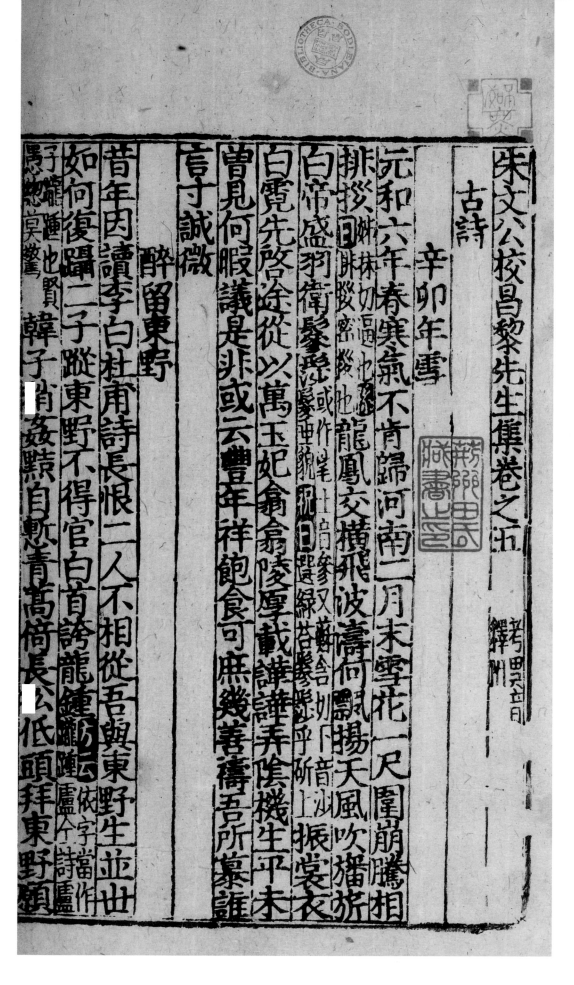

FIG. 173

Combined Collected Works of Han Yu and Liu Zongyuan
(**Han Liu er xiansheng wenji** 韓柳二先生文集)

Han Yu (768–824) and Liu Zongyuan (773–819) were Confucian scholars, major writers of prose and to a lesser extent poetry in the Tang dynasty (618–906). Han Yu had an official career but also spent time in exile for not toeing the line politically. Liu Zongyuan had an official career in the capital Chang'an (modern-day Xi'an), but was later posted far away to the south central province of Hunan and later still exiled even further away to Guangxi. In exile he wrote fables, poetry and philosophical musings. He believed that men, rather than Heaven, directed the pattern of actions: 'It is rather by our efforts than by the Decrees of Heaven that the unlucky is changed into the lucky, and the unjustifiable transformed into the justifiable'.

This classic book of the works of these two historical scholars is printed in a compressed typeface. It was printed for the use of scholars and not for the emperor. The style of printing shows continuity with that of the Yuan dynasty (1271–1368). Individuals and institutions both kept libraries full of such books, spreading literacy and culture across Ming China.

Woodblock-printed, ink on paper
1448
China
h 30 cm
Bodleian Library, Oxford
Backhouse +431

5 BELIEFS
   ## MIRACLES AND SALVATION

Marsha Haufler

On the seventh day, sweet dew fell, the colour of frozen butter.
It was fragrant and beautiful. Suddenly a five-coloured cloud was seen
and gold boughs with jade flowers that were lustrous, jewelled,
sparkling and blazing.

'MIRACLES OF THE MASS OF UNIVERSAL SALVATION CONDUCTED
BY THE FIFTH KARMAPA FOR THE YONGLE EMPEROR', 1407[1]

FIG. 174
White porcelain ewer

Based on a Yuan-dynasty prototype, the
form of this ewer is also found in Tibetan
metalwork. Connoisseurs use the term
'monk's cap ewer', as the zigzag edge of
the rim is evocative of the tall yellow hats
worn by some Tibetan priests. The Yongle
emperor commissioned these ewers, and
a large number were made at Jingdezhen
at the imperial kilns. They were probably
produced for the Yongle emperor's
requiem rituals for his parents, the Rite
for Universal Salvation, held in Nanjing
(see fig. 208).

Porcelain with incised decoration beneath a
clear glaze
Yongle era, c. 1407
Jingdezhen, Jiangxi province
Sir Percival David Collection, PDF A425

The business of belief in early Ming China went on as it had for centuries before and
would for centuries to follow. Women prayed for male children. Boys aspiring to
government service memorized Confucian classics. Buddhist monks and nuns chanted *sūtras* (scriptures) and meditated. Clouds of incense filled temples devoted to a
multitude of gods. In other words, people carried on the routines of Confucianism,
Buddhism (fig. 175) and Daoism (fig. 181), collectively known as the 'Three Teachings',
in homes and temples all across China. Islam flourished separately, often in close
proximity to these practices, although on a smaller scale demographically.

But the first half of the fifteenth century was also a time of wonders and
extravagant enterprises brought forth by a series of remarkable personalities. Along
with larger-than-life emperors, most notably Zhu Di (1360–1424), emperor of the
Yongle period (1403–1424), many of the key players on this stage were eunuchs and
monks – two groups that Chinese history has not always treated kindly. Emperors
collaborated with high-ranking court eunuchs and eminent clerics to put a personal,
often cosmopolitan, stamp on the religious cultures of the Ming capitals, Nanjing and
Beijing, and used religion to political ends at home and abroad. In his engagement
with religion, as in other aspects of his life, the famous eunuch mariner Zheng He
(1371–1433) exemplifies this age. So too, regrettably, does another eunuch, Wang
Zhen (d. 1449) (fig. 212), the imperial advisor held responsible for the military disaster
at Tumu Fort where he died and the emperor of the Zhengtong period (1436–1449)
was taken captive (see p. 24).

The activities of Zheng He and Wang Zhen chronologically bracket the
following account of religious beliefs related to the early Ming court. Rather than
a linear narrative, however, this is a collection of sketches of people, places and
events layered to evoke the range and fluidity of Ming religion. Numerous gods
appear to suggest the density of the spiritual landscape and the interplay among
the Three Teachings and the official, or state, religion (fig. 178). Emphasis is placed
not on doctrine, but on the agency of the gods, and on efforts to deploy them to
political and personal ends by material and visual means. These efforts played out
in various arenas, including the lives of the princely families of the Ming provinces
(figs 177 and 179), but nowhere more dramatically than in court-sponsored religious
spectacles.

This chapter concludes with a set of scroll paintings made on imperial order for

FIG. 175

Standing Buddha

This finely cast figure is instantly
recognizable as a Buddha because of
the set repertoire of features that it
displays. These include hair dressed
in tight curls, culminating in a jewel;
elongated earlobes representing the
Buddha's vast wisdom; draped monastic
robe and cape in folds; and the hand
positions, with palms facing the viewer.
The right hand is raised in a gesture
of reassurance, the left hand lowered
in a gesture of giving. Craftsmen cast
this figure with an imperial inscription,
'Bestowed in the Great Ming-dynasty
Xuande reign' (*Da Ming Xuande nian
shi* 大明宣德年施). Some figures were
displayed in temples and monasteries;
others were given to important priests
visiting the court, especially those from
Tibet.

Gilded bronze
Xuande mark and period, 1426–1435
h 64 cm
Musée Cernuschi, Paris, bequeathed by
Henri Cernuschi, 1896, M.C.686

Qur'an from the Great Mosque of Khanbaliq (Beijing), calligraphy by Hajji Rashad ibn 'Ali al-Sini

FIG. 176

MANY MUSLIMS lived in China in the early Ming period, and were often given the Chinese surname Ma. Some made the pilgrimage to Mecca, known as the Hajj, evidenced by the name Hajji – a title added after the journey had been made. In 1407 the Yongle emperor officially issued an edict, written in classical Chinese, Persian and Mongolian, protecting Muslim clerics within the Ming empire. Muslims were employed at the imperial court in the Bureau for Translation, as eunuchs within the palace, as part of the army, and as astronomers and mathematicians. Ambassadors from the Middle East also made frequent voyages to the Ming court and would have visited mosques in China.

From the inscription at the end of the book (colophon), we know that the writing of this Qur'an was completed by Hajji Rashad ibn 'Ali al-Sini in the Great Mosque of Khanbaliq (Beijing) on the last day of Muharram in the year 804 (9 October 1401). This mosque is commonly known as Niujie Si (Ox Street Mosque) – the largest of Beijing's three mosques in the early fifteenth century. Produced in thirty parts, this section is part twenty-nine. The manuscript was modelled on thirteenth-century Middle Eastern Qur'ans. Its existence is a testimony to the religious tolerance and cultural diversity of China in the early fifteenth century. When this Qur'an was made, the Yongle emperor was still Prince of Yan and living in Beijing, while Nanjing was the capital city.

Burnished laid paper with black-and-red ink and gold
Dated 9 October 1401
Beijing
h 24.5 cm, w 17.5 cm
Nasser D. Khalili Collection of Islamic Art,
London, QUR 974 folio 56b (colophon)
and QUR 974 fol. 1 (det)

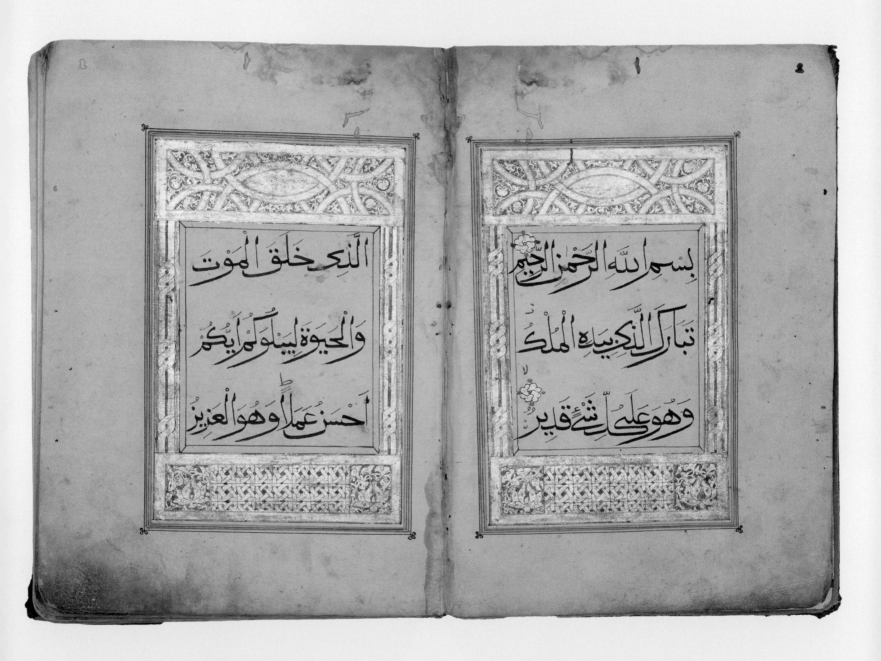

FIG. 177
Gold hat ornament of dancing deity

Daheitian (also known in Sanskrit as Mahākāla) is the protector of the *dharma* or law, who is revered in Buddhism, as it is practised in Tibet. The deity is generally depicted with a crown of five skulls, representing the five negative energies that prevent the mind from functioning properly (variously described as fear, anger, jealousy, desire and depression, or alternatively envy, greed, selfishness, anger and ignorance), which can be changed into five positive qualities or wisdoms. The iconography is based on Himalayan models, with parallels in Tibetan sculpture, Thang ka paintings and embroideries.

The Yongle and Xuande emperors received religious instruction from Tibetan

priests, and their courts absorbed Himalayan styles, which were then used for the production of religious imagery. Such a lavish gold ornament would have been made by eunuch craftsmen in the central imperial palace in the workshop for precious metals, the *Yinzuoju* (Jewellery Service). The Mahākāla figure was originally sewn on to a cloth hat as an ornament.

Gold
c. 1400–41
Nanjing or Beijing imperial workshops
h 9.4 cm, w 5.4 cm, d 1 cm
Hubei Provincial Museum, excavated from the tomb of Zhu Zhanji, Prince Zhuang of Liang, and of Lady Wei at Zhongxiang, Hubei province

FIG. 178
Vessels for state rituals

In the Yongle era copper-red glazes were perfected at the imperial kilns and stand at the top of the hierarchy of Yongle porcelain state ritual vessels. As far as we know, these red hues were achieved only in the Yongle and Xuande eras. In the Zhengtong era no single-colour copper-red glazed vessels were made. Perhaps the

Zhengtong emperor's youth meant that the services could not be performed in the same way. Recent research suggests that the glaze colour was not achieved by using pure copper oxide, but by pulverizing parts of ancient bronze vessels and adding them to the glaze. The ability to fire these fine red pots was lost from about 1450 to 1700.

Porcelain with copper-red glaze
Bowl (PDF 585): Yongle period, 1403–1424; bowl (PDF A529): Xuande mark and period, 1426–1435; Jingdezhen, Jiangxi province
Yongle bowl: h 9.7 cm, diam. 20.7 cm;
Xuande bowl: h 8.2 cm, diam. 18.7 cm
Sir Percival David Collection, PDF 585 and A529

FIG. 179
Prayer beads

Prayer beads are traditionally used to count the number of times a prayer or mantra is recited. Buddhist prayer beads are typically made with 16, 27 (as in this set), 54 or 108 beads. Sometimes these rosaries were made from human bones. A late fifteenth-century Chinese writer, Lu Rong, recorded that after the Battle of Baigou River, during the civil war in 1400, the Yongle emperor ordered the skulls of the soldiers who had died to be collected and made into strung beads for palace eunuchs, who could then say prayers to promote their reincarnation. The larger skulls were made into cups for offering pure water on a Buddhist altar.

Bone, gold and red string
Yongle period, c. 1403–1424
China
l 10.3 cm, perimeter 16.4 cm
Hubei Provincial Museum, excavated from the tomb of Zhu Zhanji, Prince Zhuang of Liang, and of Lady Wei at Zhongxiang, Hubei province

a grand Buddhist ritual, the esoteric right of salvation known as the 'Water-and-Land Dharma Assembly', or *Shuilu fahui*. Depicting gods and spirits summoned from across the Chinese religious spectrum, these scrolls offer a near summation of Ming belief.

ZHENG HE AND THE GODS

Grand Director Zheng He was born into a devout Muslim family in Yunnan province, and he remained connected with Muslim communities throughout his life (see also Chapter 1, p. 37). Through his travels and court service he came to be associated with a number of famous Islamic sites. According to a stele at the Great Mosque of Xi'an, he went there in 1413 to engage an Arabic-speaking interpreter for his fourth expedition.[2] In 1417 he prayed at the tombs of two seventh-century Muslim holy men just outside the Chinese port city of Quanzhou, seeking their blessing on his fifth voyage.[3] Zheng He also worshiped at the Great Mosque of Quanzhou, one of seven mosques that once served the large Muslim population of the city.[4]

The Xuande emperor (r. 1426–1435) ordered Zheng He back to sea near the end of the mariner's life (see Chapter 6). The imperial fleet departed Nanjing on its last voyage in the winter of 1431. The great ships sailed down the Yangtze River to Liujiagang at the river's mouth, stopped for two months, and then continued on to Changle in Fujian province, where they waited five months for favourable winds. At each place Zheng He and his crew erected a stone stele dedicated to the popular local goddess Tianfei (Celestial Consort), today best known as Mazu. The stele inscriptions record the voyages of the imperial fleet and the sailors' faith in the power of the goddess: they had only to call her name and, with the swiftness of an echo, a divine light (St Elmo's Fire) would appear atop the ship's mast and calm their fears. The stelae also tell of the great improvements they made to Tianfei temples at both moorings and a Buddhist monastery at Changle.[5] A handsome bronze temple bell with a cast inscription of their prayer for long life, safe sailing and good fortune is another remnant of their pious works at Changle (fig. 232).

The Scripture of Lord Lao, the Most High, Speaking on the Numinous Efficacy of the Celestial Consort in Relieving Distress (Taishang Laojun shuo Tianfei jiuku lingyan jing, or simply Tianfei

FIG.188

**Part of the 'Perfection of (Transcendent) Wisdom
Sūtra' (*Da ban ruo bo luo mi duo jing*
大般若波羅蜜多經)**

This Buddhist *sūtra* is from a much larger set originally
commissioned by the Ming court, probably in the Yongle or
Xuande era. The pages fold together like an accordion and
are read from right to left and from top to bottom. The indigo-
coloured paper was buffed with ivory or horn, and the images
and text applied in gold. These texts are known by their
Sanskrit name *Prajna paramita sūtra*. When they were chanted,
they would have been accompanied by striking cymbals and
bells, as well as different kinds of drums. In the early Ming,
monks would have been paid to recite this *sūtra* on behalf of
Buddhist believers.

Gold on indigo paper
Yongle or Xuande period, 1403–1435
h 40.5 cm
Private Collection

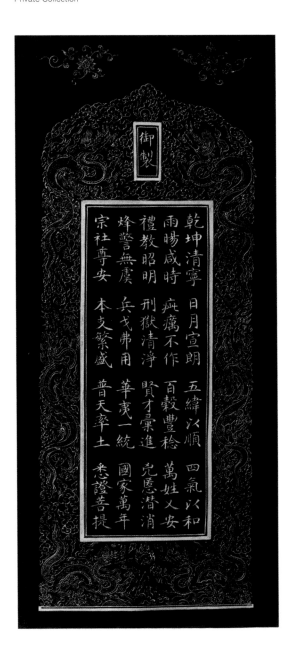

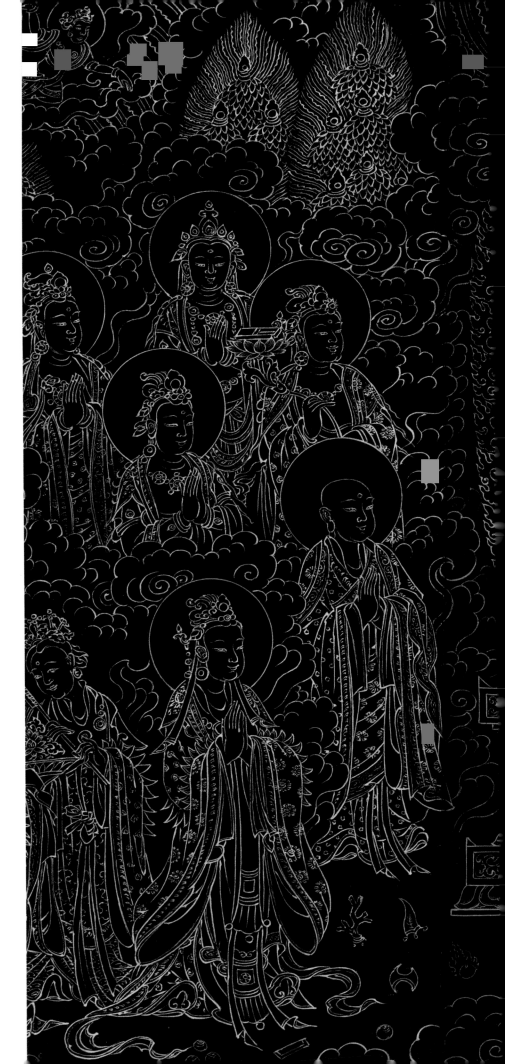

FIG.189

Jean-Joseph-Jules Defer (1803–1902), the 'Porcelain Pagoda', Nanjing

Before it was destroyed in the mid-nineteenth century, the pagoda of Da Baoen Monastery was considered one of the Seven Wonders of the World. The octagonal structure rose to a height of almost 80 metres and was faced with white porcelain bricks. Although it was constructed in the early fifteenth century, the only images of it are much later, from the seventeenth to nineteenth centuries. Plans for its reconstruction in Nanjing are underway.

Oil on canvas
h 38.1 cm, w 45.7 cm
Private Collection

FIG.190

Terminal for a roof at the Great Monastery of Filial Gratitude (*Da Baoensi* 大報恩寺)

This architectural tile is from Da Baoensi, a major Buddhist monastery patronized by the imperial family. It was extremely sophisticated and expensive to make. Most architectural tiles are of a single colour, but this has up to six colours on a single tile. Contemporary scholars have estimated that this building project would have cost £150 million in modern money. Materials to construct the edifice were drawn from a wide area: white clays were imported from Anhui province and worked in Nanjing; white porcelain tiles were brought from the imperial kilns in Jingdezhen, Jiangxi province; and local kilns at Jubaoshan in Nanjing were kept busy making building materials to reconstruct Nanjing after the battles of the early Ming period that were fought to topple the Yuan, and those of the civil war that followed. As well as the pottery and porcelain construction materials, the Buddhist monastery was decorated with stunning mural paintings executed by some of the greatest court painters of the early Ming. In 1428 the Xuande emperor ordered the eunuch commander Zheng He (1371–1433) and his officers, whose fleet was resting in Nanjing, to take command of the completion of Da Baoen Monastery.

Earthenware, moulded and sculpted with lead-fluxed glazes
Yongle to Xuande periods, 1412–31
Nanjing
h 57 cm, l 67.25 cm, d 26.5 cm
Nanjing Municipal Museum

including one in his native Yunnan, the monastery he and his men maintained in Changle in Fujian, and Jinghai (Peaceful Seas) Monastery built in his honour just west of the Tianfei Palace overlooking the Yangtze River in Nanjing.[8]

Zheng He also carried out religious construction projects in Nanjing for the court. While serving there as garrison commander between his last two voyages, he oversaw work on some very different sites. In 1426 he successfully petitioned the newly enthroned Xuande emperor to let him refurbish the state altars in Nanjing, which had grown old and shabby after the removal of the capital to Beijing.[9] In 1430 he was ordered to supervise the renovation of the Nanjing Jingjue Mosque using workmen and materials from the eunuch offices of the Nanjing palace, thereby ensuring its palatial splendour.[10] In the meantime, he was charged with completing the restoration of Da Baoen Monastery (Great Monastery of Filial Gratitude) in Nanjing, a project begun years earlier by the Yongle emperor as a filial gesture towards his parents, a theme that ran through many of his pious works.[11] The crowning jewel of Da Baoen Monastery was an octagonal nine-storey pagoda, some 80 metres high, considered one of the Seven Wonders of the World before it was destroyed in the middle of the nineteenth century (fig. 189). The pagoda glowed around the clock, by night from oil lamps burning in 146 exterior and interior niches, and by day from sunlight reflected off the white porcelain bricks that gave the tower its nickname, the 'Porcelain Pagoda'. Today we glimpse its magnificence only through writings, pictures by Chinese and Western artists, and architectural fragments. Brightly coloured glazed tiles with moulded relief images of elephants, lions, hybrid leonine goats, crocodilian *Makaras*, *Nāgas* (serpent deities) and the great winged Garuda were once assembled around the pagoda's arched doorways, turning them into 'gates of glory' (figs 190 and 191), a motif introduced from Nepal and Tibet during the Mongol-Yuan dynasty (1279–1368).[12]

Three tiles from the Great Monastery of Filial Gratitude (Da Baoensi 大報恩寺)

FIG.191

DA BAOENSI was built between 1412 and 1431 in Nanjing on the site of an earlier well-known temple. Acknowledged as an important site by the Hongwu emperor, he had it renovated but it had fallen into disrepair by the Yongle era. According to a stele of 1424 written by the Yongle emperor, it was constructed on his orders to commemorate his parents, the Hongwu emperor and Empress Ma, and to express his filial gratitude to them both. Confirming the Yongle emperor's legitimacy, it was a powerful emblem of his connections with the founders of the Ming dynasty. Often called the Porcelain Pagoda by Western writers, it stood until 1856 when Taiping Rebels dismantled it so that it could not be used as a vantage point by their enemies.

These three multi-coloured glazed tiles show images of a caparisoned elephant, a lion and a winged goat (hou). The tiles were locked into place with wooden keys and were part of a doorframe of the landmark's nine-storey octagonal pagoda, the centrepiece of the temple. Originally, there were four openings on each of the nine storeys, with bright tiles replicating the iconography of the 'revolving' *sūtra* cabinet in the scripture hall at the Zhihua si in Beijing. Nanjing's landscape would have been dominated by this building; the nine-storey pagoda soared to almost 80 metres into the sky, was lit up at night by lanterns, and bedecked with bells and chains tinkling in the wind.

Some famous religious figures travelled thousands of miles to conduct services at the emperor's behest. For example, an entourage of Buddhist priests from Tibet spent three years crossing China to reach Nanjing to conduct a requiem mass for the Yongle emperor's parents. Some of the miraculous events that occurred as a result of these rituals are recorded in early fifteenth-century paintings with texts in many languages, suggesting a multi-cultural audience for some imperial rituals. Private ceremonies were also performed by the emperor and members of the court.

Earthenware, moulded and sculpted with lead-fluxed glazes
Yongle to Xuande periods, 1412–31
Nanjing
h 51 cm, w 47.6 cm, d 39.5 cm
Nanjing Municipal Museum

FIG.192

Anonymous, calligraphy by Shen Du (沈度) (1357–1434), 'Tribute giraffe from Bengal' (*Mingren hua qilin Shen Du song* 明人畫麒麟沈度頌)

The ruler of Bengal sent a giraffe for presentation to the Yongle emperor in 1414. The animal was interpreted at court as the mythical beast *qilin*, which was supposedly seen only when a sage ruler was on the throne.

Hanging scroll, ink and colours on silk
c. 1414
Image: h 90.4 cm, w 45 cm
National Palace Museum, Taipei

THE WILL OF HEAVEN

Zheng He and his fellow mariners were obliquely connected with another aspect of Ming belief through their transport of giraffes and other exotic animals sent as tribute to the Ming court from lands visited by the imperial fleet (see also p. 257). Following ancient precedents, the Ming court believed in omens and signs, and giraffes qualified as such. They were identified according to an ancient taxonomy of wondrous creatures as *qilin*, gentle beasts whose appearance heralded a sage ruler and age of peace. The first giraffe-cum-*qilin*, a gift from the Sultan of Bengal, arrived at the Yongle court in 1414 to great acclaim, and was thoroughly documented in words and images (figs192 and 218–19).[13] Did the emperor really believe this exotic ruminant was a magical *qilin* come to express Heaven's approbation of his reign? In truth, it scarcely mattered. It was enough that this identification fitted the age-old pattern of recognizing unusual celestial and terrestrial phenomena as divine responses to human activities and as portents. Signs of Heaven's favour were especially felicitous at dynastic beginnings and turning points, and Zhu Di's deviation from the line of imperial succession was in effect both (see p. 25). Fashioning himself as the rightful holder of the Mandate of Heaven after usurping the throne from his nephew called for *qilin* and more.[14]

The giraffe joined a parade of events that signalled divine sanction of the Yongle reign. For example, in 1404 the silt-laden Yellow River ran clear, and the emperor's younger brother Zhu Su (1361–1425), Prince of Zhou, captured and presented a *zouyu*, a white tiger-like creature that, like the *qilin*, was believed to appear in times of benevolent rule (fig. 126). Two years later auspicious 'sweet dew' fell on the imperial tombs and a 'pure spring' erupted at the Divine Music Abbey, a Daoist temple near the state altars that provided music and dance for state rituals. There was a fairly standard script for celebrating auspicious signs at court: court officials congratulated the emperor, and the emperor righteously interpreted the omens in light of his relationship with Heaven and Earth, while exhorting his officials to even more strenuous efforts in aid of good government. Imperial acknowledgement of the sweet dew and pure spring followed this pattern. The Yongle emperor contended that auspicious signs were frequently seen because he reverently served Heaven and Earth on behalf of the imperial ancestors, the people and the nation. However, the signs were not due to his virtue, rather they were to be understood as Heaven's blessings on the spirits of his ancestors, and credited to the diligence of his civil and military officials, whom he asked to support his virtue so he might have the approval of Heaven forever.[15]

Heaven was the zenith of the official state religion, and the emperor served as high priest, assisted by members of his family and state officials at altars and designated temples in the capital and across

the country. Ming princes, for instance, sacrificed at altars in their fiefdoms. The offerings were received by an extended pantheon encompassing ancient nature deities, spirits of human heroes of antiquity and Daoist gods. The rites were graded according to the status of the god served, conducted on a set calendar and tightly scripted with prescribed sacrifices of food, drink and material goods, prayers and music, all offered in aid of harmonizing human society with the cosmic order to ensure the welfare of the state.[16]

The Yongle emperor initially sacrificed to Heaven and Earth in the Hall of Great Sacrifices within a sacred compound in the southeast of the Nanjing city wall. Protected from common view by vermilion walls, this imperial complex also contained altars to the sun and moon, planets and stars, sacred peaks, seas, mountains and rivers. To the west stood a smaller walled enclosure, the Altar of Mountains and Water, devoted to nature and vocational gods: Taisui (Year Star); the weather gods Wind, Cloud, Thunder (fig. 193) and Rain; the Five Sacred Mountains; Five Guardian Mountains; Four Seas; Four Great Rivers; Mount Zhong (in Nanjing); the mountains and rivers of the capital; and the Capital City God. The Altar of the First Farmer and Temple of Military Flags and Banners were here too. Sacrificial rites for the most revered human spirits, the imperial ancestors, were conducted in the Great Ancestral Temple, which was located in front of the palace to the east of the main gate, opposite the Altars of Soil and Grain on the west. For more intimate communion with the imperial forebears there was the Worshipping the Ancestors Hall inside the palace,

FIG.193

Scripture of the Jade Pivot
(**Yu shu jing** 玉樞經)

This woodblock-printed Daoist ritual document details one of the most important liturgical aspects of Daoism. It gives instructions on how to call upon thunder gods for protection against everyday calamities. Thunder gods also had the power to prevent drought and flooding.

The manuscript combines religious iconography, everyday life and the supernatural. There are images of childbirth, funerals, umbrellas, carpenters, wheelbarrows and butchery. These are shown in contrast to rains of flowers and magical meetings of deities. The pronunciation of difficult characters is written down to help its oral delivery.

Woodblock-printed book, ink on paper
Yongle period, 1403–1424
Each page: h 34 cm, w 12 cm
British Library, London ORB 99/161

FIG.194
Seated figure of Zhenwu with an inscription

The fact that the donor of this small-scale image, made in the city of Hangzhou, describes himself as a devout Buddhist but is commissioning a Daoist image indicates that devotion to different aspects of various religions was widespread in China. Worship of the Daoist god Zhenwu was not confined to the elite but was widespread.

Gilt-bronze
1439
Qiantang, Hangzhou
h 36.4 cm
The Art Institute of Chicago. Gift of Robert Sonnenschein II, 1950.1054

convenient for the emperor's residence. Confucius, the First Teacher, was served in his own temple next to the Imperial Academy in the city.[17]

More gods and spirits received state offerings in temples in the southern capital. The first Ming emperor, Zhu Yuanzhang (1328–1398), early in his reign commissioned temples to celebrate his military victory and affirm his place in the history of successive dynasties. The Temple of Meritorious Officials built in 1369 honoured the valiant men who fought beside him to found the dynasty. Four years later the Temple of Kings and Emperors was set up for the veneration of the Three Sovereigns and Five Emperors of remote antiquity and dynastic founders down to Qubilai Khan (1215–1294). Officials were also dispatched to make offerings to the spirits of local historical figures and to regional gods, including Tianfei (fig. 216), as well as to two popular deities with national stature, Lord Guan Yu and the Daoist god Zhenwu (figs 105 and 194).[18]

Guan Yu (162–220), a legendary general of the Three Kingdoms period (220–265), apotheosized as a miracle-working god, was popular at all levels of society as a divine protector. Taken into the Daoist pantheon and also embraced by Buddhism as a monastery guardian, he was another popular divinity appropriated by the state with official titles granted from the Song dynasty onwards. Lord Guan was believed to have come to the aid of both Zhu Yuanzhang and his son Zhu Di in their campaigns for the throne, and was worshipped in the Ming as a god of wealth and war.[19] Zhenwu, the Perfected Warrior, also received his first official title in the Song dynasty, but was a god of great antiquity. Originally known as Xuanwu, the Dark Warrior, he is god of the north among the deities of the cardinal directions. Like most popular gods, Zhenwu was versatile. People prayed to him for such blessings as male heirs, good weather, cures and even salvation from hell, but he was a potent god of war invoked by soldiers for victory in battle. Qubilai Khan, Zhu Yuanzhang and Zhu Di all claimed to have received signs from Zhenwu at critical junctures in their careers. When Zhu Di turned to Zhenwu in his ecumenical quest for divine legitimization, the god responded impressively. An unofficial history of the Ming tells of Zhenwu's dramatic appearance to sanction Zhu Di's rebellion as the prince was preparing to go to war. Zhu Di was anxious to launch his attack on his nephew's imperial army, but the monk Daoyan counselled patience. Finally, when Daoyan decided the time was right, the soldiers assembled and just then the prince had a vision of a figure wearing armour, his hair untied, surrounded by banners. The prince turned to his trusted advisor and asked the identity of the apparition. Daoyan replied that it was 'his teacher' Zhenwu, for whom he had been waiting. The prince loosened his own hair, put his hand on his sword and the rest is history.[20]

The Yongle emperor expressed his devotion to Zhenwu in many ways, but most magnificently by reconstructing monasteries destroyed at the fall of the Yuan dynasty on Mount Wudang in central China, home of the god's cult. The Mongols had lavishly patronized Zhenwu and his mountain as a means of legitimizing their rule, but the Yongle emperor surpassed them with essentially the same objective. For popular consumption, however, he piously hoped 'to repay the god's kindness, to serve the memory of [his] parents on high, and to ask for blessings on all who live

FIG.195

Śākyamuni, the historical Buddha

The style of this halo, or mandorla, is consistent with Ming woodblock-printed images of the Buddha from the period 1400 to 1450. Recent scientific testing at the British Museum shows that the gilded-bronze mandorla and stand were made of a different type of metalwork, added in the Qianlong era (1736–1795). The Yongle Buddha is inscribed 'Bestowed in the Yongle era of the Great Ming dynasty' (*Da Ming Yongle nian shi* 大明永樂年施), suggesting that it was either given to one of the Tibetan delegations or was presented to a Ming temple.

Gilded bronze
Yongle mark and period, 1403–1424, with Qianlong (1736–1795) mandorla and stand
Nanjing or Beijing
h 59 cm
British Museum, London 1908.0410.4

FIG. 196

Miraculous Manifestations of Zhenwu on Mount Wudang

The peak of Mount Wudang, home of the god Zhenwu who was patronized by the early Ming emperors and accredited with their rise to power, was surrounded by a 'five-coloured round radiance' and purple clouds that lingered. These illustrations of auspicious signs were probably made for the Yongle emperor's birthday and given by him to the Baiyun (White Cloud) Monastery in Beijing.

Handscroll, ink and colours on silk
1403–24
Each section: h 56 cm, w 85 cm
Baiyun (White Cloud) Monastery (Baiyun guan), Beijing

FIG. 197

'Illustrated record of the auspicious responses of the Supreme Emperor of the Dark Heaven (Zhenwu) of the Great Ming Dynasty'

Miracles were documented and descriptions widely disseminated in verbal and visual forms. These were interpreted as auspicious signs and positive omens for the emperors of the early Ming.

Printed ink on paper
1444–5
Each page: h 35 cm, w 11.3 cm
Bibliothèque Nationale de France, Paris, Chinois 9546 [952]

here below'.[21] In 1412 he charged two noblemen with the project. They led thousands of army workers in building seven major monastic complexes and many smaller ones on Mount Wudang, completing the main temples by the end of 1418. The acme of this spate of construction was the installation of the gilt-bronze Golden Hall (Jindian) in the Palace of Supreme Harmony (Taihegong) on top of the highest peak, the Pillar of Heaven. This hall enshrines the classic image of the god, robust and regal in bearing, with a long beard, unbound hair, bare feet and armour visible beneath his robe. We see it echoed in a large bronze statue in the British Museum, made some time between 1416 and 1439 (fig. 105), and in a small gilt-bronze image dated 1439 in the Art Institute of Chicago (fig. 194).[22] This image of the god resembles that of his devoted imperial patron, the Yongle emperor, as he appears in the imperial portrait made around 1424 in the National Palace Museum (fig. 29). Indeed, some see the likeness as deliberate.

Not surprisingly, the imperial enterprise on Mount Wudang was blessed with celestial and terrestrial miracles: five-coloured clouds over the Pillar of Heaven, unusually abundant *lingzhi* (mushrooms of immortality), a round five-colour radiance surrounded by purple clouds that lingered over the Golden Hall, and the fruiting of a betel-nut plum tree, a hybrid credited to Zhenwu. Like giraffes, such marvels required pictorial record, resulting in the woodblock-printed *Illustrated record of the auspicious responses of the Supreme Emperor of the Dark Heaven of the Great Ming Dynasty* (fig. 197), collected in the Ming Daoist canon. Four episodes are included in the *Illustrated album of Zhenwu's auspicious responses*, a lavish collection of coloured paintings perhaps made for imperial consumption around the time of the reconstruction.[23] More map-like illustrations of miraculous manifestations on Mount Wudang appear in a handscroll kept at Baiyun Abbey in Beijing, where tradition identifies it as a gift from the Yongle emperor (fig. 196).[24]

FIG. 198
Stoneware vase

This flower vase has an incised inscription that reads: 'Made on an auspicious day in the seventh month of the seventh year of the Xuande era [1431] for use in the *Tianshi fu* [literally Celestial Master's mansion]' (*Xuande qi nian qi yue ji ri zao tianshifu yong* 宣德七年七月吉日造天師府用). The *Tianshi fu* was the headquarters of the Celestial Masters located on Mount Longhu in Jiangxi province. They managed Daoist official lineages across China and were called upon by the early Ming emperors to perform rituals. Rituals could include ceremonies to summon good weather and control storms, or even to conduct exorcism rituals. The Celestial Master Zhang Yuchu (1361–1410) received an imperial commission in 1406 to gather texts for the official canon of Daoism, the *Daozang* (see fig. 183). The Longquan kilns in Zhejiang province, where this vase was made, were still firing court-quality objects at the end of the Xuande reign, but thereafter all high-quality production moved to Jingdezhen and heavy green celadons fell out of fashion at court.

Stoneware, incised decoration, green glaze; the neck cut-down
Longquan area, Zhejiang province
Dated 1432
h 44.2 cm
Sir Percival David Collection, PDF 239

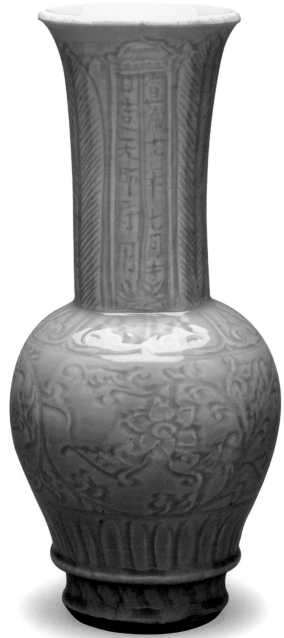

FIG. 199
The Bodhisattva Mañjuśrī

The four-armed form of Mañjuśrī, the Bodhisattva of Wisdom, was prevalent in the early Ming period. The Bodhisattva's two left hands hold a lotus, which supports the *Prajñāpāramitā sūtra* ('Perfection of Wisdom *Sūtra*'), and a bow. His upper right hand clasps a sword, and the lower right hand an arrow. In 1413 the Yongle emperor wrote that a Buddha had appeared to him in a vision with the thirty-two marks of the *chakravartin*, a 'Universal King'. Qubilai Khan of the Mongols had been regarded by the Tibetans as a reincarnation of Mañjuśrī. The Yongle emperor promoted the idea that he, too, was the earthly manifestation of Mañjuśrī and so 'Universal King'. He was not only an all-powerful Confucian Son of Heaven, but also an enlightened Buddhist lord.

Gilded bronze
Yongle period, 1403–1424
Nanjing or Beijing
h 19 cm
British Museum, London, donated by Walter Leo Hildburgh, 1953.0713.4

FIG. 200 ABOVE
Lacquered wood *sūtra* cover

In 1410, in Nanjing, the Yongle emperor ordered the printing of the Buddhist canon in Chinese and Tibetan. This is called the *Bka' 'gyur* (*Kangyur*) (the 'Translated words' or written words of the Buddha). Commissioning such a religious text was considered a pious act. He presented one set of the Bka' 'gyur, with wooden board covers decorated in red and gold *qiangjin* lacquer, to *Kun dga' grags pa* (*Kunga Dagpa*), the head of the Sa skya (Sakya) monastery in Tibet, who visited Nanjing in 1413–14. Out of the 108-volume set given to this monastery, 106 volumes are extant in Tibet. Another less elaborate set of 108 volumes was given to the Sera monastery in 1416 that was founded by Sha kya Ye shes (Shakya Yeshe) (1354–1435), a disciple of Tsongkhapa (1357–1419). Of those volumes 103 are still preserved there. The Yongle emperor was not the first leader of China to give elaborate gifts to important Tibetan officials: Qubilai Khan (1215–1294) had also done so as a way of improving diplomatic relations and as a devout act.

Each pair of red lacquer boards was made to protect a volume. The name of the particular *sūtra* is inscribed in both Chinese and Tibetan on the other side of the top board. The central motif on both boards is a triple-flaming jewel, or *Triratna* – symbolic of the three treasures of Buddhism (the Buddha, his teachings and the monastic community). This is flanked by four of the Eight Buddhist Treasures on each board. From left to right these are the wheel, banner, double fish and precious vase. The missing bottom board would have depicted the parasol, conch shell, lotus flower and endless knot. The pattern of formal petals around the border is believed to derive from Nepali traditions, while the format for the *sūtra* covers is Tibetan.

Red lacquer with engraved gold (*qiangjin*) decoration on wood board
Yongle period, *c.* 1410
Nanjing
h 26.7 cm, w 72.4 cm
British Museum, London, purchased with Brooke Sewell Permanent Fund, 1992.0129.1

FIG. 201 RIGHT
One volume of the Buddhist canon, Nanjing

Each pair of red lacquer boards was made to protect a volume like this of the Buddhist canon. The texts were printed in a series of about 108 volumes in both Chinese and Tibetan. It was printed in Nanjing in 1410 by order of the Yongle emperor.

Woodblock-printed, ink and colours on paper
First published 1410, this edition Wanli period
Harvard-Yenching Library of the Harvard College Library, Boston

Detail of fig. 200 showing the title in Chinese and Tibetan on the underside of the *sūtra* cover.

FIG. 202

Buddhist ritual sceptre

Demons and other obstacles were overcome with this Buddhist ritual sceptre. It is made of iron, and finely inlaid with designs in gold and silver, a technique known as damascening. Craftsmen introduced this metalwork technology to China from the Middle East via Tibet or Mongolia, when China was under Mongol rule.

The handle of the sceptre is surmounted by a *vajra* (thunderbolt cross) above a skull, an old and a young human head, then four leaves draping a vase of abundance, crossed *vajra* and a lotus bud.

Commissioned by the Yongle emperor, the sceptre bears the seal-script mark 'Made in the Yongle reign' (*Yongle nianzhi* 永樂年製). In 1407 Halima (see p. 233) was given, among other presents, 'two skeleton staffs' by the Yongle emperor.

Iron inlaid in gold and silver
Yongle mark and period, 1403–1424
Imperial workshop in Beijing
l 44 cm
British Museum, London, purchased with
the Brooke Sewell Permanent Fund, 1981,0207.1

VISITORS AND ENVOYS

Buddhist miracles also graced the Ming capitals and sacred mountains, and visiting Tibetan clerics produced some of the most spectacular examples. The Yongle emperor welcomed his Tibetan guests with great ceremony (fig. 208), showering them with gifts (figs 200–202), and granting them long Buddhist-inflected aristocratic titles and seals of authority. They offered gifts in return but, more importantly, provided religious instruction, initiations and ceremonies that confirmed the emperor's identity as a *cakravartin*, or Buddhist ideal universal ruler, thus internationalizing his indigenous mandate of Heaven. This exchange recalled Qubilai's famous patron–priest relationship with his Tibetan Imperial Preceptor 'Phags-pa (1235–1280), contributing to Zhu Di's efforts to cast himself in the role of the Mongol khan's spiritual heir, as well as the inheritor of Mongol political hegemony.[25]

As Ming relations with Tibetan clerics continued through the fifteenth century, the attendant flow of material goods had a profound influence on the art and taste of both cultures (figs 204, 206 and 210). The Ming emperors received Buddhist texts, images and *śarira* (Buddhist body

FIG. 203

Kneeling Bodhisattva

Avalokiteśvara is perhaps the Bodhisattva most often worshipped in China. The imperial courts of the Yongle and Xuande emperors followed Yuan-dynasty precedent, relying on Himalayan Buddhism to create a visual vocabulary to represent Buddhist deities. This figure was later mounted on a Qing-dynasty, Qianlong-era (1736–95), cloisonné base.

Gilded bronze
Xuande era 1426–1435
Beijing
h 20.3 cm
Victoria and Albert Museum, London,
275&A-1898

relics), and reciprocated with images, liturgical implements, printed scriptures, jade seals, porcelains, textiles, clothing and other luxury goods produced in imperial workshops (figs 202 and 203).[26]

In the first year of the Yongle era, 1403, an imperial delegation set out for Tibet bearing a letter from the emperor to Deshin Shekpa (1384–1415), the Fifth Karmapa, called Halima in Chinese sources, head of the Karma sub-school of the Kagyu Order. The eunuch official Hou Xian (active 1403–1427), who later sailed with Zheng He, led the party accompanied by the eminent monk Zhiguang (d. 1435). The imperial letter invited Deshin Shekpa to the Ming to 'preach' the doctrine of the Buddha for the benefit of the country and to conduct rituals to repay the kindness of the emperor's late parents and liberate the souls of the deceased. After the invitation was extended again by another delegation led by Hou Xian, Deshin Shekpa finally

FIG. 204
Mahasiddha Virupa

Mahasiddha means 'Great Adept'. Virupa was a ninth-century Indian saint revered as an enlightened being. He is depicted sitting on an antelope pelt and would have held a skull cup in his right hand. This figure, one of the largest and most spectacular metal Buddhist figures to have survived from the early fifteenth century, has a replacement left arm. The original left arm would have pointed to the sun. Virupa's legend tells that he stopped the movement of the sun so that it burned the Earth in a demonstration of his power. The sculpture expresses power through the war-like gesture and Virupa's armour. Smaller versions were made as gifts for Tibetan religious leaders visiting the Ming court.

Gilded bronze
Yongle period, 1403–1424
Nanjing or Beijing
h 79 cm, w 41 cm
Victoria and Albert Museum, London, purchased with the support of the Robert H.N. Ho Family Foundation, V&A 15-12-2010

FIG. 206

Anonymous, set of paintings from a monastery in Shigatse

This set of images may be incomplete, missing two *luohan* paintings to make the normal set of sixteen, but alternatively the attendants may complete the group. Fourteen of the images in this set represent *Dgra bcom pa* (*Dra chompa*) (known as *luohan* in Chinese or *Arhat* in Sanskrit), with two attendant figures: Dharmatala, the man with the backpack of Buddhist texts and accompanied by a tiger, also identified as the Tang Buddhist monk Xuanzang; and Hvashang, who is jolly, rotund and surrounded by children. The four remaining images are guardian figures of the four directions – North, South, East and West. These were painted with an awareness of Chinese painting styles, notably the courtly blue-and-green landscape tradition, and include Chinese objects. However, they are painted on Tibetan cloth rather than on Chinese silk or paper, and all have Tibetan inscriptions in ink on the reverse, which name the deity. Other inscriptions on the back are placed to correspond with the heart, mind and spirit of each figure on the front of the painting. By doing so, the images are given divine powers. Each image also has a Tibetan inscription on the front, describing the subject.

The *luohan* are all shown on a larger scale than their attendants. The figures are in remote mountain or forest settings, emphasizing their otherworldly nature; they are poised between our world and a more perfect place. Their seats and tables are strangely formed rocks, suggesting a mastery of nature. Blue-and-green landscapes were painted using mineral pigments from azurite and malachite, and are a staple of Tibetan art from the fifteenth century onwards. High-quality court objects were transported between Tibet and China in the late Yuan dynasty and early Ming dynasty. Some of these court objects are visible in these paintings, such as the blue cloth-bound books, scarlet and gold qiangjin lacquer boxes and trays, and gilded-bronze ritual vessels for burning incense. These are all Chinese in style and help to date the set of paintings to the late fourteenth or early fifteenth century.

The set of paintings was used in a monastic context for a daily ritual. Colonel J.C. French collected them from a monastery in Shigatse, Tibet, before 1943 and presented them to the British Museum in 1955. This monastery had direct links to the Ming court in the early fifteenth century.

Gouache on cotton
c. 1403–35, probably c. 1425
Tashi Lhunpo Monastery (the main seat of the Panchen Lamas of Gelugpa Sect), Shigatse (Xigazē) in Tsang, Tibet (Xizang) Autonomous Region
Each image: h 57 cm, w 44 cm;
Hvashang: h 63.5 cm, w 47 cm
British Museum, London, donated by J.C. French, Asia 1955, 04-16.020 to .039

arrived in Nanjing late in 1406 and conducted the requested mass of universal salvation in the second month of the next year at the great Linggu Monastery in the city. The ritual lasted fourteen days and recalled grand rites of salvation conducted for earlier imperial households. The following month, the Karmapa, by then known as the Great Treasure Dharma King (*Dabao fawang*), a title bestowed on him by the grateful emperor, left for Mount Wutai in northern China to conduct a mass for the recently deceased Empress Xu (1362–1407).[27]

Politics and belief came together in splendour in these rituals, which simultaneously affirmed the virtue of the imperial patron and the spiritual prowess of the Buddhist master. During the Karmapa's ritual and the attendant court formalities in Nanjing, and for days after his departure, Linggu Monastery was awash in amazing sights and sounds that even touched the palace and the imperial tombs. These events are depicted in a 49-metre-long horizontal scroll nearly as miraculous as its subject (fig. 208). Meticulously painted by court masters in brilliant colours on silk, the scroll unfolds in alternating texts and pictures. In scene after scene, we see the

Detail showing another *luohan* from this set with a Chinese incense burner on a red-lacquer stand.

FIG. 207
'Xylographs in Marvelous Images, Names, *Sūtras* and Dharanis of the Buddhas and Bodhisattvas' (***Zhufo pusa miaoxiang minghao jingzhou*** 諸佛菩薩妙相名號經咒)**, showing Deshin Shekpa**

Deshin Shekpa conducted further services on Mount Wutai on his return journey to Tibet. He was rewarded with titles and lavish gifts. During his visit he transmitted this text, an illustrated collection of Buddhist texts and mantras captioned in Chinese, Tibetan, Lantsa (used in Nepal and Tibet) and Mongolian. The famous monk himself is depicted among the deities, dressed in monastic robes and crown, the halo and falling heavenly flowers signifying his status as an enlightened being.

Woodblock-printed, ink on paper
1431
Each page: h 26 cm, w 16.5 cm
Musée Guimet, Paris

monastery pagoda and halls emitting and touched by wondrous illumination, variegated radiances and rays, often a brilliant sun, and auspicious five-coloured cloud formations throughout. Relics appear on top of the pagoda, heavenly flowers rain down, blue phoenixes and white cranes dance in flight, and Buddhist figures – Arhats (Buddha's enlightened disciples) and Bodhisattvas (enlightened saviours) – emerge from the sky. You can almost hear the otherworldly chanting of Sanskrit scriptures and divine music said to have come from the sky.[28] The scroll's main inscriptions are in five languages – Chinese, Persian, Tay, Tibetan and Mongolian – advertising, like the Galle stele, the international reach of the emperor's authority.[29]

When Deshin Shekpa arrived on Mount Wutai, wonder worker trod wondrous ground. Located in Shanxi province, southwest of Beijing, Mount Wutai, or Five-Terrace Mountain, is recognized as the earthly home of Mañjuśrī, Bodhisattva of Wisdom, who manifests himself there in various guises, and announces his presence through uncommon clouds and celestial illuminations. For centuries Mañjuśrī had been recognized as a special protector of emperors and the nation, and his mountain had been a magnet for imperial patronage as well as international pilgrimage. Tibetan Buddhism put down deep roots on Mount Wutai during the Yuan dynasty and flourished alongside Chinese Buddhism there henceforth. The Yuan imperial house was actively involved with this numinous landscape, spending extravagantly on the construction of monasteries there, and Qubilai Khan came to be identified as a manifestation of Mañjuśrī. Such precedents made care of the mountain's Buddhist establishments a requisite for Buddhist rulers in the Ming. In preparation for Deshin Shekpa's arrival, the Yongle emperor sent another trusted eunuch, Grand Director Yang Sheng, to renovate the Great White Stūpa built at the heart of the mountain by Qubilai's Nepalese master craftsman Anige (1245–1306) and to rebuild the mountain's oldest, most important monastery for the Karmapa's use.[30]

The Tibetan monk Shakya Yeshe (Shakya Ye shes) (1354–1439) first came to the Ming court as a substitute for his teacher Tsongkhapa (1357–1419), founder of the Gelug order of Tibetan Buddhism, who famously declined two invitations from the Yongle emperor. Upon receiving the second one, however, Tsongkhapa sent his disciple in his place. Arriving in Nanjing early in 1415, Shakya Yeshe performed esoteric Buddhist rites at imperial request over three months, producing miracles similar to those conjured earlier by Deshin Shekpa, and departed with the title Great Preceptor of State (*Da guoshi*), a gold seal, Buddhist images, scriptures and ritual implements, as well as gifts for his teacher. Before and after this visit he stopped on Mount Wutai, which must have had special meaning for him as Tsongkhapa was recognized as an emanation of its resident Bodhisattva. Shakya Yeshe returned to the mountain again at the beginning of the Xuande period and stayed there for a number of years. Over the course of these visits, through teachings, initiations, ordinations and the restoration of monasteries, he left a substantial spiritual and physical legacy on the mountain. Tibetan sources credit him with the renovation or expansion of six major sites, including Xiantong Monastery, where he lived. In 1427 the Xuande emperor invited Shakya Yeshe to the capital, and he went a few years later,

FIG. 208 ABOVE, BELOW AND OVERLEAF

Anonymous, 'Miracles of the Mass of Universal Salvation Conducted by the Fifth Karmapa for the Yongle Emperor'

The service was performed for the ritual releasing of the souls of the Yongle emperor's parents. Over fourteen days in 1407, the Tibetan monk Dezhin Shegpa/Deshin Shekpa (1384–1415), called Halima in Chinese sources, led services at Nanjing. Deities and auspicious creatures appeared. The skies filled with rainbows, showers of flowers and multi-coloured clouds. The Yongle emperor commissioned artists

to create this narrative painting in forty-nine scenes, with captions in Chinese, Persian, Tay, Tibetan and Mongolian [Whitfield 2014].

Handscroll, ink and colours on silk
1407
h 66 cm, w 4,968 cm
The Tibet Museum

FIG. 209

Anonymous, 'Portrait of Sha kya Ye shes'

This portrait depicts the senior Tibetan monk Shakya Yeshe (1354–1439) as an ageing cleric. He is sitting on a throne not unlike that used for the Yongle and Xuande emperors' portraits.

Silk tapestry
1426–35
h 108.5 cm, w 63 cm
Norbulingka Collection

around 1431. He most likely stayed at Great Ci'en (Compassion and Grace) Monastery, the foremost monastery receiving Tibetan monks in Beijing, and lived out his life there (by another account, he died in 1435 en route back to Tibet). In 1435 he presided over a momentous event, the cremation ceremony for the eminent monk Zhiguang. By then Shakya Yeshe was recognized as the 'Great Compassion Dharma King', part of the elevated title bestowed upon him a year earlier. The full title is rendered in Chinese and Tibetan on a movingly realistic portrait of the elderly master executed by Ming court artists in slit-silk tapestry and mounted in a Tibetan style (fig. 209).[31]

While some eunuch officials were carrying imperial gifts and invitations west to Tibet, others were travelling east into Jurchen lands and Korea as political envoys with different Buddhist agendas. The eunuch Yishiha, a man of Jurchen origin with a biography very like Zheng He's, led missions to the Jurchen people of far eastern Manchuria. Around 1411, with over 1,000 men on twenty-five boats, he departed from Jilin and sailed on the Sunggari and Amur Rivers to reach an Amur riverside settlement, today Tyr near Nikolayevsk-on-Amur. Upon returning there in 1413, he built the magnificent Buddhist Yongning Monastery and erected a stele documenting the political as well as the religious intentions of his expeditions. Titled 'Record of the Imperially Built Yongning Monastery', the stele is inscribed in Chinese, Mongolian, Jurchen and Tibetan. This effort at proselytization was not well received. Local peopled damaged the monastery soon after it was built and it fell into ruin. Yishiha rebuilt it on his last visit in 1432–3, and set up another commemorative stele, this one bearing a single inscription written, perhaps less provocatively, only in Chinese.[32]

Of the Ming envoys to Korea in the first half of the fifteenth century, the eunuch Huang Yan is infamous. In the Yongle period he made eleven trips to the capital of Korea's Joseon dynasty (1392–1897), modern Seoul, where he apparently served Ming interests well, but offended his hosts. In the *Annals of the Joseon Dynasty* (*Joseon wangjo sillok*) he is described as greedy, cunning and disrespectful. Among other things, he demanded Buddhist relics and images. An episode particularly galling to his Korean hosts occurred in 1406: on behalf of his emperor, who was planning a great ritual for his deceased parents, Huang Yan requisitioned three Buddhist statues from Beophwa Monastery, inconveniently located on Jeju Island off the southern tip of the Korean peninsula. Joseon officials brought the bronze statues from the island and packed them with all of their trappings in fifteen containers for transport to Nanjing. Before departing, Huang Yan asked the Korean king, Taejong (r. 1400–1418), to bow and kowtow before the statues. The king angrily refused, not wishing to bow to the Buddhist statues because his was not a Buddhist state. Buddhism had been the state religion of the preceding Goryeo dynasty (918–1392) and belief continued, even among the royal family, but the Joseon dynasty had come to power with a strong Confucian mandate and actively suppressed Buddhist influence. The Joseon court's position on Buddhism strained its dealings with Ming envoys, who shared their emperor's enthusiasm for the religion. Ming gifts of Buddhist texts and statues created particularly awkward situations.[33] Received politely but not devoutly, the images may nevertheless be related to a small group of gilt-bronze statues with early Ming Tibeto-Chinese characteristics found in Korea and datable to the early Joseon period.[34]

THE RELIGIOUS LANDSCAPE OF BEIJING

However far the imperial reach, an emperor's primary site of religious expression was inevitably his capital. The Yongle emperor put his own stamp on the religious environment of Nanjing through building projects and religious spectacles, but there he was always in negotiation with his father's legacy and shadowed by the ghost of the nephew he dethroned. Beijing, in contrast, was his domain spiritually and physically – first the heart of his principality, then an imperial construction site, and ultimately his imperial city.

Beijing received a fresh layer of ritual culture in the Yongle period with the establishment of its state altars. The imperial sacrifices in the new capital initially followed the pattern set in Nanjing, but the lesser official rites varied. The popular national gods Guan Yu and Zhenwu received state offerings in both capitals. In contrast, the founding heroes of the Ming and the local heroes of Nanjing were not conveyed to Beijing, although their offerings continued in the southern capital. Meanwhile, the northern muster grew with the addition of spirits that had special connections to Beijing or to the emperor. The inclusion of the Southern Song loyalist Wen Tianxiang (1236–1283), whose shrine was built near his Beijing execution site by people from his native place, was another instance of the state co-opting a local cult. The Daoist spirits Xu Zhizheng and Xu Zhiyi, worshipped at Lingji Palace in Beijing, were rewarded with state offerings for curing the emperor of an intractable illness. The most controversial addition to the official roster was Zhu Di's monk-advisor Daoyan, whom the Hongxi emperor recognized in 1425 as a meritorious official of his father's reign, due offerings at the Great Ancestral Temple. This arrangement lasted for over a century before disapproving Confucian scholars managed to have his rites relocated to a Beijing monastery, formerly his home.[35]

Beijing gave the Yongle emperor a cultural canvas apart from his father's, but it was far from blank. Much remained from its recent incarnation as capital of the Mongol-Yuan dynasty.[36] When the prince moved to the capital of his fief in 1380, he was heir not only to the physical and spiritual legacy of the Yuan dynasty but also to an ethnically diverse cultural geography of considerable antiquity and quite distinct from that of Nanjing.

Islamic culture had long contributed to Beijing's cosmopolitan environment. Muslims held high positions as military commanders, officials, administrators and scholars under Qubilai Khan, and thousands served in his armies.[37] This tradition

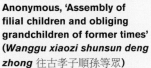

Anonymous, 'Assembly of filial children and obliging grandchildren of former times' (*Wanggu xiaozi shunsun deng zhong* 往古孝子順孫等眾)

This painting is divided into two parts. The upper section shows a man carrying an old woman, probably his mother, on his back, while holding an incense burner in his hand. He is accompanied by a young man holding a golden cup and followed by two other men – one carrying a bamboo pole with rolls of silk and hats, and the other carrying another load of silk bolts and a hat. They appear to be fleeing with their possessions.

In the main scene below, old men and women are helped by younger men and women to walk. The old lady in the centre holds a rosary with 108 beads. Another figure holds a red lacquer box and a third holds a fine book. Behind these figures comes a mother with her baby. The child is wearing a gold-embroidered red silk shirt tied at the neck and a tiny gold bangle. His mother has elaborate hair ornaments and a red silk scarf around her hair, signifying that she is married. It is inscribed with the title; the positioning instructions read 'Left fifty-five' (*zuo di wushiwu* 左第五十五).

Anonymous, 'Assembly of forlorn souls of sold and pawned bond-maids, and abandoned wives of former times' (*Wanggu gudian binu qili qizi guhun zhong* 往古雇典婢奴棄離妻子孤魂眾)

This shocking scene shows, in the foreground, three young female slaves, perhaps children, with ropes tied around their necks and bound hands. They are dressed in rags and are being led by well-dressed and well-armed men. One of the girls has a big nose and curly hair; she may be intended to represent someone foreign or from one of the conquered aboriginal tribes on the southern Chinese borders. The man in the centre wearing the fancy blue robe is holding a wad of Ming paper money. Another is studying a contract. In the scene above, a man is abandoning his lawful wife. She is holding a paper with the imprint of a hand, perhaps an early contract, and her child is clinging to her skirt. Another group of men hold a further tethered girl. This image is evidence of the slave trade in Ming China. Its position within the series is recorded as 'Fifty eight' (*wushiba* 第五十八).

Anonymous, 'Assembly of forlorn souls of a band of armed brigands' (*Bingge daozai zhu guhun zhong* 兵戈盜賊諸孤魂眾)

A gang of robbers, dressed in fine armour and riding well-decked horses, is shown destroying a home, killing the father, seizing the mother and abandoning the infant child who tries to crawl after its mother. In front of their home, all their worldly riches are collected: coins, silver ingots and artworks. All will be looted and carried off by their attackers. The position of this painting within the ritual set appears in a caption 'Right fifty one' (*you di wushiyi* 右第五十一).

Anonymous, 'Various ghosts of the souls of all shamans, shamanesses, and secular and official music performers who died violent deaths' (*Yiqie wushi shennü san yueling guanzu heng wanghun zhu gui zhong* 一切巫師 神女散樂伶官族橫亡魂諸鬼眾)

This painting of musicians is hard to interpret. It depicts four figures in the foreground: a monkey-man carrying a fan; a man holding a tambourine; a woman holding castanets and a fan; and a man with a demon-quelling sword and alms bowl. In the background is a woman holding a tray with two model figures of a man and a woman; while the next three figures carry banners. The position of this painting within the ritual set appears in a caption 'Right fifty-eight' (*you di wushiba* 右第五十八)

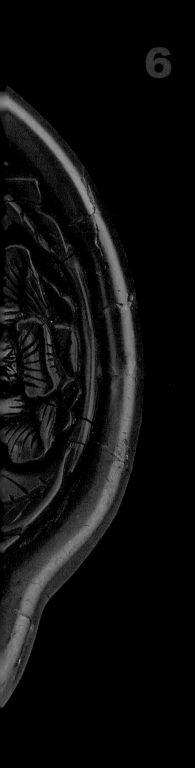

6   COMMERCE
THE MING IN THE WORLD

Timothy Brook

In the eleventh year of the Yongle period … the Grand Ancestor and Cultured Emperor issued an imperial order that the principal envoy the grand eunuch Zheng He should take general command of the treasure ships and go to the various foreign countries in the Western Ocean to read out the imperial commands and to bestow rewards.

MA HUAN, PREFACE TO *OVERALL SURVEY OF THE OCEAN'S SHORES*, 1433[1]

A MAP OF THE WORLD

The early emperors of the Ming dynasty knew that a vast world extended out in all directions beyond their realm. To the north lay the prairies of the Mongol steppe, the forbidding expanse of the Gobi Desert and beyond, an unboundable space under an ever-changing sway of khans, confederacies and nomad states. Out of that dangerous quarter had come first Chinggis Khan (*c.* 1162–1227) to attack north China, and then later his grandson Qubilai (1215–1294) to occupy the entire realm for a century under the name of the Yuan dynasty, until the forces of the rebel leader and dynastic founder Zhu Yuanzhang (1328–1398) drove the Mongols back north in 1368. To the east were to be found Korea and Japan, kingdoms that had absorbed a certain measure of Chinese culture and with which China had tended to maintain less violent relations for some time. To the south lay a scattering of smaller states around Southeast Asia, from kingdoms along China's border with present-day Vietnam to some of the furthest islands of what is now Indonesia, many strong enough to resist a Chinese invasion but none powerful enough to challenge its formal position at the top of the regional hierarchy of states. Finally, there lay the least known and most mysterious zone of all, the west: the zone into which the Daoist patriarch Laozi (traditional dates 571–480 BC) had disappeared; the site of the Western Paradise of the Buddha; the home of the supreme matriarchal deity, the Queen Mother of the West; and beyond those, the fabled realms of Tibet and India, where Siddhartha had attained enlightenment and become the Buddha. Ming China was large, but the world was even larger.

No Ming emperor ever ventured far into the world beyond these outer limits and one of the two who did, the Zhengtong emperor (1436–1449), was captured and taken hostage by the Mongols. The extent to which the emperors did know these regions was only from information gleaned from maps. One of the earliest in the court's possession was a vast map attributed to the eminent Buddhist monk Qingjun (1328–1392). The original has long since disappeared, but it was said that he completed it in 1360 while the Mongols still ruled China. Recorded as measuring 1.66 metres top to bottom and 1.75 metres across , this map depicted every part of the known world, from Siberia at one end to Spain at the other. The knowledge of the maritime world that the map displayed must have reached Qingjun via Muslim merchants and navigators who came to the Yuan dynasty to do business. Qingjun's cross-dynastic

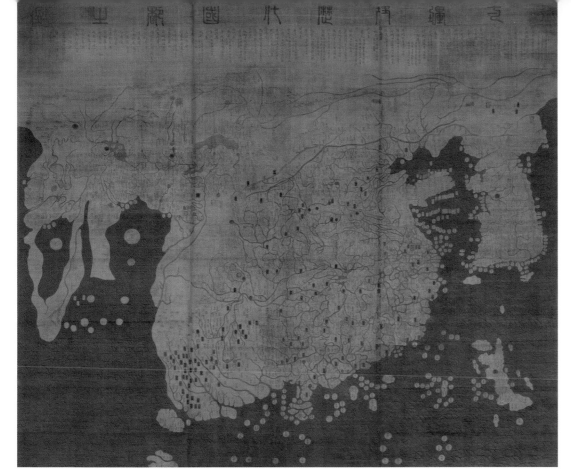

FIG. 215
'Unification map of the regions within and beyond the frontiers of the realm through the ages'
(混一疆理歷代國都之圖)

Based on an earlier map by the Buddhist monk Qingjun (1328–1392), this version by the Korean envoy Yi Hoe depicts every part of the world known to the Ming emperors in the early fifteenth century. The outlines of countries from Siberia to Spain were drawn from information given by sailors and merchants who had journeyed to the Mediterranean, the Arabian Peninsula and the east coast of Africa.

Hanging scroll, ink on silk
c. 1470 copy of 1402 version
h 158 cm, w 163 cm
Ryūkoku University Library, Kyoto

stature – the founder of the Ming dynasty honoured him as the senior Buddhist in the realm just as the Mongols had done – ensured the survival of copies of the map in China, Korea and Japan, where it sports such titles as 'The broad Dharma-wheel map of the regions within and beyond the frontiers' and 'The unification map of the Great Ming dynasty' (*Da Ming hunyi tu*). Best known is a copy dating from around 1470 of a 1402 version that a Korean envoy produced, based on a copy that he in turn had acquired in Nanjing while on a diplomatic assignment there three years earlier. This map of the world is usually referred to as the *Kangnido*, an abbreviation of its title in Korean (fig. 215).[2] This version inflates the Korean peninsula far beyond its natural size, and has allowed Southeast Asia to atrophy to nothing, but set aside these peculiarities and you can pick out the Indian Ocean, a distended Arabian peninsula, an oblong Africa hollowed out by a vast inland lake, and above the Mediterranean and Black Seas, a wobbly but recognizable Europe. Whether or not the label in the North Atlantic that reads 'Chicken Mountain' (*Ji shan*) is the British Isles is anyone's guess.

The *Kangnido* map attests to the remarkable knowledge that the Chinese had of the world in the years before Zhu Yuanzhang drove the Mongols out of China. It was knowledge acquired through China's familiarity with the maritime world of trade, and it would stand the new Ming dynasty in good stead for its first century. Yet only one version of the *Kangnido* map has survived in a Chinese court archive, and only the odd visual fragment from that map managed to escape into the realm of public knowledge.[3] Otherwise, as we shall see, after the middle of the fifteenth century the court allowed this panoramic knowledge of the world to lapse, as diplomatic priorities shifted and the concern became defending the border, not projecting power.

MING FOREIGN RELATIONS BETWEEN 1402 AND 1449

Zhu Yuanzhang founded the Ming dynasty in 1368 in the wake of a long civil war that culminated in the destruction of the Yuan dynasty. The pitch Zhu made to his new subjects to elicit support for his brand new regime was that he had released them from the cruel yoke of Mongol rule. Never mind that he took over the politics and ideology of the Mongol regime lock, stock and barrel as his own; xenophobia masked these borrowings and bathed the new regime in a satisfying moral legitimacy.

Once in power, Zhu harboured two sources of anxiety that he could never throw off: the fear that rivals within his own ranks would overthrow him, and the concern that foreign states would refuse to recognize him as the legitimate ruler of China. These two anxieties coincided disastrously in 1380 when Zhu believed he had discovered that his prime minister Hu Weiyong (d. 1380) was conspiring with a delegation from the state of Champa (today in southern Vietnam) to assassinate him. He unleashed a series of purges that led to the deaths of possibly as many as 55,000 officials at all levels over the next decade and a half, and redesigned the Ming constitution so that all power rested in his hands.[4] He also tightened foreign access to China.

Zhu Yuanzhang outlived the threats he feared, passing the throne to his grandson, the Jianwen emperor (1377–1402), in 1398 in what he thought would be a frictionless succession. It was not to be. The boy's uncle, Zhu Di (1360–1424), who commanded the forces that held the northern part of the country against the Mongols, launched an offensive to overthrow his nephew. A bitter three-year civil war ended in 1402 with the disappearance of the Jianwen emperor in a palace fire and Zhu Di's elevation as the Yongle emperor. Purges of officials loyal to Jianwen followed, claiming possibly as many victims as Yongle's father had punished during his reign.

FIG. 216

'*Sūtra* spoken from on high of the miraculous efficacy of Tianfei in salvation from distress' (*Taishang shuo Tainfi jiuku lingying jing* 太上說天妃救苦靈應經), showing Zheng He's voyages

Very few images of Zheng He's ships survive today, but these boats, which are illustrations in a *sūtra* dedicated to Tianfei, Celestial Consort, are likely to be accurate as they were made in 1420. Later illustrations are less reliable as the size of the ships is the subject of much academic debate.

Woodblock-printed, ink on paper
Dated 1420
National Library of China

FIG. 217
Two 'spirit way' figures bearing gifts

These carved stone figures once formed part of
a 'spirit way' leading to the tomb of a prince or
another member of the imperial clan. When the
figures arrived at the Victoria and Albert Museum in
1913, they were described as Korean, since Korean
noblemen wore similar wide-brimmed horsehair hats.
The men are shown presenting a scroll, possibly with
the text of an imperial edict, and a casket that might
be a container for a gift or document. The robes are
carefully carved to represent cloud-patterned silk and
the square badge of rank on their backs is carved
with a scaly dragon. Only the imperial court could
accept foreign tribute. Korean kings regularly sent
tribute to Ming China.

Marble
c. 1400–50
North China
h 215 cm, w 75 cm, d 57 cm
Victoria and Albert Museum, London, given
by The Art Fund, V&A A.1-1913 and V&A A.2-1913

If the father had reason to worry about other rulers denying his claim to the throne, the son had even greater reason. The Yongle emperor desperately needed diplomatic recognition to cover the stench of his reputation as a usurper, a regicide and a nepoticide (an uncle who kills his nephew). He opted not to sit passively and wait for foreign heads of state to send notice of their submission to him via the tribute system, by which heads of lesser states acknowledged the superior status of the emperor of China in order to legitimize their own positions and gain access to Chinese markets (see p. 275). Instead the emperor despatched trusted subordinates within the ranks of the palace eunuchs as his personal envoys to every ruler in Asia. They were usually sent at the head of a large and well-armed delegation to impose submission where it might not otherwise be voluntarily offered.

The most famous of these envoys was the Muslim eunuch Zheng He (1371–1433), who would lead seven naval expeditions to the Western Ocean (*Xi yang*) (fig. 216). The Western Ocean (*Xi yang*) was the vast avenue of water that started in what is now called the South China Sea and extended westward through the Strait of Malacca and across the Indian Ocean to the east coast of Africa. Beyond that lay what Chinese in the seventeenth century came to call the Great Western Sea, our Atlantic. Zheng He was said to be over 2 metres tall and have a waist that measured a metre and a half – impressive measurements for anyone and even more so for a war captive gelded for service in the imperial household at the age of ten. Zheng wielded an authority to match his stature. If not by persuasion then by force, he roved Asia to persuade local leaders to grant what his master most craved: recognition as the legitimate emperor of the most powerful state on the *Kangnido*, or any other map. From the rulers who saw the wisdom of acceding to Zheng's persuasion, he obtained declarations of fealty, along with some remarkable tribute gifts (fig. 217). One of the more spectacular was the giraffe that the ruler of Bengal sent to Yongle in 1414, along with its own keeper (see p. 260). The giraffe's arrival caused a great sensation at court,

Anonymous, 'Tribute giraffe with attendant' (*Ruiying qilin tu* 瑞應麒麟圖)

FIG. 218 OPPOSITE

EMBASSIES to the Chinese court bearing tribute gifts were seen as acknowledgment of the Ming emperor's dominant position in the region. Ambassadors were entertained and given lavish gifts to take home, reaffirming the relationship. Tribute trade and diplomatic exchange brought thousands of people from different cultures into contact with the Ming courts and their staff. We know the types of goods that were taken in and out of Ming China because of a variety of written texts that survive, including diaries of visiting members of the embassies, official court histories and stone stelae that list gifts in several languages. Later on in the fifteenth century fewer embassies were exchanged.

This giraffe was presented to the Ming court on 20 September 1414 in the name of Saif al-Din Hamzah Shah, ruler of Bengal (r. 1410–1412). The event was recorded in the *Veritable Records of the Ming Dynasty* (*Ming Shilu*), compiled in 1430, in which the giraffe is mentioned as a gift alongside fine horses and other local products. In return, the delegation was given silks and other textiles, porcelain and luxury goods. The giraffe was a special present bestowed partly in appreciation for the Yongle emperor's expression of condolences for the ruler of Bengal, whose father had recently died, and partly to cement the ruler of Bengal's own mandate to rule. Perhaps he also wanted China's support in the longer term.

When the giraffe was described to the court, it was assumed that it was the mythical beast *qilin* which, according to Confucius, only appeared when a sage is on the throne. So it was taken as a sign of the emperor's good governance. This phenomenon of the appearance of magical creatures or signs, known as 'Auspicious

responses' (*ruiying*), was seen as a signal of the right to rule. These magical signs were particularly sought by the Yongle emperor as he had seized the throne from his nephew, the legitimate ruler.

Several giraffes were presented to the Ming court; they were kept within the palace grounds as part of an exotic animal and bird menagerie, which included other tribute creatures such as bears, rhinoceroses, elephants and peacocks. Shen Du (1357–1434), a court calligrapher, inscribed the painting, praising the Yongle emperor's rule and stating that the *qilin*'s appearance confirmed the ruler's good governance. Other giraffes referred to in the records as *qilin* were presented in 1415 from Malindi (Mozambique) in East Africa, in 1419 from Aden and in 1433 from Mecca. Multiple images of the giraffe were produced to spread awareness of this sign of Heaven's blessing on the dynasty.

The following poem appears on the scroll:

When a sage possesses the virtue of utmost benevolence so that he illuminates the darkest places, a qilin *appears. This shows that Your Majesty's virtue equals that of Heaven; its merciful blessings have spread far and wide so that its harmonious vapours have emanated a* qilin*, as an endless bliss to the state for a myriad, myriad years.*

[Translated by Sally Church after J.J.L. Duyvendak]

Hanging scroll, ink and colours on silk
Dated 1414
h 80 cm, w 40.6 cm
Philadelphia Museum of Art, donated by John T. Dorrance

FIG. 219

'Timur receiving gifts from the Egyptian ambassadors'

African giraffes were sent to the Ming court, but were also presented to other rulers in south Asia and the Middle East. This painted illustration from a manuscript of the Zafarnama of Sharaf al-Din 'Ali Yazdi (1336–1405) depicts the historical event of a giraffe being given to Timur (Tamerlane, 1336–1405). The giraffe presented to the Yongle emperor was in fact re-gifted from Africa by the Sultan of Bengal.

Album leaf, ink, opaque watercolour and gold on paper
Dated 16 July 1436 (Dhu'l-Hijja 839)
Shiraz, Iran
h 17.8 cm, w 24 cm
Worcester Art Museum 1935.26

FIG. 223
Anonymous, 'Chinese lady'

This drawing is lightly sketched in red and black ink on paper, in a style reminiscent of Timurid court artists practising in Herat in present-day Afghanistan. The Chinese woman is dressed in layered robes with a front-fastening jacket, of a type excavated in an early fifteenth-century tomb in Zhejiang province. In one hand she holds a delicate porcelain wine cup on a silk pad. Her headdress is secured around her high-piled hair with a string of beads, perhaps suggesting that she is a married woman. Her shoes show the cotton stitching of the soles and turned-up ends, and from her waist a Chinese purse is suspended. The Ming diplomatic mission arrived in Herat, where this may have been sketched, in 1414.

There were many regular exchanges between the Ming and Timurid courts from the 1410s through the 1420s, during the reigns of the Yongle emperor (r. 1403–1424) and Shahrukh (r. 1409–1447). In 1413 a caravan of merchants from Timurid lands arrived in the capital city of Nanjing with exotic goods; the Yongle emperor sent a mission back with return gifts of plain and patterned silk. In 1408 and 1409 Tamerlane's successor, Shahrukh, sent envoys to Nanjing, and in 1410 the Chinese envoy, Fu An, was sent with an embassy to Herat. In total, the Yongle court received twenty missions from Samarqand and Herat, thirty-two from greater Central Asia, thirteen from Turfan and forty-four from Hami.

Red and black ink on paper
Herat, Afghanistan
Timurid dynasty, 1410–1440
h 25.8 cm, w 17.9 cm
British Museum, London, donated by National
Art Collections Fund, 2000,0615,0.1

FIG. 224
Anonymous, 'Two *luohan* and a tiger'

The Timurid artist who created this drawing was inspired by Chinese models that were possibly brought to Iran or Central Asia in the early 1400s. In Buddhist belief, *luohan* are enlightened beings who remain outside paradise to teach others the way to enlightenment. They are often depicted as Buddhist monks, wearing loose monastic robes.

These figures are rendered accurately from Chinese Chan Buddhist iconography. Some scholars identify them as Budai (with rounded belly) and Fenggan (with a staff). However, there are some differences between this and Chinese images: it is sketched on paper in reed pen rather than with a Chinese brush and the *luohan* wear plain, rather than patchwork, robes.

Ink and watercolour on paper
Iran or Central Asia
1420–40
h 34.5 cm, w 23.8 cm
Metropolitan Museum of Art, New York,
Rogers Fund, 1968 (68.48)

where it was deemed to be the mythical *qilin*, a beast that showed itself only when a sage ruler appeared (figs 192 and 218).[5]

The Yongle emperor looked east as well as south for ratification of his enthronement, receiving tribute missions from the Philippines, Ryūkyū (a state based on modern Okinawa), Japan (fig. 225) and Korea in quick succession. He also looked west to inner Asia, from Tibet on his western border to, beyond it, the Timurid kingdom (in what is now Iran and Afghanistan) (figs 223–4), hoping to fashion a network of relations that would weaken their ties to the Mongols and strengthen their obligations to him.[6] His expectations to the north had to be more modest. This was the near-inaccessible grassland into which his arch-enemies, the Mongols, had withdrawn and from which they continued to harass the realm, dreaming that one day one of them might claim the mantle of Chinggis Khan and return to conquer China. Holding the Mongols at bay was an enterprise that the Yongle emperor took seriously, so much so that his final act as emperor would be to lead a military expedition against them in 1424. He died while on campaign that summer.

The Yongle emperor's death did not just end that particular campaign against the Mongols. It halted the maritime embassies. Zheng He had been poised to leave on his seventh mission when the emperor died. A chorus of previously silenced voices at court called for an end to what they regarded as extravagant sops to the vanity of the emperor. These missions were expensive. Each sailing involved anywhere from fifty to two hundred vessels large and small, some built and fitted out in the Longjiang

FIG. 225
Lacquer box from the Ryūkyū Islands

This lacquer box, manufactured in the Ryūkyū Islands, has been transformed by later Japanese collectors into an incense burner by the addition of a metal liner and pierced cover. Originally the box would have had a shallow cover with a flat top. It is decorated with a delicate gold pattern of peacocks and peonies on a ground of brown lacquer. From contemporary Ming records we know that ships were sent by the court to the Liuqiu (Japanese Ryūkyū) Islands in the early Ming dynasty. In 1388 Cao Zhao, author of the *The Essential Studies of Antiquities* (*Gegu yaolun*), recorded: 'Carved red lacquer is greatly favoured by the peoples of Japan and the Ryūkyū Islands'. The quality of lacquer goods was judged by the thickness of the lacquer carving and the brightness of the red colour.

Lacquer with gold decoration and bronze cover
Box: 1400–1500; cover: Japanese, Edo period, 1603–1867
Ryūkyū Islands
h 18.4 cm, diam. 24.9 cm
British Museum, London, donated by Sir Harry and Lady Garner, 1974,0226.73

FIG. 226

Lacquer wares for foreign consumption

Chinese carved lacquer objects were highly prized in Japan and formed part of the equipment for the developing tea ceremony. Documents survive that record diplomatic gifts from the court of the Yongle emperor to the court of the Ashikaga military rulers (*shogun*) in Japan. In 1403 gifts of textiles, lacquered and gold-decorated furniture, and fifty-eight carved red lacquer wares were presented. The carved lacquer wares were in a variety of shapes and sizes, including boxes, dishes, bowls, plates, trays, a vase and a mirror case.

The Ashikaga court successfully dealt with the pirates who had been hampering trade between the two courts and making life on China's southeastern coast difficult. They also returned members of an earlier unsuccessful Ming embassy who had been detained in Japan. Another surviving letter to the *shogun* Ashikaga Yoshimochi (r. 1395–1423), dated 1407, itemizes presentation gifts and addresses the Japanese *shogun* as 'king' in recognition of the Ashikaga court as a tribute state.

Lists of presentation gifts from the Ming Yongle- and Xuande-era courts to the Ashikaga court in Japan survive for the years 1403, 1406, 1407, 1433 and 1434. They note detailed descriptions and measurements of the gifts, such that we can match surviving objects with their descriptions.

CLOCKWISE FROM TOP RIGHT:

Lobed dish with flowers of the four seasons
Yongle period, 1403–1424
l 19.6 cm, w 15.5 cm
British Museum, London, donated by
Sir Harry and Lady Garner, 1974,0226.16

Oval dish
Yongle period, 1403–1424
l 22.6 cm, h 3.4 cm
Victoria and Albert Museum, London, donated
by Sir Harry and Lady Garner, FE.28:1-1974

Bowl stand
Yongle period, 1403–1424
diam. 16.5 cm
Victoria and Albert Museum, London, donated
by Sir Harry and Lady Garner, FE23-1974

Carved red lacquer vase
Yongle period, 1403–1424
h 11.0 cm
British Museum, London, donated by
Sir Harry and Lady Garner, 1974,0226.17

Box with peonies
Yongle period, 1403–1424
diam. 18.6 cm
British Museum, London, purchased with
Brooke Sewell Permanent Fund, 1970,0413.1

Box with narcissus
Yongle period, 1403–1424
diam. 13.2 cm
British Museum, London, purchased from Soame
Jenyns with the Brooke Sewell Permanent Fund,
1970,0715.1

FIG. 228 BELOW

Collected poems of Ḥāfiẓ (Dīvān of Ḥāfiẓ) on Ming decorated paper

This Dīvān (collected poems by one particular author, in this case Ḥāfiẓ) was copied by Sulaymān Fūshanjī in 1451. The place where it was copied is not given in the colophon, but the copyist's surname suggests that it was produced in Herat, in modern Afghanistan, as Fushanj is a village near that city.

The poems are written on coloured paper that is flecked with gold, which would have been imported from Ming China. Nineteen of the pages have Chinese pictorial scenes; seven have designs of bamboo, willows, pomegranates and other plants; and twelve depict Chinese landscapes and palaces. This example shows a Chinese palace set against a background of mountains and lakes, with pine trees in the foreground. The Persian calligraphy is dated 1451 and appears to have been applied with no consideration to the direction of the Chinese design, which has been turned sideways.

High-quality Chinese paper was traded to Iran in the early fifteenth century, but this trade appears to have stopped some time after 1450. In the sixteenth century Persian paper-makers made their own substitute paper. Relatively few manuscripts using this type of Chinese paper survive. The combination of gold on a plain background may ultimately derive from patterned silk designs.

Gold-flecked and gold-painted coloured Chinese paper with Persian ink
Paper made 1403–35, Persian calligraphy dated 1451 (AH 855)
Possibly Herat, in modern Afghanistan
Each page: 17 cm, w 11 cm
British Library, London, Add 7759 (3r)

FIG. 227 ABOVE

Sharaf al-Dīn Ḥusayn, Poetry Anthology, on Ming decorated paper

This calligraphic page is from a collection of poems by twelve different authors writing from the fourteenth to the fifteenth century. This opening is part of a selection (ff. 23–41) from the *Dīvān of Maulana Kātibī* (d. 1434–6), who for a time was court poet of the ruler of Shirvan, Mirza Shaykh Ibrahim (d. 1417–18). The anthology was produced on the western shores of the Caspian Sea in Shamakhi, capital city of Shirvan, and completed in 1468. The copyist was Sharaf al-Dīn Ḥusayn; as he adds *sultānī* to his own name, we know that he was the royal scribe and produced the anthology under the patronage of Furrukh Yasār (r. 1462–1501). The stability of long-standing patronage at Shamakhi attracted some of the best artists in Herat to move there.

The miniatures and illuminated headings in this manuscript are painted on thick, heavy-glazed, polished, gold-sprinkled coloured paper. This sheet is coloured mauve, but within the anthology there are sheets of indigo, purple, bright mauve, lavender, apricot, sage green, light brown and yellow ochre, all flecked with gold. The paper was exported from China only in the early fifteenth century. It was also used at the Ming court for imperial correspondence such as the Hongxi emperor's personal edict (fig. 27). The paper may have been a diplomatic gift from court to court.

Gold-flecked and gold-painted coloured Chinese paper with Persian ink
Poems by Ḥāfiz, Amīr Khusraw, Kātibī, Bisāṭī, Jāmī, Kamāl Khujandī, Mawlānā Ashraf, Amīr Shāhī, Khayālī, Ṭāli'ī, Ṭūsī and Nāsir Bukhārā'ī (d. 1370)
Paper made 1400–50, manuscript completed in 1468
Shamakhi (Shirvan), in modern Azarbayjan
h 12 cm, w 7.5 cm
British Library, London, Add 16561 (36v)

FIG. 229
Anonymous, 'Tenjin in China'
(*Totō Tenjin* 渡唐天神)

Tenjin is an alternate name for
Sugawara no Michizane (845–903), a
court official and Japanese scholar of
Chinese literature whom the powerful
Fujiwara family successfully conspired
to have exiled to Kyūshū, where he died
a lonely death. After his death, he was
renamed Karai Tenjin and worshipped
as a Shinto deity. He is still regarded
as the patron of scholarship as well
as Japan's greatest poet writing in the
Chinese language. This image of Tenjin
wearing Chinese robes, carrying a sack
that contains his Zen priest's surplice
and holding a sprig of plum blossom, is
known by the Japanese title *Totō Tenjin*.

During the Muromachi period
(1337–1573), a revival of interest in
'*kanbun*' (classical Chinese, or Japanese
written in the manner of classical
Chinese) resulted in Tenjin being held
in even higher regard; this imaginary
portrait is from that time. Portraits of him
were created in professional painting
workshops, not at court, in Ming China
for sale to Japanese customers. This
example may have been painted and
inscribed in China, or produced in Japan
as a faithful copy of a Chinese original.
A poem at the top reads:

*In a past life was planted a celestial
body of unhindered power.
Fusang [Japan] and the red sun are
equally radiant.
How is it that the people can forever
pass on their beliefs?
A sprig of plum blossom [Tenjin]
travelled thousands of miles to
receive vestments at Mount Jing [in
China].*

[Translated by Luk Yu-ping]

夙植天身自在威
扶桑紅日並騰輝
下民以何永傳信
千里梅花雙徑衣

Hanging scroll, ink and colour on silk
1450–1500
Ningbo, China or Japan
h 71.3 cm, w 29.4 cm
British Museum, London, previous owner
Arthur Morrison, donated by Sir William
Gwynne-Evans, Bt, in 1913, 1913,0501,0.38

FIG. 230
Longjiang shipyard, number 6

FIG. 231
Shipbuilding tools

Excavations at the Longjiang shipyards outside Nanjing demonstrate the enormous size of the 'star-guided rafts' or 'treasure ships' used by Zheng He and his contemporaries for their diplomatic and trading missions. Zheng He's armada consisted of up to 250 ships, manned by 27,000 men, mostly soldiers. These ships were broad but had a very shallow draught, needing just 6–7 metres of water to sail in. They were expensive to maintain and only had a life of about ten years before needing extensive repairs out of the water. There were ten shipyards altogether and number six (see above) was excavated between 2003 and 2004. It was constructed in 1405 for the official manufacture of large ships. This set of tools includes saws, files, drills, awls, knives, nails and mallets.

Metal and wood
1405–30
l 12–48.4 cm
Nanjing Municipal Museum

shipyard just outside Nanjing (fig. 230), some in the harbours along the Fujian coast, which was traditionally the site for building ocean-going ships. The largest of these ships, known as 'star-guided rafts' or 'treasure ships', were at least 45 metres and possibly as much as 60 metres long. Enormous for the time, they were expensive vessels that had to be rebuilt at least once a decade, which usually meant two rebuildings during the three decades they were in use. The court diary known as the *Veritable Record* preserves orders to build 217 large ships for these missions. The cost in wood alone, conservatively estimated at ten large trees per foot of ship's length and then multiplied by a factor of three to cover being rebuilt twice, would have been over a million trees.[7] Given how deforested China already was by the start of the Ming dynasty, when large trees could be harvested only in the far southwest, the cost of securing the raw material for these flotillas must have been enormous. Add the cost in labour and other materials, plus the supplies for the hundreds of officials, officers and pilots, and the thousands of sailors, soldiers and labourers who were sent on these two-year-long expeditions, and the Zheng He voyages racked up an almost intolerable bill that generated no significant returns to investment.

The additional expenses involved in the Yongle emperor's decision to move the capital from Nanjing to Beijing, which included rebuilding the Grand Canal, exhausted the resources of the state. The voyages had to be suspended if the dynasty was to be financially sustainable. They were, but only temporarily. In 1430 the Yongle emperor's grandson, who reigned as the Xuande emperor from 1426 to 1435, permitted Zheng He to lead a seventh and final expedition to the Western Ocean to reconfirm alliances forged in his grandfather's time and to certify his own succession. It was too late in the year for Zheng to embark, so he ended up lingering with his fleet on the coast of Fujian. While waiting for the winds to turn, he sought divine assistance by having a bell cast for a Daoist temple, a bell that still exists today (fig. 233). The seventh voyage reached points as distant as Hormuz, Mecca and Mogadishu, bringing back a suitable menagerie of exotica, including more giraffes and even elephants (fig. 232).

The seventh would be the last expedition. Zheng He died on the return voyage, and the Xuande emperor died a year and a half later. Had he lived longer, however,

FIG. 232
Detail of a white elephant from 'Pictures of auspicious responses' (*Mingren ruiying tu* 明人瑞應圖)

White elephants were auspicious creatures, linked to the birth of the Buddha and to the rule of a wise and virtuous sovereign. This painting records miraculous happenings associated with the Yongle emperor's rule, including the Yellow River running clear and magical creatures appearing. White elephants are not albino but are born grey and turn white. They were once native to Laos, Cambodia, Thailand, Burma and Vietnam, and were given as tribute to the Ming court. This painting was commissioned by Zeng Qi (1372–1432) for his poems written in 1404–14.

Handscroll, ink and colours on paper
Dated 1414
h 30 cm, w 686.3 cm
National Palace Museum, Taipei

Bronze bell offered by Zheng He (鄭和) *(1371–1433)*

FIG. 233

THE EUNUCH COMMANDER Zheng He offered this large cast bronze bell to a Daoist temple in Changle, Fujian province, in 1431, while waiting for the winter monsoon to pass so he could begin his last expedition. The bell is covered with inscriptions, trigrams from the *Book of Changes* (*Yijing*), and designs of clouds and waves symbolizing the perils of the elements and oceans that Zheng He and his crew had to face. Eight characters adorn the upper part of the bell: 'May the country prosper and the people be at peace. May the winds be regular and the rains fall in season' (*Guo tai min an feng tiao yu shun* 國泰民安風調雨順). The lower part of the bell has information about when and why Zheng He and others had the bell cast. It reads:

Eternal and immortal offering, praying for a safe journey to and from the Western Ocean, may the fortuitous omens match what is wished for. On an auspicious day in the mid-summer of the xinhai, *the sixth year of the Xuande reign of the Great Ming, eunuchs Zheng He, Wang Jinghong and fellow military officials resolve to cast one bell.*

[Translated by Malcolm McNeil]

永遠長生供養，祈保西洋往回平安，吉祥如意者。大明宣德六年辛亥仲夏吉日，太監鄭和、王景弘等同官軍人等，發心鑄造鐘一口。

This text is particularly interesting as it confirms that the ships were manned by the army. Zheng He's Daoist, Buddhist and Islamic patronage is illustrative of the multi-faith tolerance in the early Ming period and the way in which people drew from different religions for different aspects of their lives.

The largest of the ships used to travel to the east coast of Africa from China had nine masts, featured compasses for navigation, watertight bulkheads and sternpost rudders to facilitate steering. The exact appearance of these 'treasure ships' is the subject of passionate debate. Illustrations for a religious text published in 1420, entitled '*Sūtra* spoken from on high of the miraculous efficacy of Tianfei in salvation from distress' (*Taishang shuo Tianfei jiuku lingying jing*) (fig. 216), which describes the rescue of sailors by Tianfei, the goddess to whom Zheng He and his entourage prayed for safe voyages, show deep-water, three-masted ships, similar to those in the stellar diagrams of the Mao Kun map. As these illustrations would have been contemporary with the voyages they may support the argument that Zheng He's ships were of a more modest size than the colossal vessels that have sometimes been imagined: in other words, three-masted *fuchuan* rather than *shachuan* boats.

Cast bronze
Dated 1431
h 83 cm, diam. of mouth 49.0 cm, weight 77 kg
National Museum of China, excavated in Nanping, Fujian province

the emperor would have been unlikely to support a proposal for an eighth voyage. His greater strategic concern was instability on the northern border. That, he knew, was where he had to concentrate his government's resources. He thought of himself accordingly as a hard-riding emperor in the Mongol style and had himself depicted as one (fig. 125). He was also a painter in his own right, the only Ming emperor to distinguish himself in any of the arts. Perhaps his animated rendering of two salukis, hounds native to Persia and best suited for hunting swift grassland animals, tells us in what direction his imagination roamed (fig. 122). The steppe, not the ocean, beckoned.

The Xuande emperor was succeeded in 1436 by his hapless eldest son, Zhu Qizhen (1427–1464), installed as the Zhengtong emperor at the age of eight. He too fancied himself in the persona of a Mongol khan. At the age of twenty-two he was persuaded – or at least not dissuaded – by his senior eunuch Wang Zhen (d. 1449) to command a massive army against the Mongols. The adventure ended in the year 1449 in the fiasco known as the Tumu Incident, when the Ming forces were annihilated and the emperor fell into the hands of the Western Mongol (Oirat) khan, Esen (d. 1455) (see also Chapter 3, p. 119). It was the dynasty's single greatest military humiliation, a failure that haunted the Ming to its final days. Rather than pushing on to Beijing and installing the captive Zhengtong emperor as his vassal, as he might have, Esen withdrew and used the emperor as a pawn to negotiate for indemnities and trade concessions. The court adroitly sidestepped the crisis of an absent emperor by dethroning Zhengtong and installing his younger half-brother, Zhu Qiyu (1428–1457), as the Jingtai emperor, thereby depriving Esen of his advantage. The khan ended up giving his captive back to the Ming without ransom after a year. Seven years later, in 1457, in the wake of the worst climate crisis of the fifteenth century, bringing unusually harsh winters and poor crops, the returned hostage overthrew his half-brother and re-ascended the throne as the Tianshun emperor.

The first half of the fifteenth century thus ended for China as it had begun: with a massive political crisis provoked by yet another member of the royal family defying the rules of patrilineal descent set down by the founder. Official historiography combed the crises of 1402 and 1449 out of the standard story of the dynasty, recasting Yongle from nepoticidal usurper to dynamic second founder, and Zhengtong from callow adolescent to victim of eunuch manipulation. This manipulation of the history of the first half of the fifteenth century ignores more than the treachery of ambitious rulers and a Chinese cultural preference for political restabilization at any cost. It sets aside the fact that both crises were handled, even resolved, not by domestic responses but through foreign policy. Both had an enormous impact on China's situation in the world. In striving to rescue himself from the charge of usurpation by investing enormously in the system of tribute relations, the Yongle emperor after 1402 ended up despatching tens of thousands of Chinese out into the maritime world, many of whom stayed on in niches of new trading networks, meshing the Chinese economy with the rest of Asia. The Zhengtong emperor's reckless escapade northward into Mongol territory in 1449 had the opposite effect. The dynasty pulled back inside its borders, reducing rather than enlarging its interactions with the world.

FIG. 234

Poh San Teng Temple built at Bukit Cina, Melaka, to honour Zheng He in 1795

Parameswara (1344–1424), ruler of the city-state of Malacca in modern Malaysia, accepted the establishment of tribute relations with the Yongle emperor's court in 1403. Bukit Cina was a hill used as a symbol for China's protection. In 1411 Parameswara visited Nanjing himself with a retinue of 540 men. According to Malay popular history, the Yongle emperor married one of his daughters to Parameswara, resulting in the arrival of a large number of Chinese people. Later Bukit Cina, China Hill, became the cemetery of Melaka's Chinese community. It is the largest and oldest Chinese graveyard outside China, with over 12,500 graves.

TRIBUTE AND TRADE

The Ming dynasty organized its relations with the outside world according to two mechanisms: tribute and trade. The tribute system was the official structure behind the country's foreign relations. It revolved around the emperor, whom it positioned at the pinnacle of a pyramid that spread downward through China to the rest of the world and pointed upward through him to the sole connection with Heaven. Being the Son of Heaven, the emperor supposed that all other rulers were subordinate to him and should acknowledge their obedience to Heaven by submitting tribute to him. That was the ritual logic of the tribute system, but it also embodied a practical logic – to funnel trade with foreign countries through agencies of the imperial household. The tribute system both choreographed diplomatic protocol and monopolized trade. It was a regulatory system that was geared less to stimulating trade than to ensuring that it never escaped the watchful eye of the government.

For foreign states, trade concerns tended to dominate how they participated in the tribute system, though diplomatic recognition also gave rulers implicit Ming backing against domestic and regional rivals. A device that several Southeast Asian rulers used early in the fifteenth century to confirm their fealty to the Ming empire – which Chinese envoys probably put them up to – was to ask the Ming emperor for a patent of investiture declaring a local hill to be a defender of that empire. Parameswara (1344–1424), who ruled the city-state of Melaka (or 'Malacca'), a key trading nexus in modern Malaysia between the South China Sea and the Indian Ocean, received a visit from one of the Yongle emperor's eunuch envoys in 1403 proposing the setting up of tribute relations. Parameswara had only recently been enthroned and was happy to become a tributary in his struggle to fend off Siam, a state roughly contiguous with modern Thailand. The envoy he sent to Nanjing requested that a hill back at home be invested as a 'Mountain for the Protection of the State' – a hill that even today recalls this diplomatic moment by bearing the name of Bukit Cina, China Hill (fig. 234). Parameswara's early link served him well, for whenever a Ming armada passed through the Strait of Malacca, he dispatched yet another delegation to China to reap the benefits of direct trade. Finally

FIG. 235

Spirit way from the tomb of 'Abd al-Majid Hasan, Nanjing, 1408

'Abd al-Majid Hasan (1380–1408) was the Sultan of Brunei, Borneo, who died while on a tribute mission to the Yongle emperor in Nanjing in 1408. The Yongle emperor had him buried in Nanjing following imperial funerary rites. A carved stone spirit way led up to the tomb, lined with animals and figures in pairs.

FIG. 236 OPPOSITE

A courtly scene in a garden, left folio of a double-page frontispiece (recto) illustration from the *Shahnama* (*Book of Kings*) of Abu'l-Qasim Manur Firdawsi (c. 934 – c. 1020)

The *Shahnama* is the Iranian national epic poem that combines legend and historical fact to narrate Persian history from the earliest times to the Arab invasions of 651. At least three illustrated royal Timurid copies survive from the reign of Shahrukh (r. 1409–1447) as fragments or as complete manuscripts. This sheet shows three Ming courtiers at the Timurid court, with blue-and-white ceramics on tables in the foreground.

Opaque watercolour, gold and silver on paper
c. 1444
Shiraz, Iran
h 32.7 cm, w 22 cm
Cleveland Museum of Art

he (along with 540 retainers) obtained passage on Zheng's third homeward voyage to pay his respects in person to the emperor in 1411.[8]

The same year that the Melakan envoy sought investiture for Bukit Cina, 'Abd al-Majid Hasan (1380 –1408), the Sultan of Brunei on the northwest coast of Borneo, sent a tribute envoy to Nanjing to seek the Yongle emperor's protection against a competitor in the neighbouring state of Sulu. That envoy likewise proposed that a hill in Brunei be elevated as a 'Mountain for the Eternal Tranquility and Protection of the State'.[9] The Ming emperor was gratified to incorporate a piece of Brunei ritually into the Chinese pantheon of sacred sites and agreed. The twenty-eight-year-old maharaja decided to express his thanks in person, and thereby cement the relationship through personal ties, by travelling with his family to the Ming court three years later, in 1408. Sadly for him, he died in Nanjing before he could return home. On his sickbed he asked to be buried in China so as to be closer to Heaven. The Yongle emperor acceded to his request, honouring him with imperial funerary rites and building him a tomb complex outside the capital. The burial mound and spirit way – an approach between paired lines of human and animal statues arranged from small to large – still stand today as tangible reminders of this foreigner who participated in the Ming tribute system (fig. 235).

CURRENCIES AND COMMODITIES

Ming China's presence in the world beyond its borders has left much tangible evidence (fig. 236). Ming copper-alloy coins (figs 237 and 238), for example, circulated widely throughout Asia, and provided the models for coinage produced on the same pattern (round with square holes) in Japan, Korea and Vietnam (figs 239 and 240). As the Yongle emperor was the ruler most aggressive about projecting Ming power into the Indian Ocean, coins bearing his reign mark outnumber those of any other fifteenth-century reign in archaeological digs as far afield as east Africa (although the length of time over which these coins continued to circulate means they may have arrived there in later centuries, so their specific archaeological contexts have to be taken into account). The reputation of these coins was so high that Japanese goldsmiths cast copies in gold to make what may have been high-denomination currency, but which more likely served as talismans or badges of status (fig. 241).

Coins were not the only form of Ming money to go abroad. We know from entries in the Veritable Records that Ming paper currency (fig. 243) was presented as gifts to foreign rulers, who may have seen it as a continuation of the practice under Mongol rulers, famous for giving out paper money that could be exchanged for valued goods within China's borders. Ming notes were intended to be non-convertible, so would have been of little use outside of China. It is therefore not surprising that none appears to have survived in the areas to which they were sent. However, there are specimens in museum collections around the world, which were acquired in the Qing dynasty or later.

Ironically, while the Yongle emperor was bestowing paper currency on foreign dignitaries as tokens of his esteem, its value inside China was falling. So far did it fall

FIG. 237

Copper-alloy coin with Yongle inscription

This follows the standard format for inscriptions on Chinese coins, and reads: 'Circulating treasure of the Yongle era' (*Yongle tongbao* 永樂通寶). Coins with this inscription were first cast around 1410 in the new northern capital of Beijing, but were distributed widely. For example, the China–Kenyan Lamu Islands Archaeological Project (launched in 2010 by the National Museum of China, Peking University, and the Kenya National Museum) has found similar coins in Kenya in an early fifteenth-century context, which may have been brought by Chinese ships. Alternatively, coins minted in China may have come to Africa, having changed hands through traders in the Middle East.

Copper-alloy
1403–24
Beijing
diam. 2.5 cm, weight 3.42 g
British Museum, London CH.57

FIG. 238

Copper-alloy coin with Xuande inscription

The four characters on this coin read: 'Circulating treasure of the Xuande era' *Xuande tongbao* 宣德通寶). The minting and circulation of standardized coins was a demonstration of imperial power. Coins were mass-produced in moulds and then strung together. In the final years of the Xuande reign (1426–1435), the Ming government abandoned its attempt to enforce the use of paper money, and allowed all transactions to be carried out using copper coins and silver valued by weight. No coins at all were cast by the state in the following Zhengtong reign (1436–1449), and poor-quality 'private coinage' caused increasing difficulties for the Ming economy. Coins such as these circulated beyond the Ming empire: a Korean ambassador to Japan in 1429, for example, was surprised at their prevalence there.

Copper-alloy
1426–35
Beijing
diam. 2.4 cm, weight 2.79 g
British Museum, London 1882,0601.445

FIG. 239

Vietnamese coins

During the period of Ming occupation, from 1407 to 1428, *Yongle tongbao* coins circulated in northern Vietnam. Later, after independence from the Ming, new coinage was issued bearing the names of the Vietnamese rulers. These were made in the Chinese style: circular, with a square hole in the centre and four characters, including two that mean 'circulating treasure'. This was a format established in the Tang dynasty (618–906) that even the Vietnamese coins of the tenth century followed. The earlier of these two coins is marked 'Circulating treasure of Thieu Binh'

(*Thieu Binh thong bao* 紹平通寶), minted in the reign of Lê Thai Tông (r. 1434–1440). The second is marked 'Circulating treasure of Dai Hoa' (*Dai Hoa thong bao* 大和通寶), minted in the reign of Lê Nhân Tông (r. 1443–1450).

Copper-alloy
1434–40 and 1443–50
Vietnam
diam. 2.4 cm, weight 2.85 g
diam. 2.4 cm, weight 3.28 g
British Museum, London, purchased, 1883,0802.2940 (left) and anonymous gift, 1979, 0304.47(right)

FIG. 240

Korean coin

Song-dynasty coins (960–1279) had circulated in Korea in the Goryeo period (918–1392). Korea issued its first paper money in the year 1401. This coin was minted in 1443, following the Chinese traditional coin with a square hole in the centre. It carries the inscription 'Circulating treasure of the Joseon era' (*Joseon tongbo* 朝鮮通寶), following the Chinese model. Coins with this inscription were made from 1423. Eventually they went out of circulation because the exchange rate fell to less than the intrinsic value of the coin.

Copper-alloy
Joseon period (1392–1897), minted in 1443
Hanseong (modern-day Seoul), Korea
diam. 2.4 cm, weight 3.65 g
British Museum, London, Tamba Collection, 1884,0511.1211

FIG. 241

Gold coin minted in Japan in imitation of Yongle coins

Bronze coins with the inscription 'Circulating treasure of the Yongle era' (*Yongle tongbao* 永樂通寶, or *Eiraku tsūhō* in Japanese) were issued in China during the Yongle era (1403–1424). These Chinese coins were sought after in Japan because they were of a higher quality than most Japanese coins. Local issues of the bronze coins were also made in Japan until their private minting was banned in the early 1600s. Gold and silver coins with this inscription were made in Japan as well, mainly for special use – such as rewarding soldiers for bravery; they were also used in payments on account of their gold and silver content.

Gold
Japan
1400–1700
diam. 2.5 cm, weight 4.39 g
British Museum, London, Tamba Collection, 1884,0511.207

FIG. 242
Silver ingot

In the early Ming, the *Nei Chengyun ku* was the imperial palace storehouse for treasure, so we know from the inscription on this ingot that it was personally given by the imperial court to Prince Zhuang of Liang. At that time the courts collected taxes in the form of grain twice a year, in summer and in autumn. From 1436 onwards peasants living south of the Yangtze River were ordered to pay taxes in silver rather than grain. Silver was of paramount importance to the Ming government but it was mined in regions far from the courts, and under the jurisdiction of local officials shaped into ingots to pay taxes. Some silver mines were worked illegally but there were strict punishments for this. From the mid-fifteenth century the importance of silver increased and that of paper money declined. Trade became less centralized and more dependent on local enterprise than state sponsorship. The ingot is inscribed: 'Top-grade silver [weight] 50 *liang* [1865.9 g] from the Imperial Treasury' (內承運庫 花銀伍拾兩 嚴一等).

Silver
c. 1424–41
China
l 14.8 cm, w 11 cm, d 5.2 cm
Hubei Provincial Museum, excavated from the tomb of Zhu Zhanji, Prince Zhuang of Liang, and of Lady Wei at Zhongxiang, Hubei province

FIG. 243
Metal printing plate and paper money

Ming paper money is large and flexible. In everyday use the notes would have been folded for convenience. Early Ming paper money was printed following a standard layout and stamped with red seals. All Ming paper money was printed with the reign period Hongwu (1368–1398) in the inscription, even in the following Yongle (1403–1424) and Xuande (1426–1435) eras. Paper money is frequently referred to in texts as a reward for both Ming subjects and foreigners. Chinese paper money circulated to foreigners, distributed by official ambassadors for the emperor such as Zheng He, but it could only be spent in China or exchanged for Chinese goods. Between 1400 and 1450 the value of paper money declined dramatically. In 1436 the government began collecting land taxes in silver, and paper money stopped being so important, except for small-scale transactions. However, early Ming paper money was still in circulation until the late 1400s. The small printing plate (on the left) is for 30 wen (coins). The large paper note (on the right) is for 100 wen (coins).

Bronze printing place
Issued in 1375
l 21.5 cm, w 11.9 cm, d 3.7 cm
Shanghai Museum

Paper money
Ink on paper
Issued in 1375
h 34.1 cm, w 22.2 cm
British Museum, donated by Emily Georgina Hingley, 1942,0805.1

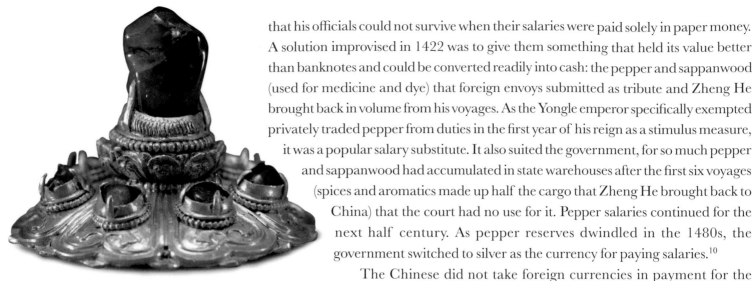

FIG. 244

Gold hat-top ornament

Gems were imported to China from Southeast Asia, India and Sri Lanka, and set in gold at the imperial workshops in the *Yinzuoju* (Jewellery Service). They were then sewn on to the tops of hats for princes. Before 2002 this ornament lay undiscovered in Prince Zhuang of Liang's tomb in Hubei. Such hat ornaments were fashionable at the imperial Mongol court and demonstrate continuity with the earlier regime.

Gold decorated with gem stones
c. 1420–41
Nanjing
h 3.9 cm, w 5.2 cm
Hubei Provincial Museum, excavated from the tomb of Zhu Zhanji, Prince Zhuang of Liang, and of Lady Wei at Zhongxiang, Hubei province

that his officials could not survive when their salaries were paid solely in paper money. A solution improvised in 1422 was to give them something that held its value better than banknotes and could be converted readily into cash: the pepper and sappanwood (used for medicine and dye) that foreign envoys submitted as tribute and Zheng He brought back in volume from his voyages. As the Yongle emperor specifically exempted privately traded pepper from duties in the first year of his reign as a stimulus measure, it was a popular salary substitute. It also suited the government, for so much pepper and sappanwood had accumulated in state warehouses after the first six voyages (spices and aromatics made up half the cargo that Zheng He brought back to China) that the court had no use for it. Pepper salaries continued for the next half century. As pepper reserves dwindled in the 1480s, the government switched to silver as the currency for paying salaries.[10]

The Chinese did not take foreign currencies in payment for the manufactures they sold abroad. Rather, they collected payment in the concrete forms of gems and precious metals. The jewels that stud the gold hat bobbles found in the tomb of Prince Zhuang of Liang (1411–1441), buried with him on his death, probably arrived from abroad during the Zheng He voyages (figs 47 and 244). The prince was also buried with gold ingots intended to cover his expenses in the afterlife. One of these carries an inscription that acknowledges the foreign origin of the gold: 'one ingot weighing 50 ounces of 80 per cent pure gold purchased in the Western Ocean and other locations, cast on __ day in the fourth month of the seventeenth

FIG. 245

Gold ingot

Prince Zhuang of Liang (1411–1441) was probably presented with this gold bar, one of two found in his tomb, by the Yongle emperor on the occasion of his second marriage to Lady Wei (d. 1451). A calligrapher at the *Yinzuoju* (Jewellery Service) inscribed the gold bar in clear characters. The text reads: 'On a day in the fourth month of the seventeenth year of the Yongle reign [1419], purchased from the Western Ocean and other places, 80 per cent pure gold [weighing] one *ding* and 50 *liang*.' (永樂十七年四月 日西洋等處買到 八成色金壹錠伍拾兩重). From this we can surmise that the ingot was made partly from gold brought back by one of the expeditions under the leadership of Zheng He.

Gold
Dated 1419
Excavated at the tomb of Zhu Zhanji, Prince Zhuang of Liang (1411–1441)
h 13 cm, max. w 10 cm, d 1.5 cm, weight 1,937 g
Hubei Provincial Museum, excavated from the tomb of Zhu Zhanji, Prince Zhuang of Liang, and of Lady Wei at Zhongxiang, Hubei province

FIG. 247 BELOW
Patterned silk fragment

This ivory-coloured fragment of silk is patterned with sprays of pomegranates on a chequered ground. Pomegranates are auspicious and represent a desire for many sons, because of the many seeds within the fruit. The words for sons and seeds are, in fact, the same in Chinese.

Silk damask
1300–1600
Nanjing, Suzhou or Hangzhou
h 19.0 cm, w 14 cm
Victoria and Albert Museum, London, donated by the
Reverend Dr Franz Bock (1823-99), V&A 7052-1860

FIG. 246 ABOVE
Silk cut for a tunic

Textiles were one of the most important commodities exchanged with east Asia, the Middle East and Africa. This section of a tunic, showing an armhole and a trimmed neck, is part of a group of Chinese silks that came from the medieval urban centre of Fustat in Egypt. The pattern of this silk consists of circular medallions with the stylized Chinese character *shou*, meaning 'longevity', and a motif of a flaming jewel that fills the spaces in between the medallions. The tailor has used the cloth upside-down, misunderstanding the pattern. Similar textiles have not been found in China so it is possible that this blue silk damask was woven especially for the Mamluk (1250–1517) court in Egypt, either by Chinese weavers or by local weavers who appropriated a Chinese pattern. A similar fragment in the Metropolitan Museum of Art (Fletcher Fund 46.156.20) is said to be from Al-Azam, also in Egypt.

Silk damask
1300–1450
Nanjing, Suzhou or Hangzhou
h 53 cm, w 30.5 cm
Victoria and Albert Museum, London, V&A 754-1898

FIG. 248 ABOVE
Yellow silk damask fragment

Small-scale motifs were favoured in the late Yuan and early Ming dynasties. Such textiles were exported to the Middle East, Africa and Europe, and used in royal and religious contexts. The colours would have been bright, and the material soft to the touch, with a glossy sheen and delicate pattern. Damasks were often later embroidered in the West, as the two-tone pattern provided an outline for further stitching.

This example of yellow silk damask has a design of trailing flowers against a diamond background. These small motifs seem to have been popular in Ming China for clothing and book covers, but they were also exported to Europe and used in Christian church treasuries as vestments and to wrap relics. This example is believed to have been found in Cairo. Similar textiles have been excavated from the Yuan-dynasty tomb of Qian Yu in Wuxi, Jiangsu province (*c.* 1320), and Li Yu'an in Zhou county, Shandong province (*c.* 1350).

Silk damask
1320–1450
Nanjing, Suzhou or Hangzhou
h 20.0 cm, w 11.5 cm
Victoria and Albert Museum, London, donated by the
Reverend Dr Franz Bock (1823-99), V&A 7056-1860

year of the Yongle reign', that is, May 1419 (fig. 245). Since the Western Ocean covered the maritime space from Sulu in the east to Zanzibar in the west, the gold could have come from any of the numerous places between them where it was mined. Once again, Zheng He is the likely agent transferring this material back to Ming China.

Most of what the Chinese brought home, from gold to spices, has disappeared, having been transmuted into other things: gold into bracelets, for example, and spices into food. So, too, has much of what they carried abroad to trade, such as silk fabric (figs 246–8). Fragments of export commodities, however, have survived through re-purposing: Chinese silk, for instance, could be used as backing for banners or armour. Ornamental papers were traded in the Middle East, where they were used

FIG. 250
Stoneware bottle collected in India

Kilns in the Longquan area of Zhejiang province produced finely made ceramics with glossy, green glazes in the early fifteenth century. The kilns by that point had been producing fine quality celadons for centuries both for the domestic and export markets. After the 1450s these kilns stopped making high-quality products. This bottle was exported and found in India.

Stoneware with celadon glaze
c. 1400–50
Longquan area, Zhejiang province
h 33.5 cm
British Museum, William Cummins collection, 1963,0520.9

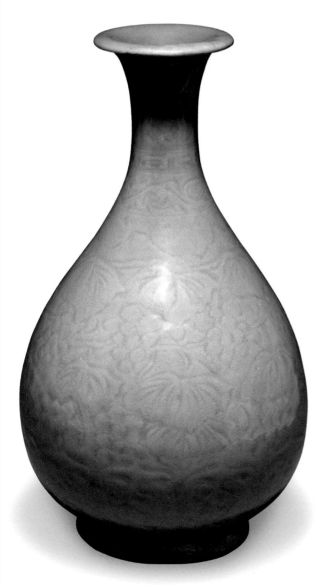

to produce books and manuscripts (figs 227, 228). In Korea and Japan there was a thriving market for Chinese books and paintings, and some paintings even found their way to the Timurid courts of Iran; very little of this survives. But in far-flung locations throughout the Western Ocean world – in communities along its coasts as far as Egypt, and even more frequently on the seabed under the navigation routes that radiated from the southern port of Quanzhou – one export item has survived the ravages of time if in rather partial condition: ceramics.

Export ceramics in the early Ming were dominated, as they have been ever since, by blue-and-white porcelain – which we call 'china'. It so happens that the china that is now thought of as quintessentially Chinese, is in fact the outcome of a century-long interaction during the Yuan dynasty between potters and consumers in west Asia and porcelain makers in China. One effect of the Mongol conquest in the 1270s was that the Mongols linked China with other Mongol regimes to the west as far as the edge of Europe. Along the Silk Road came enterprising traders such as Marco Polo (1254–1324), and with them came new tastes, designs, technologies, raw materials and demands. Persian traders far outnumbered Europeans on the Silk Road; for these dealers Chinese potters began to incorporate the Persian taste for white ceramics painted in blue symmetrical patterns. The Persians also brought cobalt, the key ingredient for decorating blue-and-white ceramics, which in its Persian form was much superior to the native cobalt available to Chinese potters. The kilns that responded most energetically to the foreign demand for this style, which the Chinese called 'Muslim blue', were situated in the town of Jingdezhen, close to clay deposits south of the Yangtze River. Jingdezhen is still the symbolic centre of China's porcelain industry.

The more Jingdezhen potters produced for this market, the better they were able to mould, decorate and glaze their new products. This stimulated even greater demand for their wares, which were not just conveyed back to Persia but stowed on ships and bundled on carts for transport throughout the Asian world, and even as far as the Mediterranean and Italy (fig. 263). Chinese kilns continued to turn out other forms of ceramic products, including porcelain with the jade-green glaze later known in Europe as celadons (figs 250 and 251), and these continued to be highly prized in Asian markets (figs 252–4); but it was blue-and-white that came to dominate world taste.[11] As the exotic became domestic, the repeating lattice-like patterns and vegetative scrollwork that must once have looked foreign to the Chinese eye gained popularity in the domestic market as well (fig. 252).

The far west was not the only destination for Ming export porcelain. Markets opened wherever Chinese merchants arrived with such marvellous wares, as modern-day treasure hunters and archaeologists diving along the coasts of Southeast Asia are increasingly showing us by bringing these commodities to the surface in ever greater numbers. These shipwrecks not only reveal the popularity of porcelain in Southeast Asia; they also help us to understand changing taste in the ceramics trade. Much of what is being recovered is not the fine blue-and-whites that graced court tables, but inexpensive everyday ware. At that level, too, it seems, Chinese manufactures dominated the international market. On ships that sank between

1368 and the 1420s, Chinese ceramics account for between 30 and 50 per cent of the cargo (silks, now long perished, would have made up much of the rest). From the 1420s and continuing for the next half century, however, the percentage of Chinese ceramics in shipwreck cargoes falls to less than 5 per cent. Chinese wares no longer supplied Southeast Asia, leaving a void that Thai (fig. 253) and later Vietnamese potters exploited to their advantage (figs 256, 259–61).[12] Archaeologists call this 'the Ming gap', and it correlates perfectly with the end of Zheng He's voyages. It attests to China's partial withdrawal from foreign contact and maritime trade from the 1430s. Chinese ceramics re-enter maritime trade networks towards the end of the fifteenth century as officials negotiated a loosening of restrictions along the south coast, though that partially reopened door was slammed shut in 1525 when yet another beleaguered Ming emperor closed the coast to trade. Not until 1567, when a new emperor reopened designated ports for maritime trade, did Ming ceramics resurge in regional markets and spread around the globe.

FIG. 251
The Katzenelnbogen bowl

Celadons and blue-and-white porcelains that made their way to Europe in the early fifteenth century were regarded as rare treasures. Philip the Elder, Count of Katzenelnbogen (1402–1479), purchased this bowl while on pilgrimage to the Holy Land between 14 July 1433 and 3 May 1434. On returning home from the Middle East, he had it mounted in a Rhenish workshop. It is recorded in an inventory of 1483.

Porcelain, incised with celadon glaze and with gilded metal mounts
Bowl: Longquan kilns, Zhejiang province, 1403–33
Mount: Rhineland, Germany, 1434–53
h 20.6 cm
Hessisches Landesmuseum, Staatliche Kunstsammlungen, Kassel

FIG. 252

Stoneware dish discovered in Borneo

Local copies of court green wares made at the Longquan kilns were exported to Southeast Asia and beyond. This dish was collected in Borneo in Indonesia in the 1890s. It would have been shipped there from Zhejiang where it was made. The design is similar to court wares, but the potters used poorer-quality materials to make it. Many similar dishes have been found on shipwrecks with cargoes dating to the early fifteenth century.

Stoneware with green glaze
1400–50
Zhejiang province
diam. 21.7 cm
British Museum, London, donated by Sir Augustus Wollaston Franks, Franks.3090

FIG. 253

Thai dish imitating Longquan stoneware

Copies of these green wares from the Longquan kilns were made across Asia. This example was made in the villages of Ban Ko Noi and Ban Pa Yang, along the Yom River north of the old city of Si Satchanalai in Sukhothai province, Thailand. The dish was shipped to customers in Indonesia where it was found. In the mid-fifteenth century Thai and Vietnamese merchants increased their volume of exported ceramics as numbers traded from China declined.

Stoneware with green glaze
1430–1500
Sawankhalok (Si Satchanalai), Thailand
diam. 25.8 cm
British Museum, London, donated by Angus Forsyth, 2009,3016.1

FIG. 254

Mamluk imitation of a Chinese dish

Blue-and-white copies of Chinese porcelain made in the Middle East are well known but celadons were also imitated in local materials at sites where they were exported. A dish similar to the one found in Borneo (fig. 252) must have travelled to Egypt where it inspired Mamluk potters to produce their own version of the design using locally sourced materials. The body material was fired to a lower temperature than the Chinese dish and as a result is not so hard. The glaze is similar in colour, but the texture is quite different as the Chinese glaze was applied in up to seven layers.

Earthenware with green glaze
1400–50
Egypt
h 7.7 cm, diam. 36.5 cm
British Museum, London, donated by Prof. J.M. Rogers, 2000,0727.1

FIG. 255
Stoneware dish collected in India

The stoneware dish is drilled with four Middle
Eastern owner's marks. On the base are two
marks engraved in fine Arabic script, which gives
the weight of the dish. These are Mughal Indian
coin and jewellers' weights. The second gives the
owner's name, A'zam Khan. There is more than
one person of this title. It is possible that the dish,
by then an antique, belonged to Mir Muhammad

Baqir, who was appointed Prime Minister in
1628, given this title in 1630 and died in 1649.

Stoneware with celadon glaze
c. 1400–50
Longquan area, Zhejiang province
diam. 44.7 cm
British Museum, William Cummins collection,
1963,0520.12

FIG. 256

Large dish with design of a chrysanthemum flower

Although the design on this dish is blue on a white ground, the body is made of local Vietnamese stoneware, which could not withstand the higher temperature firings of the Chinese kilns in Jingdezhen. Thus the body is not white but putty-coloured.

Vietnam was run as part of the Ming empire from 1407 to 1428. After it regained independence, the Chu Dau and other kilns in the Red River Delta started producing ceramics in competition with the blue-and-white wares exported from China in the early decades of the fifteenth century. Their designs, while original, showed some stylistic continuity with both the previous Mongol Yuan dynasty and the early fifteenth-century products of the Yongle and Xuande emperors' reigns.

This particular dish was found on the Indonesian island of Sulawesi in the early 1960s. From shards excavated in Trowulan, east Java – centre of the Majapahit kingdom of the thirteenth to fifteenth centuries – we know that the Indonesian kingdom ordered blue-and-white tiles from Vietnam in a variety of shapes, as well as other stonewares. Some of these tiles survive as wall decoration at the Great Mosque of Demak. Other tiles have been found in Sulawesi (Celebes).

Stoneware with underglaze cobalt-blue painting
Chu Dau kilns, Red River Delta, Vietnam
c. 1430–80
diam. 36.9 cm
British Museum, London, Brooke Sewell Permanent Fund,
2009,3014.5

FIG. 257
Porcelain dish with design of melons

Chinese blue-and-white wares ordered by the court were exported all over the world and inspired local copies wherever they were traded. They have been described as the world's first truly global product. Court-commissioned pieces such as this one are generally distinguished by the carefully selected materials used in their manufacture and the fine painting of their designs.

Porcelain painted in underglaze cobalt blue
Yongle period, 1403–1424
Jingdezhen, Jiangxi province
h 7 cm, diam. 37.3 cm
British Museum, London, donated by
Mrs Winifried Roberts in memory of
A.D. Brankston, 1954,0420.1

FIG. 258
Porcelain flask

There are few surviving examples in Chinese porcelain of this rare form: this one is in the Palace Museum, Beijing; another is in the Shanghai Museum; and a third is in the Freer Gallery of Art and Arthur M. Sackler Gallery, Washington DC. The Ministry of Works (*Gong bu*) controlled production for courts at Jingdezhen in the early fifteenth century. By 1402 there were twelve kilns under imperial supervision, employing at least 300 regular workers. These factories divided up labour tasks to increase efficiency: preparing the clay, forming the objects, decorating, firing, finishing, packing and distributing them.

Porcelain with underglaze cobalt-blue decoration
Yongle period, 1403–1424
Jingdezhen, Jiangxi province
h 46 cm, w 35 cm
The Palace Museum, Beijing

FIG. 259

Jar and twenty-four white cups from the Hoi An shipwreck

These stoneware cups were packed within the larger jar for safe and compact transportation. The white stoneware cups imitate Yongle-period white porcelain in their form, with everted rim and decoration. As the Vietnamese white wares were fired at a lower temperature, the body material is softer and the glaze less glossy than the Chinese examples. Blue-and-white decoration on the jar, with outsize birds, is distinctively Vietnamese.

Stoneware with underglaze cobalt-blue glaze; stoneware with moulded decoration and clear glaze
1430–60
Chu Dau kilns, Red River Delta, Hai Duong province, Vietnam
Hoi An shipwreck
h of cups 5.3 cm, h of jar 19.3 cm
British Museum, London, purchased with the Brooke Sewell Permanent Fund, cups 2000,1212.9 to 33

FIG. 260

Stoneware dragon ewer from the Hoi An shipwreck

The dragon was a popular motif in Vietnam, but the shape of this particular ewer is very unusual. The potters moulded the vessel for use as a rice wine pourer, the liquor being poured out of the opening in the dragon's jaws. It was part of a cargo of Vietnamese, Thai, Cham and Chinese ceramics that was taken by a Thai ship to trade in markets in Southeast Asia. Merchants overloaded their craft and the boat sank under the weight of its cargo. In 2000, after the Vietnamese government had made a selection of the recovered cargo for museums in Vietnam, the remaining items were auctioned in San Francisco: this ewer was one of only three dragon ewers to be included in the auction.

Stoneware with underglaze cobalt-blue
1430–60
Chu Dau kilns, Red River Delta, Vietnam
h 22.4 cm
British Museum, London, purchased with the Brooke Sewell Permanent Fund, 2000,1212.1

FIG. 261

Two stoneware pouring vessels from the Hoi An shipwreck

Monochrome blue stoneware ceramics were first made in Vietnam in the fifteenth century at the Chu Dau kilns, Hai Duong province. Until the sixteenth century the Vietnamese ceramics trade was dominated by the export of wares to neighbouring countries in Southeast Asia and to customers in the Middle East. Many of these plain blue wares are made in shapes specifically for the Southeast Asian trade market, such as these kendi or water pourers. These are quite different in form from the Chinese kendi, with a much longer spout and condensed body. A chocolate-coloured slip has been applied to the base.

Stoneware with single-colour blue glaze and iron-brown glazed base
1430–60
Chu Dau kilns, Red River Delta, Vietnam
Hoi An shipwreck
h 14.1 cm
British Museum, London, purchased purchased with the Brooke Sewell Permanent Fund, 2000,1212.2 and 3

THE PARTIAL DISAPPEARANCE OF THE WORLD

In 1370 the imperial founder decreed that his officials should produce a national catalogue of the places and people over whom he ruled. It would be entitled *The Unification Gazetteer of the Great Ming Dynasty* (*Da Ming yitong zhi*) – in direct imitation of a similar publication that the Mongols had ordered for the Yuan dynasty. The same ideal of unification was also expressed using the term for 'mixing together' (*hunyi*), which is the language employed in the title of the *Kangnido* map of 1472.[13]

Zhu Yuanzhang died before the gazetteer could be produced. Indeed, the work may never have been started, for his son the Yongle emperor issued another decree calling for its compilation in 1418. Still no luck. The Jingtai emperor repeated the order in 1454, by which time much of the work, and possibly even some of the engraving of the blocks, had already been done. The unwieldy publication finally lumbered into print seven years later. Oddly for a geographical reference book, it contains only one national map, labelled 'The unification map of the Great Ming dynasty' (fig. 262). Nothing could be more unlike the ambitious reach of the *Kangnido* map. It offers the merest sketch of the realm. The Indian Ocean makes an appearance in the lower lefthand corner, but no place west of China is indicated except for Hami, home of the Oirat Mongols who had captured the Zhengtong emperor in 1449. Korea, Japan and Ryukyu are off to the right, and Annam (Vietnam) down at the bottom, all in positions that defy our sense of geography, and that lay beyond the reach and knowledge of most Chinese.

The *Kangnido* map provided the early Ming emperors with a broad vision of the position of their domain within the world. The national gazetteer map of 1461 displayed a shrunken realm unconnected to any but China's immediate neighbours, and perhaps not even to them. The world had not changed, but China had. Some Chinese still travelled abroad to trade and some foreigners still banged on the gates, but the court now limited its concern to what lay within the borders, not what lay beyond. It is too simple to look back and judge this retrenchment as misguided, or worse to deplore the fact that the Ming empire was withdrawing just at the time that Portugal and Spain were setting sail, or to complain that what the Chinese did in the fifteenth century they failed to do in the sixteenth. Who knew what was to come? What we can affirm is that, for a half century, Chinese inhaled and even celebrated influences from a wider world, influences that would linger in Chinese culture all the way to the present. That in itself was a remarkable accomplishment.

FIG. 262

'The Unification map of the Great Ming dynasty', at the beginning of *The Unification Gazetteer of the Great Ming Dynasty* (*Da Ming yitong zhi* 大明一统志)

By the mid-fifteenth century Ming China was no longer interested in sending extravagant court-sponsored voyages around the world, and knowledge of foreign countries and their geography appears to have declined.

Woodblock-printed, ink on paper
Dated 1461
Each page: h 26.4 cm, w 17.5 cm
Harvard-Yenching Library

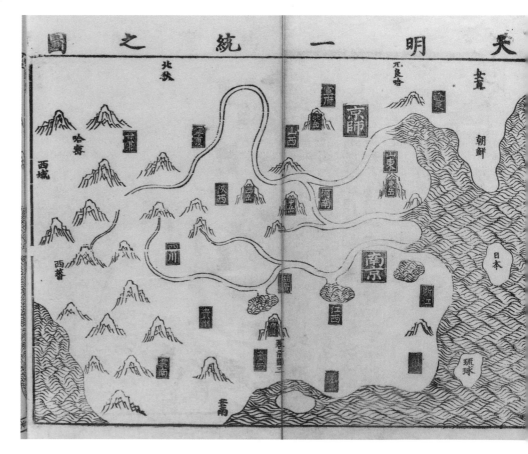

Andrea Mantegna (1431–1506), *'Adoration of the Magi'*

FIG. 263 OPPOSITE

IN THE COURSE of a long and successful career, the Italian painter Andrea Mantegna worked for a range of religious and aristocratic patrons in a number of cities, including Padua and Rome. His work included major altarpieces and more intimate religious subjects, as here in this depiction of a popular story taken from the Gospel according to St Matthew, the visit of the Three Wise Men to the infant Christ. Three Wise Men travelled, following a star, to acknowledge the birth of the king of kings. Jesus Christ, his mother, the Virgin Mary, and her husband, Joseph, have haloes and wear simple garments, while the Magi are dressed in exotic clothing and jewels, and bear exquisite gifts. Caspar, bearded and bareheaded, presents the Christ Child with a rare Ming blue-and-white porcelain bowl from China, filled with gold. Melchior, the younger bearded king behind Caspar, holds a Turkish censer for perfuming the air with incense. On the right, Balthasar carries a covered agate cup.

Ming porcelain did appear in Europe in the early fifteenth century, but it was very rare indeed; perhaps Mantegna's patrons, such as the Gonzaga Marquises of Mantua, or Pope Innocent VIII, owned some examples. Porcelain from the imperial factory at Jingdezhen confirms that the bowl in the painting is a court product made in the Yongle reign (1403–1424). Bowls and cups of this form, with this type of delicate floral motif, have been excavated in the Yongle strata.

The court-sponsored voyages of Zheng He and the global exchanges of Chinese commodities took place long before Christopher Columbus (c. 1450–1506) crossed the Atlantic in 1492, or Vasco da Gama (c. 1460–1524) went to India in 1497–8. There were few Chinese commodities in Europe in the early fifteenth century, beyond some silk and porcelain. These were mostly in the possession of royal courts and aristocrats, having been purchased in the Middle East during pilgrimages, or presented as gifts. The shield of Henry V of England (r. 1413–1422), now kept at the Palace of Westminster, is backed with Chinese silk. Later in the fifteenth century several large gifts of Ming porcelain were made from the courts in Egypt to Italian courts. In 1487 the Sultan of Egypt sent twenty porcelains to Lorenzo de Medici (1449–1492). Not until the sixteenth century did direct trade open between Europe and China.

Distemper on linen
1495–1505
Italy
h 48.6 cm, w 65.6 cm
The J. Paul Getty Museum, 85.PA.417

NOTES

CHAPTER 1 A SECOND FOUNDING: MING CHINA
1400–1450

1   Translated by Kathlyn Liscomb, Liscomb 1988/9, p. 128, with minor modifications by the author.
2   *Ming Taizong shilu* 12/3/*wuyin*, after Wu et al. 1992, p. 1,061.
3   Sung 2004.
4   Since the lunar calendar was used in China, the equivalence is not exact: see Hazelton 1984.
5   Clunas 2007, p. 23.
6   Hucker 1998, p. 17.
7   Barnhart 1993, p. 137.
8   Brook 2010, p. 94.
9   The chart in Tong 1991, p. 47, suggests that the years 1403–50 were the most peaceful of the entire dynasty.
10   Shin 2006, p. 44; Heijdra 1998, pp. 428–33.
11   Okada 1999, p. 266.
12   The term 'second founding' (*zai zao*, 再造) was already in use by the Yongle reign in the mid-Ming: see Farmer 1976, pp. 98–133.
13   Chan 1988, p. 238.
14   Ibid., p. 239.
15   Ibid., p. 239.
16   Ibid., p. 226 and Franke 1968, p. 210, for contemporary texts.
17   Clunas 2007, p. 140.
18   Liu 1997, p. 132.
19   Liscomb 2002, pp. 143 and 147.
20   Atwell 2002, p. 85.
21   Wu et al. p. 71.
22   Ibid., p. 712.
23   Chan 1988, pp. 226 and 285.
24   *Ming Taizong shilu* 12/3/*bingshen* after Li and Zhang 1995, p. 44.
25   *Ming Taizong shilu* 12/3/*wuxu* after Li et al. 1992, p. 133.
26   Franke 1968, p. 30.
27   Chan 1988, pp. 239 and 252.
28   Farmer 1976; Elman 2000, p. 191.
29   Wang 1998, p. 47.
30   Chan 1988, p. 260 and Zhang 2006, p. 59.
31   Naquin 2000, p. 109; Brook 1998, p. 648.
32   Chan 1988, p. 241; Chu 2008.
33   Chan 1988, p. 282.
34   Ibid., p. 242.
35   Ibid., p 321.
36   Hammond 2001, p. 193.
37   Wu 1968, p. 279.
38   Wang 1998, p. 25; Weidner 2001, p. 130.
39   Shin 2006, p. 8.
40   The exact nature of Ming-dynasty 'mandarin' (*guanhua*) remains controversial among historians of linguistics: see Coblin 2000, also Mai and Zhu 2012.
41   von Glahn 1996, pp. 48–82.
42   Shin 2006, pp. 51–2.
43   Atwell 2002, pp. 84 and 86.
44   Naquin 2000, p. 201.
45   Atwell 2002, pp. 86–7.
46   von Glahn 1996, pp. 75–6.
47   Atwell 2002, p. 89.
48   Ibid., p. 91.
49   Ibid., pp. 93–8.
50   Ibid., p. 98.
51   *Ming Taizong shilu* 12/12/*jiaxu* after Xu et al. 1995, p. 311.
52   Whitmore 2010, p. 109.
53   Kauz 2011.
54   Clunas 2013.
55   Wade 2010, p. 23.

CHAPTER 2 COURTS: PALACES, PEOPLE AND OBJECTS

1   Translated by David Robinson in Robinson 2013, p. 293.
2   Farmer 1976.
3   Paludan 1981, pp. 201–13.
4   Nanjing Museum 1996, p. 35.
5   Eng 2008, pp. 336–49.
6   Park Hyun Kyu 2011.
7   Mote 1977, pp. 101–54.
8   Brook 2010, p. 31.
9   Roxburgh 2010.
10   Thackston 2001, p. 59.
11   Watt and Leidy 2005; Tsai 2001.
12   Mote 1977a, p. 202. Jurchen recipes were published in the *Shi lin guang ji*. For Korean and Jurchen relations with Ming, see Twitchett and Mote 1998, pp. 279–99.
13   Lam 2008.
14   Wang 1998.
15   Ching 2011a.
16   Soulliere 1987.
17   Ibid., pp. 92–109.
18   Soulliere 1987.
19   For a day in the life of the Yongle emperor's court, see Tsai 2001, pp. 3–20.
20   Liew-Herres and Grabowsky 2008, pp. 97–116.
21   See National Museum of China and private collection. China Guardian Auction 2012. http://www.cguardian.com/tabid/95/Default.aspx?old=495759
22   Whitfield 2011.
23   Clunas 2013 and Yang 2012.
24   Goodrich and Fang 1976, p. 782; and Shandong sheng bowuguan 1972.
25   Goodrich and Fang 1976, p. 429; Zhongguo shehui kexueyuan 1978, pp. 306–13.
26   Hubei sheng bowuguan 2003.
27   Ropp, Zamperini and Zurndorfer 2001; Waltner 1981.
28   Choi Eun-so 2003.
29   Clunas 2013.
30   Robinson 2001.
31   Naquin 2000, p. 123.
32   Lam 1998.
33   Allsen 2004, pp. 172–3; Ho Peng-Yoke 1969.
34   Shi Yunli 2012.
35   Serruys 1961.
36   Mair, Steinhardt and Goldin 2005, p. 507.
37   Mote 1977a, p. 212.
38   Mote 1977a, p. 215.
39   Chang Foundation 1996.
40   Rawski and Rawson 2006.
41   Schaefer and Kuhn 2002.
42   Vainker 2004, p. 145.
43   David 1971, pp. 151–2.
44   Ibid.
45   Ibid.
46   Attributions which are made to identify pieces as Yuan, including 6,000 pieces in the Palace Museum, are based on stylistic analysis: see Zhang Rong 2012, p. 151.
47   Brinker and Lutz 1989, no. 5a–d.
48   Lu Pengliang 2012, p. 63.
49   Guoli gugong bowuyuan 1999, p. 180.
50   Chang Foundation 1998.
51   Wood 1999, pp. 66–7.
52   Liu 1995.
53   Fung Ping Shan Museum 1992, cat. no. 228.
54   Harrison-Hall 2001, pp. 143–7; Liu 1994, pp. 55–61.
55   Guoli gugong bowuyuan 1999; Li 2008; Gugong bowuyuan 2013; Eskenazi 2013.
56   Brown 2009; Brown and Sjostrand 2000.
57   Ye and Hua 2005; Zhejiang sheng wenwu kaogu yanjiusuo et al. 2009.

58   David 1971, p. 140.
59   He 2012.
60   Lee 1972, p. 23. *Jiaxing fu zhi* ('Gazetteer of Jiaxing district') of 1685 recorded the Yongle emperor's summons of Zhang Cheng to the capital. As Zhang Cheng had died his son went in his place.
61   Thackston 2001, p. 55.
62   Ibid., p. 56.
63   Mino 1980, p. 11.

CHAPTER 3 *WU*: THE ARTS OF WAR

1   Translated by David Robinson in Robinson 2013, p. 38.
2   Mote and Twitchett (eds) 1988, pp. 99–103; Wada 1959; Yun 2008, pp. 91–6.
3   Veit 2009, pp. 157–65. The Three Guards are also referred to as the Uriyangkhad.
4   Yang 2006, pp. 60–1.
5   Ibid.
6   Dreyer 1982, pp. 174–82; Chan 1988, pp. 222–9.
7   Morris Rossabi, 'Esen', in Goodrich and Fang 1976, pp. 416–20; Mote 1974; de Heer, 1986.
8   *Ming Taizong shilu*, 103.3b-4a (8/4/*jiayin*).
9   For early Ming security on the northern border see Waldron 1990, pp. 72–86.
10   Serruys 1959 and 1961.
11   Dreyer 2007.
12   Wade 2005.
13   Sen 2006.
14   Whitmore 1985, pp. 98, 109, 112 and 118. Numbers fluctuated over time.
15   Ibid.; Lo 1970.
16   Sun 2006.
17   Robinson 2001, pp. 37–41; Liew 1984.
18   Serruys 1959, 1961, 1966 and 1968.
19   Serruys 1975 and 1955; Rossabi 1982.
20   Rossabi 1982, pp. 1–36.
21   Robinson 2014.
22   Yu 1981, p. 308.
23   The following paragraphs draw from Robinson 2013.
24   Gommans 2002.
25   My thinking about hunting and rulership has benefited greatly from Allsen 2006.
26   Hu 1995–7, p. 173.
27   Ibid., p. 170.
28   Ibid., p. 168.
29   Zeng 1995–7, p. 159.
30   *Ming Taizong shilu* 37.2b (2/12/*bingxu*).
31   Jin 1993, p. 301.
32   *Ming Taizong shilu* 249.1b (20/5/*yichou*).
33   Ibid. 249.1b (20/5/*dingmao*).
34   Ibid. 249.1b (20/5/*wuchen*).
35   Ibid. 46.6a (3/8/*guisi*).
36   Tan 1958, vol. 2, p. 1,206.
37   The scroll is held at the Palace Museum, Beijing, and is reproduced in Li and Knight 2008, p. 209.
38   Allsen 2006, p. 215.
39   Liang 1987–99, p. 317; *Ming Taizong shilu* 34.2a-b (2/9/*bingwu*).

CHAPTER 4 *WEN*: THE ARTS OF PEACE

1   Translated by Jonathan Chaves in Mair 1994, p. 269.
2   Elman 1993.
3   Ditmanson 2007, pp. 114–21. Only in 1424 was clemency and release from slavery granted to their families.
4   Zhang 1995, pp. 719–68.
5   Ong 2010, pp. 154–65.
6   Chan 2005.
7   Franke 1968, p. 30.

8   Elman 2000, p. 114.

9   Brook 1998, pp. 652–9.

10 Clunas 2007, p. 99.

11 McCausland 2012.

12 Brook 1998, pp. 655–6. Rare examples in Franke 1968, pp. 126 and 260.

13 Brook 1998, p. 652.

14 Chan 1988, p. 303, and Brook 1998, p. 652.

15 See Liscomb 2002, p. 158, for the translation of *taige ti* as 'Eminent Court Official Style'.

16 Harrist and Fong 1999, pp. 148–9.

17 Mote and Chu 1989, pp. 122–6.

18 von Glahn 1996, p. 74.

19 Gugong bowuyuan 2009, p. 114.

20 Goodrich and Fang 1976, pp. 157–9.

21 Barnhart 1993, p. 60.

22 Liscomb 2002, pp. 142–6.

23 Idema 1981.

24 Idema 1984.

25 Nienhauser 1986, p. 777.

26 Zainie 1978.

27 Elman 2000, p. 650.

28 Whitmore 2010, p. 109.

29 Elman 2000, p. 241

30 Dardess 1986, p. 182.

31 Elman 2000, p. 329.

32 Ibid., p. 191.

33 Whitmore 2010, p. 109.

34 Hucker 1998, p. 37, and Dardess 1986, p. 156.

35 Dardess 1986, p. 159.

36 Ibid., p. 143.

37 Ibid., pp. 31 and 116.

38 Ibid., p. 179.

39 Chan 1988, p. 241; Chu 2008.

40 Dardess 1986, p. 88.

41 Coblin 2000; but see Chapter 1, n. 39.

42 Dyer 1983, pp. 305 and 311.

43 Dardess 1986, p. 155.

44 Clunas 2007, p. 93.

45 Nienhauser 1986, pp. 743–4; Yoshikawa 1989, pp. 122–3; Chang and Owen 2010, pp. 15–19.

46 Yin 2007.

47 Sung 1987, pp. 73–115, esp. p. 79.

48 Wang 1998, p. 329.

49 Barnhart 1993, p. 159; Wang 1998, p. 331.

50 Clunas 2013, pp. 459–74.

51 Brook 1998, p. 664. For the counter argument that books were hard to come by in the period 1400–1450, see Chia 2002, pp. 175, 183.

52 Clunas 2007, p. 54.

53 Chia 2002, pp. 176–7; Chang and Owen 2010, pp. 9–10.

54 Su 2004, p. 61.

CHAPTER 5 BELIEFS: MIRACLES AND SALVATION

1   Translated by Patricia Berger in Weidner 2001, p. 162.

2   Zhongguo guojia bowuguan 2005, pp. 26–7.

3   Gladney 1996, pp. 266–8, 285 and 379, n. 61.

4   Yang 2012, pp. 27–8.

5   Duyvendak 1939, pp. 341–55; Dreyer 2007, pp. 191–9.

6   Boltz 1986, pp. 214–31; Watson 1985, pp. 293, 299; Ptak 1994, p. 86.

7   Robinson 2008, pp. 374–6.

8   Zhongguo guojia bowuguan 2005, pp. 23–5; Chen 2008, pp. 4–8.

9   *Ming Xuanzong shilu*, j. 14, p. 389.

10 Zhongguo guojia bowuguan 2005, p. 27.

11 Ge 1976, pp. 210–11; *Ming Taizong shilu*, j. 269, pp. 2,441–3; *Ming Xianzong shilu*, j. 44, p. 1,083.

12 Zhang 193, *passim*; Thorp 1988, pp. 114–15. Fine Yuan examples are found on the ends of the marble arched passageway of the Cloud Terrace *stūpa* platform at Juyoung Pass northwest of Beijing; Kamay 1975, p. 25.

13 Duyvendak 1939, pp. 399–412; Church 2004, pp. 21–2.

14 Liscomb 2002, pp. 140–51; Schneewind 2006, pp. xvii–xx.

15 Duyvendak 1939, p. 402, ns. 1 and 2; *Ming Taizong shilu*, j. 35, p. 614, j. 34, pp. 599–600, and j. 61, pp. 882–3; Liscomb 2002, pp. 140–51.

16 Taylor 1998, pp. 840–47.

17 Li 1989, pp. 208–43, 251–9.

18 Ibid., pp. 248–51, 256, 258, 261–2.

19 Duara 1988, pp. 778–83.

20 Chao 2011, pp. 1–2, 97, 104–14 and 134–5, n. 30.

21 Lagerway 1992, pp. 299–300; Chao 2011, pp. 96–9.

22 Giuffrida 2008, pp. 147–9, 388 and 390.

23 Xiao 2007, pp. 352–3.

24 Little 2000, pp. 302–5; Giuffrida 2008, pp. 182–98.

25 Robinson 2008, p. 373.

26 Jiang and Zheng 2000, vol. 3.

27 Qujie 2012, pp. 33–50; Goodrich and Fang 1976, pp. 482 and 522; Karmay 1975, pp. 75–9; on Yuan and early-Ming precedents, see Stevenson 2001, p. 46.

28 Berger 2001, pp. 145–52 and 158–66; and, for a full translation of the Chinese inscriptions, pp. 162–6; the scroll is completely reproduced in colour in Jiang and Zheng 2000, vol. 3.

29 Whitfield 2014. The five languages have also been identified as Chinese, Chaghatai Mongolian, Tay Tibetan and Uyghur Mongolian, see Daniels 2012, p. 155.

30 Sen 2003, pp. 76–86; Jing 1994, pp. 54–6; Debreczeny 2011, pp. 1–11, 16–26; Zhencheng 1989, pp. 36, 82.

31 Chen 2004(b), pp. 99–101; Chen 2005, pp. 189 and 206–9; Debreczeny 2011, pp. 25–6; Ching 2008, pp. 346–50, figs 7.8 and 7.9.

32 Rossabi 1976, pp. 6–15; Tsai 1996, pp. 129–30; Wang 2008, pp. 56–7.

33 Mote and Twitchett 1988, pp. 268–9; Han 1996, pp. 41–6; *Joseon wangjo sillok Taejong*, j. 11 (19 and 20/4/ 6th year); j. 12 (16 and 18/5/6th year); j. 15 (19 and 22/4/8th year). I am indebted to Myenghee Son for locating and translating these records.

34 Pak and Whitfield 2002, pp. 388–93.

35 Naquin 2000, pp. 144–8, 176–7; Davis 2002, p. 151.

36 Naquin 2000, pp. 113–15.

37 Norris 2001, p. 131; Tong 2003, pp. 16–17.

38 Tong 2003, p. 227; Norris 2001, p. 128; Peng 1997, p. 21.

39 Debreczeny 2003, pp. 52–8 and 68–70; Du 2011, pp. 125–6; Zhang et al. 2012.

40 Jing 1994, pp. 46, 49–52; Yang 2012, p. 31.

41 McKeown 2010, pp. 111–54; Charleux 2006, pp. 121–6.

42 Wang 2007, pp. 128–40; Naquin 2000, pp. 179–86; Hammond 2001, p. 199.

43 Li 1963, pp. 37–41; Debreczeny 2003, pp. 49–52 and 61–2; Chen 2005, pp. 187–9; Guo 2010, pp. 69–79.

44 Hammond 2001, p. 198; Lam 2008, pp. 308–9.

45 Hammond 2001, pp. 195–7. The ceilings are now in the Philadelphia Museum of Art and the Nelson-Atkins Museum of Art in Kansas City.

46 Yan 2009, pp. 211–15.

47 Goodrich and Fang 2006, pp. 1,347–9; Hammond 2001, p. 201.

48 Lu 1985, j. 2, p. 15; Timothy Brook kindly provided this reference.

49 Wu 2010, pp. 44–7.

50 Shanxi 1985, p. 217.

51 Stevenson 2001, pp. 50–4.

52 The entire set is reproduced in Shanxi 1985.

53 Ibid., p. 52.

CHAPTER 6 COMMERCE: THE MING IN THE WORLD

1   Translation modified by Craig Clunas from Ma 1970, p. 69.

2   Ledyard 1994, pp. 244–9. For a recent analysis that situates this map in the global history of cartography, see Brotton 2012, pp. 114–45. The only existing copy of Qingjun's original map is a *c.* 1472 engraving of a 1452 copy, reproduced in Brotton 2012, p. 136. The most intriguing feature of the Qingjun map is a sea route leaving the south coast of Fujian and extending into the Indian Ocean. A note on the map tells the viewer that the voyage to Hormuz takes over 200 days.

3   One Chinese copy of the *Kangnido* map, tentatively dated 1389, has survived, though it was embargoed and did not circulate beyond the court. This map has since been reprinted in Cao 1994, pl. 1. Elements of the *Kangnido* map can be seen in *Xinan haiyi tu* (*Map of Maritime Foreigners to the South and West*) in the 1547 geography, *Huangyu kao* (*Study of the Imperial Realm*), 12.45a-b. No other surviving Ming atlas makes visual reference to this lost ancestor.

4   Farmer 1995.

5   Zheng He has been the subject of much myth-making and exaggeration, fuelled in part by an offended nationalist temper among some Chinese, in part by unnecessary Columbus envy, and more loosely by the widespread temptation to inflate the impressive into the unimaginable. For a sensible corrective, see Wade 2005.

6   Abru 1970 provides an account of a Timurid embassy of 1419–22 based on the embassy's official diary. Aspects of this embassy are presented in Brook 1998, pp. 34–9.

7   The best analysis of the size of Zheng He's ships, and a helpful corrective to popular misconceptions, is Church 2005. She points out that the standard 'official' length of 44 *zhang*, or 450 feet, derives from a novel published in 1597, a century and a half after the events it fictionalized. In reality, the ships were probably a third that length. Church's estimate of 6 million trees is a hypothetical exercise based on estimates of ship size that she disproves in the article; I have recalculated that estimate using her revised ship size.

8   The Melaka investiture is recorded in *Ming Taizong shilu*, 24.5b. On Parameswara, see Wang 1968 and Wade 1997.

9   Wang 2008, pp. 256–7.

10 I am grateful to Noa Grass for allowing me to share this information from her forthcoming doctoral dissertation; see also Yan and Hui 2008, p. 183.

11 Finlay 2010, pp. 133–74.

12 'The Ming gap' was coined by Tom Harrisson in 1958 and revived more recently in Brown 2005.

13 On the significance of, and confusion surrounding, the concept of unification, see Brook 2008, pp. 27–9.

BIBLIOGRAPHY

Allsen, Thomas, *Culture and Conquest in Mongol Eurasia*, Cambridge, 2004.

Allsen, Thomas, *The Royal Hunt in Eurasian History*, Philadelphia, 2006.

Atwell, William S., 'Time, money, and the weather: Ming China and the "Great Depression" of the mid-fifteenth century', *Journal of Asian Studies*, vol. 61, no. 1, 2002, pp. 83–113.

Barnhart, Richard M. with essays by Mary Ann Rogers and Richard Stanley-Baker, *Painters of the Great Ming: The Imperial Court and the Zhe School*, Dallas, 1993.

Beer, Robert, *The Encyclopedia of Tibetan Symbols and Motifs*, Boston, 1999.

Berger, Patricia, 'Miracles in Nanjing: an imperial record of the Fifth Karmapa's visit to the Chinese capital', in Marsha Weidner (ed.), *Cultural Intersections in Later Chinese Buddhism*, Honolulu, 2001, pp. 145–69.

Berkowitz, Alan J., 'Account of the Buddhist Thaumaturge Baozhi', in Donald S. Lopez, Jr (ed.), *Buddhism in Practice*, Princeton, 1995, pp. 578–85.

Birnbaum, Raoul, 'Light in the Wutai Mountains', in Matthew T. Kapstein (ed.), *The Presence of Light: Divine Radiance and Religious Experience*, Chicago, 2004, pp. 195–226.

Boltz, Judith M., 'In homage to T'ien-fei', *Journal of the American Oriental Society*, vol. 106, no. 1, 1986, pp. 211–32.

Boltz, Judith M, 'Notes on modern editions of the Taoist Canon', *Bulletin of the School of Oriental and African Studies*, vol. 56, no. 1, 1993, pp. 87–95.

Brinker, Helmut and Albert Lutz, *Chinese Cloisonné: The Pierre Uldry Collection*, New York, 1989.

Brook, Timothy, *The Confusions of Pleasure: Commerce and Culture in Ming China*, Berkeley, 1998.

Brook, Timothy, 'Communications and commerce', in Denis C. Twitchett and Frederick W. Mote (eds), *The Cambridge History of China: Volume 8, The Ming Dynasty, 1368–1644, Part 2*, Cambridge, 1998, pp. 579–707.

Brook, Timothy, *The Troubled Empire: China in the Yuan and Ming Dynasties*, Cambridge, MA, and London, 2010.

Brotton, Jerry, *A History of the World in Twelve Maps*, London, 2012.

Brown, Roxanna, 'Ming Ban–Ming Gap: Southeast Asian shipwreck evidence for shortages of Chinese trade ceramics', in Cheng Pei-kai, Guo Li and Chui Ki Wan (eds), *Proceedings of the International Conference: Chinese Export Ceramics and Maritime Trade, 12th–15th Centuries*, Hong Kong, 2005, pp. 78–104.

Brown, Roxanna, *The Ming Gap and Shipwreck Ceramics in Southeast Asia: Towards a Chronology of Thai Trade Ware*, Bangkok, 2009.

Brown, Roxanna and Sten Sjostrand, *Turiang: A Fourteenth-Century Shipwreck in Southeast Asian Waters*, Pasadena, 2000.

Bureau for the Collation of Tripitaka under China Tibetology Research Center, 'An account of the various editions of Kangyur and the results of their collation', *China Tibetology*, 2006, pp. 71–82, 92.

Campell, Aurelia, 'The impact of imperial and local patronage on early Ming temples at the Sino-Tibetan frontier', PhD thesis, University of Pennsylvania, 2011.

Cao Wanru 曹婉如 (ed.), *Zhongguo gudai ditu ji. Mingdai* 中國古代地圖集. 明代 (*An Atlas of Ancient Maps in China. The Ming dynasty*), Beijing, 1994.

Carr, Dawson William, *Andrea Mantegna: The Adoration of the Magi*, Los Angeles, 1997.

Chan Hok-lam, 'The Chien-wen, Yung-lo, Hung-hsi and Hsüan-te reigns', in Denis Twitchett and Frederick W. Mote (eds), *The Cambridge History of China: Volume 7, The Ming Dynasty, 1368–1644, Part 1*, Cambridge, 1988, pp. 182–304.

Chan Hok-lam, 'Xie Jin (1369–1415) as imperial propagandist: his role in the revisions of the "Ming Taizu Shilu"', *T'oung Pao*, vol. 91, nos 1/2, 2005, pp. 58–124.

Chan Hok-lam, *Legends of the Building of Old Peking*, Hong Kong, 2008.

Chang Foundation, *Imperial Hongwu and Yongle Porcelain Excavated at Jingdezhen*, Taipei, 1996.

Chang Foundation, *Xuande Imperial Porcelain Excavated at Jingdezhen*, Taipei, 1998.

Chang Kang-i Sun and Stephen Owen (eds), *The Cambridge History of Chinese Literature, Volume II: from 1375*, Cambridge, 2010.

Chang Kwang-chih, and E. N. Anderson et al, *Food in Chinese Culture*, New Haven and London, 1977.

Chao Shin-yi, *Daoist Rituals, State Religion, and Popular Practice: Zhenwu Worship from Song to Ming (960–1644)*, New York and Abingdon, 2011.

Charleux, I., 'Copies de Bodhgayā en Asie orientale: les stūpas de type Wuta à Pékin et Kökeqota (Mongolie-Intérieure)', *Arts Asiatiques – L'autre en regard*, volume en hommage à Madame Michèle Pirazzoli-t'Serstevens, vol. 61, 2006, pp. 120–42.

Chase, Kenneth, *Firearms: A Global History to 1700*, Cambridge and New York, 2003.

Chen Junji 陳俊吉, '*Baoningsi shuiluhua de huihua zhizuo niandai yu shangci niandai tanjiu*' 寶寧寺水陸畫的繪畫 製作年代與賞賜年代探究 ('A study of the dates of the execution and bestowal of the *shuilu* painting of Baoning Temple'), *Shuhua yishu xuekan* 書畫藝術學刊 (*Thesis of Department of Painting and Calligraphy*), no. 6, 2009, pp. 357–93.

Chen Nan 陳楠, '*Mingdai Daci Fawang Shijia Yeshi zai Beijing huodong kaoshu*' 明代大慈法王釋迦也失在北京活 動考述 ('Textual research on the activities of the Ming-dynasty Great Compassion Dharma King Shakya Yeshe in Beijing'), *Zhongyang minzu daxue lishi xuebao* 中央民族大學學報 (*Journal of the Central University for Nationalities*), vol. 31, no. 4, 2004(a), pp. 91–7.

Chen Nan 陳楠, '*Shijia yeshi zai Nanjing, Wutaishan ji qi yu Ming Chengzu guanxi shishi kaoshu*' 釋迦也失在南京、五台山及其 與明成祖關係史實考述 ('Historical materials about the relationship between Shakya Yeshe and Ming Chengzu and Shakya Yeshe's time in Nanjing and Wu-tai shan areas'), *Tibetan Studies*, no. 3, 2004(b), pp. 99–106.

Chen Nan 陳楠, *Mingdai Daci Fawang yanjiu* 明代大慈法王研究 (*Research on the Great Compassion Dharma King of the Ming Dynasty*), Beijing, 2005.

Chen Nan, 'The influence of Tibetan Buddhism on the hinterland in the Ming dynasty', *China Tibetology*, no. 2, 2008, pp. 1–18.

Chia Lin Sien and Sally K. Church (eds), *Zheng He & the Afro-Asian World*, Melaka, 2012.

Chia, Lucille, *Printing for Profit: The Commercial Publishers of Jianyang, Fujian (11th–17th Centuries)*, Cambridge, MA, and London, 2002.

China Culture Relics Protection Foundation, '*Beijing yi Jindai Guandi miao shixiu yanzhong wenwu zhuanjia kaifang baohu*' 北京一金代關帝廟失修嚴重 文物專家 開方保護 ('A Beijing Jin-dynasty Guandi Temple is in a serious state of disrepair, cultural preservation experts prescribe protection'). http://www.ccrpf.org.cn/tabid/73/InfoID/616/Default.aspx

China Guardian autumn 2012 auction results: http://www.cguardian.com/tabid/95/Default.aspx?oid=495759

Ching, Dora C.Y., 'Tibetan Buddhism and the Ming imperial image', in David M. Robinson (ed.), *Culture, Courtiers, and Competition: The Ming Court (1368–1644)*, Cambridge, MA, 2008, pp. 321–64.

Ching, Dora C.Y., 'Icons of rulership: imperial portraiture during the Ming dynasty (1368–1644)', PhD thesis, Princeton University, 2011.

Ching, Dora C.Y., 'The Ming imperial image: the transformation from Hongwu to Hongzhi', in Jerome Silbergeld, Dora C.Y. Ching, Judith G. Smith and Alfreda Murck (eds), *Bridges to Heaven: Essays on East Asian Art in Honor of Professor Wen C. Fong*, Princeton, 2011a, pp. 307–35.

Choi Eun Soo 최은수, '*Byeonsu (1447–1524) myo chulto yoseoncheollik e gwanhan yeongu*' 변수(邊脩 : 1447–1524)묘 출토 요선철릭에 관한 연구 ('A Research on waist lined coat with pleats based on the excavated costume from the Byun-su (1447–1524) Tomb'), *Boksik* 服飾 (*Journal of the Korean Society of Costume*), vol. 53, no. 4, (2003), pp. 163–76.

Chu Hung-lam, 'Textual filiation in Li Shimian's biography: the part about the palace fire in 1421', *East Asian Library Journal*, vol. 13, no. 1, 2008, pp. 66–126.

Church, Sally K., 'The giraffe of Bengal: a medieval encounter in Ming China', *The Medieval History Journal*, vol. 7, no. 1, 2004, pp. 1–37.

Church, Sally K., 'Zheng He: an investigation into the plausibility of 450-ft treasure ships', *Monumenta Serica*, vol. 53, 2005, pp. 1–43.

Clunas, Craig, 'Some literary evidence for gold and silver vessels in the Ming period (1368–1644)', in Michael Vickers (ed.), *Pots and Pans. A Colloquium on Precious Metals and Ceramics in the Muslim, Chinese and Graeco-Roman Worlds*, Oxford, 1987, pp. 83–7.

Clunas, Craig, 'Wine foaming in gold, tea brewing in jade: drinking culture in Ming dynasty China', *Oriental Art*, vol. 44, no. 2, 1998, pp. 8–10.

Clunas, Craig, 'The other Ming tombs: kings and their burials in Ming China', *Transactions of the Oriental Ceramic Society*, vol. 70, 2005–6, pp. 1–16.

Clunas, Craig, *Empire of Great Brightness: Visual and Material Cultures of Ming China, 1368–1644*, London, 2007.

Clunas, Craig, 'Antiquarian politics and the politics of antiquarianism in Ming regional courts', in Wu Hong (ed.), *Reinventing the Past: Archaism and Antiquarianism in Chinese Art and Visual Culture*, Chicago, 2010, pp. 229–54.

Clunas, Craig, *Screen of Kings: Royal Art and Power in Ming China*, London, 2013.

Clunas, Craig, 'Art as lineage in the Ming and Qing', in Jerome Silbergeld and Dora C.Y. Ching (eds), *The Family Model in Chinese Art and Culture*, Princeton, 2013, pp. 459–74.

Clunas, Craig, 'Going Shopping with "The Old Chinese" in early Ming Beijing,' *Orientations*, Sept 2014 (forthcoming).

Coblin, W. South, 'The evolution of mandarin', *Journal of the American Oriental Society*, vol. 120, no. 4, 2000, pp. 537–52.

Cowen, Jill S., 'Muslims in China: the mosques', Saudi Aramco World, vol. 36, no. 4, 1985. http://www.saudiaramcoworld.com/issue/198504/muslims.in.china-the.mosques.htm

Dardess, John W., *A Ming Society: T'ai-ho County, Kiangsi, in the Fourteenth to Seventeenth Centuries*, Berkeley, Los Angeles and London, 1986.

Daniels, Christian, 'Script without Buddhism: Burmese Influence on the Tay (Shan) Script of Mäng² Maaw² as Seen in a Chinese Scroll Painting of 1407', *The International Journal of Asian Studies*, vol. 9, no. 2, July 2012, pp. 147–76.

David, Sir Percival (trans.), *Chinese Connoisseurship: The Ko Ku Yao Lun: The Essential Criteria of Antiquities*, London, 1971.

Davis, Edward L., 'Arms and the Dao, 2: the Xu brothers in Tea Country', in Livia Kohn and Harold David Roth (eds), *Daoist Identity: Cosmology, Lineage, and Ritual*, Honolulu, 2002, pp. 149–64.

de Heer, Philip, *The Care-taker Emperor*, Leiden, 1986.

Debreczeny, Karl, 'Sino-Tibetan artistic synthesis in Ming dynasty temples at the core and periphery', *The Tibet Journal*, vol. 28, 2003, pp. 49–108.

Debreczeny, Karl, 'Wutai shan: pilgrimage to Five-Peak Mountain', *Journal of the International Association of Tibetan Studies*, vol. 6, 2011, pp. 1–33.

Ditmanson, Peter, 'Venerating the martyrs of the 1402 usurpation: history and memory in the mid and late Ming dynasty', *T'oung Pao*, vol. 93, nos. 1/2, 2007, pp. 110–58.

Dreyer, Edward L., *Early Ming China*, Stanford, 1982.

Dreyer, Edward L., *Zheng He, China and the Oceans in the Early Ming Dynasty, 1405–1433*, New York, 2007.

Du Changshun 杜常順, '*Mingdai Minzhou Houshi jiazu yu Da Chongjiaosi*' 明代岷州后氏家族與大崇教寺 ('The Hou family of Minzhou in Ming dynasty and the Da Chongjiao Temple'), *Qinghai Minzu Yanjiu* 青海民族研究 (*Nationalities Research in Qinghai*), no. 1, 2011, pp. 123–9.

Duara, Prasenjit, 'Superscribing symbols: the myth of Guandi, Chinese god of war', *Journal of Asian Studies*, vol. 47, no. 4, 1998, pp. 778–95.

Duyvendak, J.J.L., 'The true dates of the Chinese maritime expeditions in the early fifteenth century', *T'oung Pao*, vol. 34, nos. 1/2, 1938, pp. 341–412.

Dyer, Svetlana Rimsky-Korsakoff, *Grammatical Analysis of the* Lao Ch'i-ta, *with an English Translation of the Chinese Text*, Canberra, 1983.

Elman, Benjamin, '"Where is King Ch'eng?": civil examinations and Confucian ideology in the early Ming, 1368–1415', *T'oung Pao*, vol. 79, nos. 1/2, 1993, pp. 23–68.

Elman, Benjamin, *A Cultural History of Civil Examinations in Late Imperial China*, Berkeley, Los Angeles and London, 2000.

Eng Sunchuan Clarence, 'The use of ceramic in Chinese late imperial architecture', PhD thesis, School of Oriental and African Studies, University of London, 2008.

Eskenazi, Giuseppe, Robert D. Mowry, Sarah Wong and Eskenazi Ltd, *Junyao: 31 October–22 November 2013*, exh. cat., London, 2013.

Farmer, Edward L., *Early Ming Government: The Evolution of Dual Capitals*, Cambridge, MA, 1976.

Farmer, Edward L., *Zhu Yuanzhang and Early Ming Legislation: The Reordering of Chinese Society Following the Era of Mongol Rule*, Leiden, 1995.

Figgess, John, 'A letter from the court of Yung Lo', *Transactions of the Oriental Ceramic Society*, vol. 34, 1962–3, pp. 97–100.

Finlay, Robert, *The Pilgrim Art: Cultures of Porcelain in World History*, Berkeley, 2010.

Franke, Wolfgang, *An Introduction to the Sources of Ming History*, Kuala Lumpur, 1968.

Fung Ping Shan Museum, *Ceramic Finds from Jingdezhen Kilns (10th–17th Century)*, exh. cat., Hong Kong, 1992.

Ge Yinliang 葛寅亮, *Jinling fancha zhi* 金陵梵刹志 (*Records of the Buddhist temples of Jinling*), repr. Taipei, 1976.

Gimello, Robert M., 'Chang Shang-ying on Wu-t'ai Shan', in Susan Naquin and Chün-fang Yü (eds), *Pilgrims and Sacred Sites in China*, Berkeley, 1992, pp. 89–149.

Gimello, Robert M., '"Environments" worldly and other-worldly: Wutaishan and the question of what makes a Buddhist mountain "Sacred"', Learning Ace, 2006, http://www.learningace.com/doc/5650459/85205c8aeb90ffdc83ef07a7a44fd215/gimello

Giuffrida, Noelle, 'Representing the Daoist god Zhenwu, the Perfected Warrior, in late imperial China', PhD thesis, University of Kansas, 2008.

Gladney, Dru C., *Muslim Chinese: Ethnic Nationalism in the People's Republic*, Cambridge, MA, 1996.

Gommans, Jos, 'Warhorses and post-nomadic empire in Asia, *c.* 1000–1800', *Journal of Global History*, vol. 2, 2002, pp. 1–21.

Goodrich, Carrington and Chaoying Fang (eds), *The Dictionary of Ming Biography*, New York, 1976.

Gugong bowuyuan 故宮博物院 (Palace Museum, Beijing), *Mingdai gongting shuhua zhenshang* 明代宮廷書畫珍賞 (*Court Painting and Calligraphy of the Ming Dynasty*), Beijing, 2009.

Gugong bowuyuan 故宮博物院 (Palace Museum, Beijing), *Junci yaji: Gugong bowuyuan zhencang ji chutu junyao ciqi huicui* 鈞瓷雅集: 故宮博物院珍藏及出土鈞窯瓷器薈萃 (*Selection of Jun Ware – The Palace Museum's Collection and Archaeological Excavation*), Beijing, 2013.

Guo Liping 郭麗平, '*Beijing Fahaisi bihua zhong de zangchuan fojiao yishu yinsu tanxi* 北京法海寺壁畫中的藏傳佛教藝術因素探析' ('Analysis of elements of Tibetan Buddhist art in the murals of Fahai Monastery in Beijing'), *Zhongguo Zangxue* 中國藏學 (*Chinese Tibetology*), no. S1, 2010, pp. 69–79.

Guoli gugong bowuyuan 國立故宮博物院 (National Palace Museum, Taipei), *Gugong cangci daxi: Junyao zhi bu* 故宮藏瓷大系:鈞窯之部 (*A Panorama of Ceramics in the Collection of the National Palace Museum: Chun Ware*), Taipei, 1999.

Ḥāfiz, Abrū, *A Persian Embassy to China; Being an Extract from Zubdatu't Tawarikh of Hafiz Abru*, New York, 1970.

Hall, David A., 'Marishiten: Buddhism and the warrior goddess', PhD thesis, University of California, Berkeley, 1990.

Hammond, Kenneth J., 'Beijing's Zhihua Monastery: history and restoration in China's capital', in Marsha Weidner (ed.), *Cultural Intersections in Later Chinese Buddhism*, Honolulu, 2001, pp. 189–208.

Han U-gŭn , 'Policies toward Buddhism in Late Koryŏ and Early Chosŏn', in Lewis R. Lancaster and and Chai-shin Yu (eds), *Buddhism in the Early Chosŏn: Suppression and Transformation*, Berkeley, 1996, pp. 1–58.

Harrison-Hall, Jessica, *Ming Ceramics – A Catalogue of the Late Yuan and Ming Ceramics in the British Museum*, London, 2001.

Harrison-Hall, Jessica, '"Ming: 50 years that changed China" at the British Museum' *Orientations*, Sept 2014 (forthcoming).

Harrisson, Tom, '"The Ming gap" and Kota Batu, Brunei'. *The Sarawak Museum Journal* vol. 8, 1958, pp. 273–277.

Harrist, Jr, Robert E. and Wen C. Fong, *The Embodied Image: Chinese Calligraphy from the John B. Elliott Collection*, Princeton, 1999.

Hazelton, Keith, *A Synchronic Chinese–Western Daily Calendar 1341–1661 A.D.*, Minneapolis, 1984.

Heijdra, Martin, 'The socio-economic development of rural China during the Ming', in Denis C. Twitchett and Federick W. Mote (eds), *The Cambridge History of China: Volume 8, The Ming Dynasty, 1368–1644, Part 2*, Cambridge, 1998, pp. 417–578.

He Zhenji 何振紀, 'Guoyuan chang xiao xi 果園廠小析' ('Brief analysis of the Orchard Factory'), *Zhongguo sheng qi* 中國生漆 (*Journal of Chinese Lacquer*), vol. 31, no. 4, Dec 2012, 39–42.

Heller, N., 'From imperial glory to Buddhist piety: the record of a Ming ritual in three contexts', *History of Religions*, vol. 51, no. 1, 2011, pp. 59–83.

Helliwell, David, 'Holdings of Yongle Dadian in United Kingdom libraries', in Zhongguo guojia tushuguan 中國國家圖書館 (National Library of China) (ed.), *Yongle dadian bianzuan 600 zhounian guoji yantaohui lunwenji* 永樂大典編纂600周年國際研討會論文集 (*Collected papers from the international conference on the 6th centennial of the compilation of the Great Canon of the Yongle Reign*), Beijing, 2003, pp. 264–306.

Helliwell, David, '*Yongle da dian*', *Arts of Asia*, Nov/Dec 2014 (forthcoming).

Ho Peng-Yoke, 'The Astronomical Bureau in Ming China', *Journal of Asian History*, vol. 3, no. 2, 1969, pp. 135–57.

Höllmann, Thomas O., *The Land of the Five Flavors: A Cultural History of Chinese Cuisine*, New York, 2013.

Hong Kong Museum of Art, *Heavens' Embroidered Cloths: One Thousand Years of Chinese Textiles*, exh. cat., Hong Kong, 1995.

Hou Wei 侯偉 and Wang Jianmin 汪建民 (eds), '*Beijing mingsheng guji kaolue – Beijing guta zhi er, Zhenjuesi Jingang baozuo ta*' 北京名勝古跡考略 – 北京古塔之二，真覺寺金剛寶座塔 ('Overview of Beijing's famous ancient sites – Beijing's ancient pagodas two – Diamond Throne Pagoda of Zhenjue Monastery'), *Shifandaxue Xuebao (Shehui Kexue ban)* 師範大學學報（社會科學版）*Journal of Capital Normal University, Social Science edition*, vol. 98, no. 3, 1994, pp. 133–6.

Hubeisheng bowuguan 湖北省博物館 (Hubei Provincial Museum), '*Hubei Zhongxiang Mingdai Liangzhuangwang mu fajue jianbao* 湖北鐘祥明代梁莊王墓發掘簡報' ('Short report on the excavation of the Ming tomb of Prince Zhuang of Liang at Zhongxiang, Hubei'), *Wenwu* 文物 (*Cultural Relics*), no. 5, 2003, pp. 4–23.

Hu Guang 胡廣, *Hu Wenmu gong wenji* 胡文穆公文集 (*Collected official documents of Hu Wenmu*), in *Siku quanshu cunmu congshu* 四庫全書存目叢書 (*Extant compendia from the Complete Library of the Four Treasuries*), repr. Jinan, 1995–7, *ji* 29.

Huang Hao 黃顥, '*Beijing Fahaisi Zangzu zhuyuan sengren kao*' 北京法海寺藏族助緣僧人考 ('Study of the Tibetan donor monks of Fahai Monastery in Beijing'), in *Lasa Zangxue taolunhui wenxuan* 拉薩藏學討論會文選 (*Selected Works from the Lhasa Tibetan Studies Symposium*), Lhasa, 1987.

Hubeisheng bowuguan 湖北省博物館 (Hubei Provincial Museum), '*Hubei Zhongxiang Mingdai Liangzhuangwang mu fajue jianbao*' ('Short report on the excavation of the Ming tomb of Prince Zhuang of Liang at Zhongxiang, Hubei'), *Wenwu* 文物 (*Cultural Relics*), no. 5, 2003, pp. 4–23.

Hubeisheng bowuguan 湖北省博物館 (Hubei Provincial Museum), *Liangzhuangwang mu: Zheng He shidai deguibao* 梁莊王墓：鄭和時代的瑰寶 (*The Tomb of Prince Liangzhuang: Treasure of the Era of Zheng He*), Beijing, 2007.

Hucker, Charles O., 'Ming government', in Denis C. Twitchett and Federick W. Mote (eds), *The Cambridge History of China: Volume 8, The Ming Dynasty, 1368–1644, Part 2*, Cambridge, 1998, pp. 9–105.

Idema, W.L., 'The capture of the Tsou-yü', in W.L. Idema (ed.), *Leyden Studies in Sinology: Papers Presented at the Conference Held in Celebration of the Fiftieth Anniversary of the Sinological Institute of Leyden University, December 8–12, 1980*, Leiden, 1981, pp. 57–74.

Idema, W.L., 'The story of Ssu-ma Hsiang-ju and Cho Wen-chün in vernacular literature of the Yüan and early Ming dynasties', *T'oung Pao*, vol. 70, nos. 1/2, 1984, pp. 60–109.

Jiang Cheng'an and Zheng Wenlei (eds), *Precious Deposits: Historical Relics of Tibet, China*, vol. 3, 2000, Beijing.

Jiang Yonglin, *The Mandate of Heaven and the Great Ming Code*, Seattle, 2011.

Jin Shan 金善, *Beizheng lu* 北征錄 (*Record of the Northern Campaigns*), in Deng Shilong 鄧士龍 (ed.), *Guochao diangu* 國朝典故 (*Classical Anecdotes of the States and Courts*), vol. 1, Beijing, 1993.

Jing Anning, 'The Portraits of Khubilai Khan and Chabi by Anige (1245–1306), A Nepali Artist at the Yuan Court', *Artibus Asiae*, vol. 54, nos. 1/2, 1994, pp. 40–86.

Joseon wangjo sillok 朝鮮王朝實錄 (Annals of the Joseon Dynasty). National Institute of Korean History. http://sillok.history.go.kr/main/main.jsp

Karmay, Heather, *Early Sino-Tibetan Art*, Warminster, 1975.

Kauz, Ralph, 'Gift exchange between Iran, Central Asia and China under the Ming dynasty, 1368–1644', in Linda Komaroff and Sheila S. Blair (eds), *Gifts of the Sultan – The Arts of Giving at the Islamic Courts*, Los Angeles and New Haven, 2011, pp. 115–22.

Kerr, Rose, *Later Chinese Bronzes*, London, 1990.

Komaroff, Linda and Sheila S. Blair (eds), *Gifts of the Sultan – The Arts of Giving at the Islamic Courts*, Los Angeles and New Haven, 2011.

Lagerway, J., 'The pilgrimage to Wu-tang shan', in Susan Naquin and Chün-fang Yü (eds), *Pilgrims and Sacred Sites in China*, Berkeley, 1992, pp. 293–332.

Lam, Joseph S.C., *State Sacrifices and Music in Ming China Orthodoxy, Creativity, and Expressiveness*, New York, 1998.

Lam, Joseph S.C., 'Imperial agency in Ming music culture', in David M. Robinson (ed.), *Culture, Courtiers, and Competition: The Ming Court (1368–1644)*, Cambridge, MA, 2008, pp. 269–320.

Lam, Peter (ed.), *Layered Beauty: The Baoyizhai Collection of Chinese Lacquer*, Hong Kong, 2010.

LaRocca, Donald J. (ed.), *Warriors of the Himalayas: Rediscovering the Arms and Armor of Tibet*, exhib. cat., New York, 2006.

Ledyard, G., 'Cartography in Korea', in J.B. Harley and David Woodward (eds), *The History of Cartography* vol. 2, bk. 2 Chicago, 1994.

Lee King-tse and Hu Shih-chang, 'Carved lacquer of the Hongwu period', *Oriental Art*, vol. 47, no. 1, 2001, pp. 10–20.

Lee Soyoung, with essays by JaHyun Kim Haboush, Sunpyo Hong and Chin-Sung Chang, *The Art of the Korean Renaissance, 1400–1600*, New York, 2009.

Lee Yu-kuan, *Oriental Lacquer Art*, Tokyo, 1972.

Lee Yu-kuan, *Oriental Lacquer Art*, Tokyo and New York, 1972.

Lentz, Thomas and Glenn Lowry, *Timur and the Princely Vision: Persian Art and Culture in the Fifteenth Century*, Los Angeles and Washington DC, 1989.

Li Baoping, 'Numbered Jun wares: controversies and new kiln site discoveries', *Transactions of the Oriental Ceramic Society*, vol. 71 no. 1, 2008, pp. 65–77.

Li Guoxiang 李國祥 et al. (eds), *Ming shilu leizuan: Gongting shiliao juan* 明實錄類纂: 宮廷史料卷 (*An Anthology of Historical Materials from the* Veritable Records of the Ming: *Ming Court*), Wuhan, 1992.

Li He and Michael Knight (eds), *Power and Glory: Court Arts of China's Ming Dynasty*, San Francisco, 2008.

Li Qiongying 李瓊英 and Zhang Yingchao 張穎超 (eds), *Ming shilu leizuan: Zongfan guiqi juan* 明實錄類纂：宗藩貴戚卷 (*An Anthology of Historical Materials from the* Veritable Records of the Ming: *Princes and Relatives*), Wuhan, 1995.

Li Song 李松, '*Beijing Fahaisi lishi jianzhu bihua*' 北京法海寺歷史建築壁畫 ('Beijing Fahai Monastery: history, architecture and murals'), *Xiandai foxue* 現代佛學 (*Contemporary Buddhist Studies*), no. 4, 1963, pp. 37–42.

Li Dongyang 李東陽 and Shen Shixing 申時行 (eds), *Da Ming huidian* 大明會典 (*Collected Statues of the Great Ming*), repr. Taipei, 1963.

Liang Qian 梁潛, *Boan xiansheng wenji* 泊菴先生文集 (*Collected writings of the gentleman of the hut at the shore*), in *Beijing tushuguan guji zhenben congkan* 北京圖書館古籍珍本叢刊 (*Beijing Library Antiquarian Rare Books Compendium*) vol. 100, Beijing, 1988.

Liang Zhu 梁柱 (ed.), *Liangzhuangwang mu* 梁莊王墓 (*Mausoleum of Prince Liang Zhuangwang*), 2 vols, Beijing, 2007.

Liew Foon Ming, 'Tuntian farming of the Ming Dynasty', PhD thesis, University of Hamburg, 1984.

Liew-Herres, Foon Ming and Volker Grabowsky, in collaboration with Aroonrut Wichienkeep, *Lan Na in Chinese Historiography: Sino-Thai Relations as Reflected in the Yuan and Ming Sources (13th to 17th Centuries)*, Bangkok, 2008.

Lin Fu-shih, 'The cult of Jiang Ziwen in medieval China', *Cahiers d'Extrême-Asie*, vol. 10, 1998, pp. 357–75.

Linrothe, Rob, *Paradise and Plumage: Chinese Connections in Tibetan Arhat Painting*, exh. cat., New York, 2005.

Liscomb, Kathlyn, 'The Eight Views of Beijing: Politics in Literati Art', *Artibus Asiae*, vol. 49, 1988/9, pp. 127–52.

Liscomb, Kathlyn, 'Foregrounding the symbiosis of power: a rhetorical strategy in some Chinese commemorative art', *Art History*, vol. 25, no. 2, 2002, pp. 135–61.

Little, Stephen with Shawn Eichman, *Taoism and the Arts of China*, Chicago, 2000.

Liu Jiuan 劉九庵, *Song Yuan Ming Qing shuhuajia chuanshi zuopin nianbiao* 宋元明清書畫家傳世作品年表 (*Chronological index of extant works by calligraphers and painters of the Song, Yuan, Ming and Qing dynasties*), Shanghai, 1997.

Liu Xinyuan (Laurie Barnes trans.), 'Amusing the emperor: the discovery of Xuande period cricket cages from the Ming imperial kilns', *Orientations*, vol. 26, no. 8, 1995, pp. 62–77.

Liu Yi 劉毅, 'Mingdai Jingdezhen ciye "kongbaiqi" yanjiu' 明代景德鎮瓷業空白期研究 ('Research on the 'blank period' of Jingdezhen porcelain industry in the Ming dynasty'), *Nanfang wenwu* 南方文物 (*Relics from South*), no. 3, 1994, pp. 55–61.

Lo Jung-p'ang, 'Intervention in Vietnam: a case study of the foreign policy of the early Ming government', *Tsinghua Journal of Chinese Studies*, vol. 8, nos 1–2, 1970, pp. 154–82.

Loew Beer, F. and O. Maenchen-Helfen, 'Carved red lacquer of the Ming period', *The Burlington Magazine for Connoisseurs*, vol. 69, no. 403, 1936, pp. 166–7, 170–2.

Luk Yu-ping, 'Teachings of the Way: Daoist objects in the exhibition "Ming: 50 years that changed China" at the British Museum' *Orientations*, Sept 2014 (forthcoming).

Luk Yu-ping and Jin Xian Qiu, 'Conserving two Ming paintings', *Arts of Asia*, Nov/Dec 2014 (forthcoming).

Lu Pengliang, 'Beyond the women's quarters: meaning and function of cloisonné in the Ming and Qing dynasties', in Beatrice Quette (ed.), *Cloisonné: Chinese Enamels from the Yuan, Ming and Qing Dynasties*, New York, Paris, New Haven and London, 2012, pp. 63–80.

Lu Pengliang, 'Xuande bronzes: a legend reexamined', *Arts of Asia*, Nov/Dec 2014 (forthcoming).

Lu Rong 陸容, *Shuyuan zaji* 菽園雜記 (*Miscellaneous Records of the Bean Garden*), repr. Beijing, 1985.

Luo X.W., 'China', in Martin Frishman and Hasan-Uddin Khan (eds), *The Mosque: History, Architectural Development and Regional Diversity*, London, 1994, pp. 209–12, 216.

Ma Huan (J.V.G. Mills trans.), *Ying-yai sheng-lan: 'The Overall Survey of the Ocean's Shores')[1433]*, Cambridge, 1970.

Mai Yun 麥耘 and Zhu Xiaonong 朱曉農, 'Nanjing fangyan bushi Mingdai guanhua de jichu 南京方言不是明代官話的基礎 ('Refutation of Nanjing Dialect as Base of Standard Speech in Ming Dynasty'), *Yuyan kexue* 語言科學 (*Linguistic Sciences*), vol. 11, no. 4, July 2012, pp. 337–58.

Mair, Victor (ed.), *The Columbia Anthology of Traditional Chinese Literature*, New York, 1994.

Mair, Victor H., Nancy S. Steinhardt and Paul R. Goldin, *Hawai'i Reader in Traditional Chinese Culture*, Honolulu, 2005.

McCausland, Shane, 'Copying and transmitting, knowledge and nonsense: from the *Great Encyclopaedia* to *A Book From the Sky*', in Nicholas Pearce and Jason Steuber (eds), *Original Intentions: Essays on Production, Reproduction and Interpretation in the Arts of China*, Gainesville, FL, 2012, pp. 236–63.

McKeown, Arthur P., 'From Bodhgayā to Lhasa to Beijing: the life and times of Sariputra (*c.* 1335–1426), last abbot of Bodhgayā', PhD thesis, Harvard University, 2010.

McNeill, Malcolm, 'Two Chinese Buddhist wanderers with a tame tiger: identifying iconography and the power of names', *Arts of Asia*, Nov/Dec 2014 (forthcoming).

Meskill, John (trans.), *Ch'oe Pu's Diary: A Record of Drifting across the Sea*, Tucson, 1965.

Fei Hsin (J.V.G. Mills trans., Roderich Ptak ed.), *Hsing-ch'a sheng-lan: The Overall Survey of the Star Raft*, Wiesbaden, 1996.

Peng Nian 彭年, '*Wubainian cangsang wushinian huihuang de gusi – Beijing Dongsi Qingzhensi jiansi 550 zhounian jinian*' 五百年滄桑五十年輝煌的古寺—北京東四清真寺建寺550周年紀念 ('An ancient temple with five hundred years of vicissitudes and fifty years of glory – the 550th anniversary of Dongsi Mosque in Beijing'), *Zhongguo Musilin* 中國穆斯林 (*Chinese Muslims*) no. 4, 1997, pp. 21–3.

Ming Renzong shilu 明仁宗實錄 (Veritable Records of Ming Renzong), repr. Taipei, 1961–6.

Ming Taizong shilu 明太宗實錄 (Veritable Records of Ming Taizong), repr. Taipei, 1961–6.

Ming Xianzong shilu 明憲宗實錄 (Veritable Records of Ming Xianzong), repr. Taipei, 1961–6.

Ming Xuanzong shilu 明宣宗實錄 (Veritable Records of Ming Xuanzong), repr. Taipei, 1961–6.

Mino, Yutaka, *Freedom of Clay and Brush through Seven Centuries in Northern China: Tz'u-chou (Cizhou) Type Wares 960–1600 A.D.*, exh. cat., Indianapolis, 1980.

Mote, Frederick W., 'The T'u-mu incident of 1449', in Frank Kierman (ed.), *Chinese Ways in Warfare*, Cambridge, MA, 1974, pp. 243–72.

Mote, Frederick W., 'The transformation of Nanking, 1350–1400', in George William Skinner, *The City in Late Imperial China*, Stanford, CA, 1977, pp. 101–54.

Mote, Frederick W., 'Yuan and Ming', in K.C. Chang (ed.), *Food in Chinese Culture: Anthropological and Historical Perspectives*, New Haven and London, 1977a.

Mote, Frederick W. and Denis C. Twitchett (eds), *The Cambridge History of China: Volume 7, The Ming Dynasty, 1368–1644, Part 1*, Cambridge, 1988.

Mote, Frederick W. and Hung-lam Chu, ed. by Howard L. Goodman, *Calligraphy and the East Asian Book*, Boston and Shaftesbury, 1989.

Moule, A.C., 'Some foreign birds and beasts in Chinese books', *Journal of the Royal Asiatic Society of Great Britain and Ireland*, vol. 2, 1925, pp. 247–61.

Moule, A.C., 'An introduction to the *I yü tu chih*: or "Pictures and Descriptions of Strange Nations" in the Wade collection at Cambridge', *T'oung Pao*, vol. 27, nos 2/3, 1930, pp. 179–88.

Murray, Julia K., '"Idols" in the temple: icons and the cult of Confucius', *Journal of Asian Studies*, vol. 68, no. 2, 2009, pp. 371–411.

Museum of Far Eastern Antiquities, *Chinese Gold and Silver in the Carl Kempe Collection*, Ulricehamn, 1999.

Nan Bingwen 南炳文 et al., *Fodao mimi zongjiao yu Mingdai shehui* 佛道秘密宗教與明代社會 (Buddhist and Daoist secret religions and Ming Society), Tianjin, 2002.

Nanjing Museum, *A Legacy of the Ming – Ceramic Finds from the Site of the Ming Palace in Nanjing*, Hong Kong, 1996.

Nanjingshi bowuguan 南京市博物館 (Nanjing Municipal Museum), *Baochuanchang yizhi: Nanjing Ming baochuanchang Liuzuotang kaogu baogao* 寶船廠遺址：南京明寶船廠六作塘考古報告 (Ming Dynasty Baochuanchang Shipyard in Nanjing), Beijing, 2006.

Naquin, Susan, *Peking: Temples and City Life, 1400–1900*, Berkeley, Los Angeles and London, 2000.

Nara Kokuritsu Hakubutsukan 奈良国立博物館 (Nara National Museum), *Seichi Ninpō: Nihon Bukkyō 1300-nen no genryū* 聖地寧波：日本仏教1300年の源流 (Sacred Ningbo, gateway to 1300 years of Japanese Buddhism), exh. cat., Nara, 2009

Nienhauser, Jr, William H. (ed.), *The Indiana Companion to Traditional Chinese Literature*, Bloomington, IN, 1986.

Norris, H.T., 'The Mushaf in Beijing's (*Bikīn's*) oldest mosque', *Journal of Qur'anic Studies*, vol. 3, no. 1, 2001, pp. 123–4, 127–34.

Okada, Hidehiro, 'China as a successor state to the Mongol empire', in Reuven Amitai-Preiss and David O. Morgan (eds), *The Mongol Empire and its Legacy*, Leiden, Boston and Cologne, 1999, pp. 260–72.

Ong Eng Ann, Alexander, 'Contextualising the book-burning episode during the Ming invasion and occupation of Vietnam', in Geoff Wade and Sun Liachen (eds), *Southeast Asia in the Fifteenth Century: The China Factor*, Singapore, 2010, pp. 154–168.

Pak Youngsook and Roderick Whitfield, *Buddhist Sculpture: Handbook of Korean Art*, Seoul, 2002.

Paludan, Ann, *The Imperial Ming Tombs*, New Haven and Hong Kong, 1981.

Park Hyun Kyu 朴現圭, 'Jejudo beobhwasa samjon bulsang gwa namgyeong daeboeunsa ui gwangye' 제주도 법화사(法華寺) 삼존불상(三尊佛像)과 남경(南京) 대보은사(大報恩寺)의 관계 ('The Relationship between the three Statues of Buddha of Beophwa-sa in Jejudo and Dabaoen-si in Nanjing', *Jungguksa yeongu* 中國史研究 (Journal of Chinese Historical Research), vol. 58, no. 2, 2009, pp. 129–54.

Park Hyun Kyu 朴現圭, '*Song Jocheongaek gwiguk sijangdo ui jejak sigi wa Jocheongaek bunseok*' 送朝天客歸國詩章圖의 제작 시기와 朝天客분석 ('Analysis on the age of "Seeing off Korean envoys returning to their country" and on "Korean envoys"), *Jungguksa yeongu* 中國史研究 (Journal of Chinese Historical Research), vol. 70, no. 2, 2011, pp. 169–93.

Peng Nian 彭年, '*Wubainian cangsang wushinian huihuang de gusi – Beijing Dongsi Qingzhensi jiansi 550 zhounian jinian*' 五百年滄桑五十年輝煌的古寺—北京東四清真寺建寺550周年紀念 ('An ancient temple with five hundred years of vicissitudes and fifty years of glory – the 550th anniversary of Dongsi Mosque in Beijing'), *Zhongguo Musilin* 中国穆斯林 (Chinese Muslims) no. 4, 1997, pp. 21–3.

Pierson, Stacey, *Collectors, Collections and Museums: The Field of Chinese Ceramics in Britain, 1560–1960*, Oxford and New York, 2007.

Pierson, Stacey, *From Object to Concept – Global Consumption and the Transformation of Ming Porcelain*, Hong Kong, 2013.

Ptak, Roderich, Review of *T'ien-fei hsien-sheng lu, Die Aufzeichnungen von der manifestierten Heiligkeit der Himmelsprinzessin: Einleitung Übersetzung, Kommentar* by Gerd Wädow, *Journal of the American Oriental Society*, vol. 114, no. 1, 1994, pp. 85–7.

Quan Jinyun 全錦雲 (ed.), *Beijing wenwu jingcui daxi. Guzhong juan* 北京文物精粹大系.古鐘卷 (Series of the Gem of Beijing Cultural Relics. Ancient Bells), Beijing, 2000.

Quanzhou Yisilan wenwu baohu weiyuanhui 泉州伊斯蘭文物保護委員會 (Committee for Protecting Islamic Historical Relics in Quanzhou) and Zhongguo wenhua shiji yanjiu zhongxin 中國文化史跡研究中心 (Research Centre for the Historical Relics of Chinese Culture) (ed), *Quanzhou Yisilan shiji* 泉州伊斯蘭史跡 (Islamic Historic Relics in Quanzhou), Fujian, 1985.

Quette, Beatrice (ed.), *Cloisonné: Chinese Enamels from the Yuan, Ming and Qing Dynasties*, New York, Paris, New Haven and London, 2012.

Qujie, Suolang, 'Reconciliation and legitimization: the Fifth Karmapa Deshin Shegpa's trip to Ming China', MA thesis, University of British Columbia, 2012.

Rawski, Evelyn S. and Jessica Rawson (eds), *China: The Three Emperors, 1662–1795*, exh. cat., London, 2006.

Robinson, David M., *Bandits, Eunuchs, and the Son of Heaven: Rebellion and the Economy of Violence in Mid-Ming China*, Honolulu, 2001.

Robinson, David M., 'The Ming court and the legacy of the Yuan Mongols', in David M. Robinson (ed.), *Culture, Courtiers, and Competition: The Ming Court (1368–1644)*, Cambridge, MA, 2008, pp. 365–421.

Robinson, David M., *Martial Spectacles of the Ming Court*, Cambridge, MA, and London, 2013.

Robinson, David M., 'Chinese border garrisons in a transnational context: Liaodong under the early Ming dynasty', in Peter Lorge and Kaushik Roy (eds), *Chinese and Indian Warfare – from the Classical Age to 1870*, unpublished manuscript.

Rogers, Mary Ann, 'Visions of grandeur: the life and art of Dai Jin', in Richard M. Barnhart, *Painters of the Great Ming: The Imperial Court and the Zhe School*, Dallas, 1993, pp.127–194.

Ropp, Paul Stanley, Paola Zamperini and Harriet Thelma Zurndorfer (eds), *Passionate Women: Female Suicide in Late Imperial China*, Leiden and Boston, 2001.

Rossabi, Morris, *China and Inner Asia: From 1368 to the Present Day*, New York, 1975.

Rossabi, Morris, 'Two Ming envoys to Inner Asia', *T'oung Pao*, vol. 62, nos 1/3, 1976, pp. 1–34.

Rossabi, Morris, *The Jurchens in the Yüan and Ming*, Ithaca, 1982.

Rossabi, Morris, 'The Ming and Inner Asia', in Denis C. Twitchett and Frederick W. Mote (eds), *The Cambridge History of China: Volume 8, The Ming Dynasty, 1368–1644, Part 2*, Cambridge, 1998, pp. 222–71.

Rousmaniere, Nicole (ed.), *Kazari: Decoration and Display in Japan, 15th–19th Centuries*, London, 2002.

Roxburgh, David, 'The "Journal" of Ghiyath al-Din Naqqash, Timurid envoy to Khan Baligh, and Chinese art and architecture', in Lieselotte E. Saurma-Jeltsch and Anja Eisenbeiß (eds), *The Power of Things and the Flow of Cultural Transformations: Art and Culture Between Europe and Asia*, Berlin, 2010, pp. 90–113.

Sabban, Françoise, 'Cuisine à la cour de l'empereur de Chine au XIV siècle: les aspects culinaires du Yinshan Zhengyao de Hu Sihui', *Médiévales*, vol. 5, 1983, pp. 32–56.

Sagaster, K., 'The history of Buddhism among the Mongols', in A. Heirman and S.P. Bumbacher (eds), *The Spread of Buddhism*, Leiden and Boston, 2007, pp. 379–432.

Schaefer, Dagmar and Dieter Kuhn, *Weaving an Economic Pattern in Ming Times (1368–1644)*, Heidelberg, 2002.

Schneewind, Sarah, *A Tale of Two Melons: Emperor and Subject in Ming China*, Indianapolis, 2006.

Scott, Gregory A., 'Conversion by the book: Buddhist print culture in early Republican China', PhD thesis, Columbia University, 2013.

Sen, Tansen, *Buddhism, Diplomacy, and Trade: The Realignment of Sino-Indian Relations, 600–1400*, Honolulu, 2003.

Sen, Tansen, 'The formation of Chinese maritime networks to southern Asia, 1200–1450', *Journal of the Economic and Social History of the Orient*, vol. 49, 2006, pp. 421–53.

Serruys, Henry, *Sino-Jürčed Relations during the Yung-lo Period, 1403–1424*, Wiesbaden, 1955.

Serruys, Henry, 'Mongols ennobled during the early Ming', *Harvard Journal of Asiatic Studies*, vol. 22, 1959, pp. 209–60.

Serruys, Henry, 'Foreigners in the Metropolitan police during the 15th century', *Oriens Extremus*, vol. 8, no. 1, 1961, pp. 59–83.

Serruys, Henry, 'Land grants to the Mongols in China, 1400–1450', *Monumenta Serica*, vol. 25, 1966, pp. 394–405.

Serruys, Henry, *Sino-Mongol Relations During the Ming, III. Trade Relations: The Horse Fairs, 1400–1600*, Bruxelles, 1975.

Shandong sheng bowuguan 山東省博物館 (Shandong Museum), '*Fajue Zhu Tan mu ji shi* 發掘朱檀墓紀實' ('Record of the Excavation of Zhu Tan's Tomb'), *Wenwu* 文物 (*Cultural Relics*), no. 5, 1972, pp. 25–36.

Shanxi sheng bowuguan 山西省博物館 (Shanxi Museum), *Baoningsi mingdai shuilu hua* 寶寧寺明代水陸畫 (*Baoning Monastery Ming Dynasty Water-and-Land Paintings*), Beijing, 1985.

Shi Shouqian 石守謙 and Ge Wanzhang 葛婉章 (eds), *Da han de shiji: Meng Yuan shidai de duoyuan wenhua yu yishu* 大汗的世紀: 蒙元時代的多元文化與藝術 (*Age of the Great Khan: Pluralism in Chinese Art and Culture under the Mongols*), Taipei, 2001.

Shi Yunli, 'Islamic astronomy in the service of Yuan and Ming monarchs', paper presented at the International Congress on 'China and the Muslim World: Cultural Encounters', Beijing, 2012.

Shin, Leo Kwok-yueh, *The Making of the Chinese State: Ethnicity and Expansion on the Ming Borderlands*, Cambridge, 2006.

Silk, Jonathan A., 'Notes on the History of the Yongle Kanjur', in Michael Hahn, Jens-Uwe Hartmann and Roland Steiner (eds), *Suh r̥lekhāḥ; Fesbage für Helmet Eimer*, Swisttal-Odendorf, 1996, pp. 153–200.

Sommer, Deborah, 'Destroying Confucius: iconoclasm in the Confucian temple', in T.A. Wilson (ed.), *On Sacred Grounds: Culture, Society, Politics, and the Formation of the Cult of Confucius*, Cambridge, MA, 2002, pp. 95–133.

Soulliere, Ellen Felicia, 'Palace women in the Ming dynasty: 1368–1644', PhD thesis, Princeton University, 1987.

Sperling, E., 'The 1413 Ming embassy to Tsong-kha-pa and the arrival of Byams-chen Chos-rje Shakya Ye-shes at the Ming court', *Journal of the Tibet Society*, vol. 2, 1982, pp. 105–8.

Sperling, E., 'Early Ming policy toward Tibet: an examination of the proposition that the early Ming emperors adopted a "divide and rule" policy toward Tibet', PhD thesis, Indiana University, 1983.

Sperling, E., 'The Fifth Karma-pa and some aspects of the relationship between Tibet and the early Ming', in *The History of Tibet: Volume 2, The Medieval Period: c. AD 850–1895, The Development of Buddhist Paramountcy*, New York, 2003, pp. 473–482. (Reprinted from Michael Aris and Aung San Suu Kyi (eds), *Tibetan Studies in Honour of Hugh Richardson*, Warmister, 1979, pp. 280–89).

Stevenson, Daniel B., 'Text, image, and transformation in the history of the *Shuilu fahui*, the Buddhist Rite for Deliverance of Creatures of Water and Land', in Marsha Weidner (ed.), *Cultural Intersections in Later Chinese Buddhism*, Honolulu, 2001, pp. 30–70.

Stoddard, Heather, *Early Sino-Tibetan Art*, Singapore, 2008. Ströber, Eva, *Ming: Porcelain for a Globalised Trade*, Stuttgart, 2013.

Stuart, Jan, 'Dressing Chinese tables and chairs: furnishing textiles in imperial China', *Oriental Art*, vol. 47, no. 4, 2001, pp. 38–46.

Stuart, Jan and Evelyn S. Rawski, *Worshipping the Ancestors: Chinese Commemorative Portraits*, Washington DC, 2001.

Sturman, Peter, 'Cranes above Kaifeng: the auspicious image at the court of Huizong', *Ars Orientalis*, vol. 20, 1990, pp. 33–68.

Su Heng-an, *Culinary Arts in Late Ming China: Refinement, Secularization and Nourishment*, Taipei, 2004.

Sun Laichen, 'Ming–Southeast Asian overland interactions, 1368–1644', PhD thesis, University of Michigan, 2000.

Sun Laichen, 'Chinese gunpowder technology and Dai Việt, ca. 1390–1497', in Nhung Tuyet Tran and Anthony Reid (eds), *Việt Nam Borderless Histories*, Madison, 2006, pp. 72–119.

Sung Hou-mei Ishida, 'Early Ming painters in Nanking and the formation of the Wu school', *Ars Orientalis*, vol. 17, 1987, pp. 73–115.

Sung Hou-Mei, 'Tiger with cubs: a rediscovered Ming court painting', *Artibus Asiae*, vol. 64, no. 2, 2004, pp. 281–93.

Sung Hou-mei, *Decoded Messages: The Symbolic Language of Chinese Animal Painting*, New Haven, 2010.

Tan Qian 談遷, *Guoque* 國榷 (*An Evaluation of the State of Our Dynasty*), repr. Beijing, 1958.

Taylor, K.W., *A History of the Vietnamese*, Cambridge, 2013.

Taylor, R., 'Official religion in the Ming', in Denis Twitchett and Frederick W. Mote (eds), *The Cambridge History of China: Volume 8, The Ming Dynasty, 1368–1644, Part 2*, Cambridge, 1998, pp. 840–92.

Thackston, Wheeler McIntosh, *Album Prefaces and Other Documents on the History of Calligraphers and Painters*, Leiden and Boston, 2001.

Thorp, Robert L., *Son of Heaven: Imperial Arts of China*, exh. cat., Seattle, 1988.

Titley, Nora M., *Persian Miniature Painting and Its influence on the Art of Turkey and India*, London, 1983.

Tong, James, *Disorder Under Heaven: Collective Violence in the Ming Dynasty*, Stanford, CA, 1991.

Tong Xun 佟洵 (ed.), *Yixilan jiao yu Beijing Qingzhensi wenhua* 伊斯蘭教與北京清真寺文化 (*Islam and the Culture of Beijing Mosques*), Beijing, 2003.

'Trilingual inscription of Admiral Zheng He', *LankaLibrary Forum*, 2005. http://www.lankalibrary.com/phpBB/viewtopic.php?t=1022Tsai Shih-shan Henry, *The Eunuchs in the Ming Dynasty*, New York, 1996.

Tsai Shih-Shan Henry, *Perpetual Happiness – The Ming Emperor Yongle*, Seattle and London, 2001.

Tseng, Lillian Lan-ying, *Picturing Heaven in Early China*, Cambridge, MA, 2011.

Twitchett, Denis C. and Frederick W. Mote (eds), *The Cambridge History of China: Volume 8, The Ming Dynasty, 1368–1644, Part 2*, Cambridge, 1998.

Vainker, Shelagh, *Chinese Silk: A Cultural History*, London, 2004.

Veit, Veronika, 'The eastern steppe: Mongol regimes after the Yuan (1368–1636)', in Nicola di Cosmo, Allen Frank and Peter Golden (eds), *The Cambridge History of Inner Asia: The Chinggisid Age*, Cambridge, 2009, pp. 157–65.

von Glahn, Richard, *Fountain of Fortune: Money and Monetary Policy in China, 1000–1700*, Berkeley, Los Angeles and London, 1996.

von Glahn, Richard, *The Sinister Way: The Divine and the Demonic in Chinese Religious Culture*, Berkeley, CA, 2004.

Wada Sei 和田清, *Tōashi kenkyū (Mōkohen)* 東亜史研究(蒙古篇) (*East Asian Historical Research (Mongol Edition)*), Tokyo, 1959, pp. 8–20.

Wade, Geoff, 'The Zheng He voyages: a reassessment', *Journal of the Malaysian Branch of the Royal Asiatic Society*, vol. 78, part one, no. 228, 2005, pp. 37–58.

Wade, Geoff, 'Melaka in Ming dynasty texts', *Journal – Malaysian Branch of the Royal Asiatic Society*, vol. 70, no. 1, 1997, pp. 31–70.

Wade, Geoff, 'Engaging the south: Ming China and Southeast Asia in the fifteenth century', *Journal of the Economic and Social History of the Orient*, vol. 51, 2008, pp. 578–638.

Wade, Geoff, 'Southeast Asia in the 15th Century', in Geoff Wade and Sun Laichen (eds), *Southeast Asia in the Fifteenth Century: The China Factor*, Singapore, 2010, pp. 3–43.

Waldron, Arthur, *The Great Wall of China*, Cambridge, 1990.

Waley-Cohen, Joanna, *The Culture of War in China: Empire and the Military under the Qing Dynasty*, London, 2006.

Waltner, Ann, 'Widows and remarriage in Ming and early Qing China', in *Historical Reflections/Réflexions Historiques*, vol. 8, no. 3, 1981, pp. 129–46.

Wang Cheng-hua, 'Material culture and emperorship: the shaping of imperial roles at the Court of Xuanzong (r. 1426–35)', PhD thesis, Yale University, 1998.

Wang Guangyi 王廣義, 'Dongbei "Zheng He" – Yishiha' 東北 '鄭和' – 亦失哈 ('Zheng He' of the Northeast – Yishiha), *Baike zhishi* 百科知識 (*Encyclopaedic Knowledge*), no. 17, 2008, pp. 56–7.

Wang Gungwu, 'The first three rulers of Malacca', *Journal – Malaysian Branch of the Royal Asiatic Society*, vol. 41, no. 1, 1968, pp. 11–22.

Wang, Helen, 'Money in the Ming dynasty', *Orientations*, Sept 2014 (forthcoming)

Wang, Richard G., *The Ming Prince and Daoism: Institutional Patronage of an Elite*, Oxford, 2012.

Wang Xuemei 王雪梅, '*Mingdai Beijing chengnei huanguan yingjian simiao de dili fenbu yanjiu*' 明代北京城内宦官营建寺廟的地理分布研究 ('Research on the geographical distribution of monasteries and temples constructed by eunuchs in Ming-dynasty Beijing'), in *Beijing lishi yu wenhua lunwen ji* 北京歷史與文化論文集 (*Collected Articles on Beijing History and Culture*), Beijing, 2007, pp. 128–40.

Wang Zhenping, 'Reading Song–Ming records on the pre-colonial history of the Philippines', *Journal of East Asian Cultural Interaction Studies*, vol. 1, 2008, pp. 249–60.

Watson, James, 'Standardizing the gods: the promotion of T'ien Hou ("Empress of Heaven") along the South China Coast, 960–1960', in D. Johnson, A. Nathan and E.S. Rawski, *Popular Culture in Late Imperial China*, Berkeley, 1985, pp. 292–324.

Watt, James C.Y., 'The giraffe as the mythical *qilin* in Chinese art: a painting and a rank badge in the Metropolitan Museum', *Metropolitan Museum Journal*, vol. 43, 2008, pp. 111–15.

Watt, James C.Y. and Barbara Brennan Ford, *East Asian Lacquer: The Florence and Herbert Irving Collection*, New York, 1991.

Watt, James C.Y. and Wen Fong, *Possessing the Past: Treasures from the National Palace Museum, Taipei*, exh. cat., New York, 1996.

Watt, James C.Y. and Anne E. Wardwell, *When Silk Was Gold: Central Asian and Chinese Textiles in The Cleveland and Metropolitan Museums of Art*, New York, 1997.

Watt, James C.Y. and Denise Patry Leidy, *Defining Yongle: Imperial Art in Early Fifteenth-Century China*, exh. cat., New York, 2005.

Weidner, Marsha (ed.), *Latter Days of the Law: Images of Chinese Buddhism 850–1850*, exh. cat., Lawrence, KS and Honolulu, 1994.

Weidner, Marsha, 'Imperial engagements with Buddhist art and architecture: Ming variations on an old theme', in Marsha Weidner (ed.), *Cultural Intersections in Later Chinese Buddhism*, Honolulu, 2001, pp. 117–44.

Weidner, Marsha, 'Portraits and personalities in the temples of Ming Beijing: responses to portraits of the monk Daoyan', in Naomi Noble Richard and Donald E. Brix (eds), *The History of Painting in East Asia: Essays on Scholarly Method*, Taipei, 2008, pp. 224–42.

Whitfield, Roderick, 'The Lioness Painting' in Sotheby's Hong Kong, Friday 8 April 2011, sale catalogue.

Whitfield, Roderick, 'Ming Pyrotechnics: the Xiaoling and the Linggusi in the 1407 Scroll', *Arts of Asia*, Nov/Dec 2014 (forthcoming).

Whitmore, John K., *Vietnam, Hô Quý Ly, and the Ming (1371–1421)*, New Haven, 1985.

Whitmore, John K., 'Paperwork: the rise of the new literati and ministerial power and the effort towards legibility in Đai Viet', in Geoff Wade and Sun Laichen (eds), *Southeast Asia in the Fifteenth Century: The China Factor*, Singapore, 2010, pp. 104–25.

Wilson, Verity, 'An enthusiastic cleric and five silk fragments from China', *Oriental Art*, vol. 44, no. 2, 1998, pp. 62–5.

Wilson, Verity, *Chinese Textiles*, London, 2005.

Wood, Nigel, *Chinese Glazes: Their Origins, Chemistry and Recreation*, London and Philadelphia, 1999.

Wu Bosen 吳柏森 et al. (eds), *Ming shilu leizuan: Wenjiao keji juan* 明實錄類纂:文教科技卷 (*An Anthology of Historical Materials from the* Veritable Records of the Ming: *Cultural Education, Science and Technology*), Wuhan, 1992.

Wu Chengshan 吳承山, '*Youyu Baoning si shuilu hua chutan*' 右玉寶寧寺水陸畫初探 ('Preliminary study of the water-and-land paintings of Baoning Monastery in Youyu'), *Wenwu shijie* 文物世界 (*World of Antiquity*), no. 6, 2010, pp. 44–7.

Wu Silas, 'Transmission of Ming memorials, and the evolution of the transmission network, 1368–1627', *T'oung Pao*, vol. 54, nos. 4/5, 1968, pp. 275–87.

Xiao Haiming 肖海明, *Zhenwu tuxiang yanjiu* 真武圖像研究 (*Research into Zhenwu Illustrations*), Beijing, 2007.

Xie Jisheng 謝繼勝 and Jia Weiwei 賈維維, '*Yuan Ming Qing Beijing zangchuan fojiao yishu de xingcheng yu fazhang*' 元明清北京藏傳佛教藝術的形成與發展 ('The form and development of Yuan, Ming, and Qing Tibetan Buddhist art in Beijing'), *Zhongguo Zangxue* 中國藏學 (*China Tibetology*), vol. 1, 2011, pp. 149–61.

Xiong Mengxiang 熊夢祥, *Xijin zhi jiyi* 析津志輯佚 (*Collected Omissions from the Gazetteer of Xijin*), repr. Beijing, 1983.

Xu Shiduan 徐適端 et al. (eds), *Ming shilu leizuan: Funü shiliao juan* 明實錄類纂：婦女史料卷 (*An Anthology of Historical Materials from the* Veritable Records of the Ming: *Historical material on women*), Wuhan, 1995.

Yamane, Yukio 山根幸夫, *Seitoku Damin kaiten* 正德大明会典 (*Zhengde-period Collected Statues of the Great Ming*), Tokyo, 1989.

Yan Xiaoqing 嚴小青 and Hui Fuping 惠富平, '*Zheng He xia xiyang yu Mingdai xiangliao chaogong maoyi*' 鄭和下西洋與明代香料朝貢貿易 ('The Zheng He voyages to the Western Sea and aromatic substances given in trade and tribute to the Ming dynasty'), *Jianghai xuekan* 江海學刊 (*Jianghai Academic Journal*), no. 1, 2008, pp. 180–5.

Yan Xue 閆雪, '*Beijing Zhihua chansi zhuanluncang chutan – Mingdai Hanzang fojiao jialiu yi li*' 北京智化禪寺轉輪藏初探 – 明代漢藏佛教交流一例 ('A preliminary study of the rotating scripture cabinet for Buddhist texts of the Zhihua Temple in Beijing – equal exchange between Han and Tibetan Buddhism in the Ming dynasty', *Zhongguo Zangxue* 中國藏學 (*China Tibetology*), no. 1, 2009, pp. 211–15.

Yang, Eveline S, '*Zhufo pusa*', Wiki Scholars http://lamas-and-emperors.wikischolars.columbia.edu/Zhufopusa.

Yang Guiping, *Islamic Art in China*, Beijing, 2012.

Yang Rong 楊榮, *Beizheng ji* 北征記 (*Records of the Northern Campaign*), in Bo Yinhu 薄音湖 and Wang Xiong 王雄 (eds), *Mingdai Menggu Hanji shiliao huibian* 明代蒙古漢籍史料彙編 (*Compendium of Historical Materials on Mongols from Han Chinese Records*), vol. 1, Hohhot, 2006.

Yang Xiaolin 楊小琳, '*Yuan Dadu Da Shengshou Wan'ansi yu Baita jianzhu buju xingzhi chutan*' 元大都大聖壽萬安寺與白塔建築佈局形制初探 ('Preliminary study of the architectural layout and form of the Yuan Dadu Da Shengshou Wan'an Monastery and White Pagoda'), PhD thesis, The Central University for Nationalities, 2012.

Yang Xiaoneng, 'Archaeological perspectives on the princely burials of Ming dynasty enfeoffments", *Ming Studies*, vol. 65, 2012, pp. 93–118.

Yang Xiaoneng, 'Chinese Archaeology of the Ming Dynasty: from archaeological policies to revealing spirit worlds', *Arts of Asia*, Nov/Dec 2014 (forthcoming).

Yang Xinhua 楊新華 (ed.), *Nanjing Ming gugong* 南京明故宮 (*Nanjing's Ming Imperial Palace*), Nanjing, 2009.

Ye Yingting 葉英挺 and Hua Yunong 華雨農, *Faxian: Da Ming Chuzhou Longquan guanyao* 發現：大明處州龍泉官窯 (*Discovery: Longquan Official Kilns at Chuzhou of the Great Ming*), Hangzhou, 2005.

Yin Ji'nan 尹吉男, '*Mingdai gongting huajia Xie Huan de yeyu shenghuo yu fang Mi shi yunshan huihua*' 明代宮廷畫家謝環的業餘生活與仿米氏雲山繪畫 (*The extra-professional life of Ming dynasty court painter Xie Huan and his emulation of Mi family cloudy mountain paintings*), *Yishushi yanjiu* 藝術史研究 (*The Study of Art History*), no. 9, 2007, pp. 101–26.

Yoshikawa Kōjirō, *Five Hundred Years of Chinese Poetry, 1150–1650*, Princeton, 1989.

Young Kyun Oh, *Engraving Virtue: The Printing History of a Premodern Korean Moral Primer*, Leiden and Boston, 2013.

Yu Jideng 余繼登, *Diangu jiwen* 典故紀聞 (*Record of Quotations*), repr. Beijing, 1981.

Yü Chün-fang, 'Ming Buddhism', in Denis C. Twitchett and Frederick W. Mote (eds), *The Cambridge History of China: Volume 8, The Ming Dynasty, 1368–1644, Part 2*, Cambridge, 1998, pp. 893–952.

Yun Eun Suk 尹銀淑, '*Bugwon gwa myeong ui daerip* – yodong munje reul jungsim euro' 北元과 明 의대립 – 遼東 문제를중심으로('Conflict Between North Yuan and Ming Dynasty'), *Dongyang sahak yeongu* 東洋史學研究 (*Journal of Asian Historical Studies*), vol. 105, 2008, pp. 91–6.

Yutaka Mino, *Freedom of Clay and Brush through Seven Centuries in Northern China: Tz'u-chou (Cizhou) Type Wares 960–1600 A.D.*, exh. cat., Indianapolis, 1980.

Zainie, Carla M., 'The *Muromachi Dono Gyōkō Okazari ki*: a research note', *Monumenta Serica*, vol. 33, 1978, pp. 113–18.

Zeng Qi 曾棨, *Ke Zeng xishu xiansheng ji* 刻曾西墅先生集 (*Record of Ke Zeng, gentleman of the western villa*), in *Siku Quanshu cunmu congshu* 四庫全書存目叢書 (*Extant compendia from the Complete Library of the Four Treasuries*), repr. Jinan, 1995–7, *ji* 30.

Zhang Chuanxi 張傳璽 (ed.), *Zhongguo lidai qiyue huibian kaoshi* 中國歷代契約會编考釋 (*Collated Philological Study of Charters from Successive Chinese Dynasties*), 2 vols, Beijing, 1995.

Zhang Hongxing (ed.), *Masterpieces of Chinese Painting 700–1900*, London, 2013.

Zhang Huiyi 張惠衣, *Jinling Da Baoensi ta zhi* 金陵大報恩寺塔志 (*Gazetteer of Nanjing's Great Baoen Monastery and Pagoda*), Beijing, 1937.

Zhang Linsheng 張臨生, '*Zhongguo gudai de jing jin gongyi*' 中國古代的精金工藝 ('Refined goldworks in ancient China'), *Gugong wenwu yuekan* 故宮文物月刊 (*The National Palace Museum Monthly of Chinese Art*), no. 14, 1984, pp. 48–67.

Zhang Rong, 'Cloisonné for the imperial courts', in Beatrice Quette (ed.), *Cloisonné: Chinese Enamels from the Yuan, Ming and Qing Dynasties*, New York, Paris, New Haven and London, 2012, pp. 151–70.

Zhang Runping 張潤平, Su Hang 蘇航 and Luo Zhao 羅炤, *Xitian fozi yuanliu lu: wenxian yu chubu yanjiu* 西天佛子源流錄:文獻與初步研究 (*Record of the Origins of a Western Disciple of Buddha: Literature and Preliminary Research*), Beijing, 2012.

Zhang Wende 張文德, *Ming yu Tiemuer wangchao guanxi shi yanjiu* 明與帖木兒王朝關係史研究 (*Research on the Historical Relationship Between the Ming and Timurid Dynasty*), Beijing, 2006.

Zhang Zhengxiang 張正祥, '*Mingdai Nanjing Jubaoshan liuli yao*' 明代南京聚寶山琉璃窯 ('The glazed pottery kilns at Jubaoshan, Nanjing, in the Ming period'), *Wenwu* 文物 (*Cultural Relics*), no. 2, 1962, pp. 41–8.

Zhao Feng, *Treasures in Silk: An Illustrated History of Chinese Textiles*, Hangzhou, 1999.

Zhao Feng, 'Female Costume and Silk from the Tai Lake Region in Early Ming (1403–1424)', *Orientations*, Sept 2014 (forthcoming).

Zhao Qichang 趙其昌, '*Mingdai de Yuenan taijian Song Wenyi yu Ruan An*' 明代的越南太監宋文毅與阮安 ('Ming dynasty Vietnamese eunuchs Song Wenyi and Nguyen An'), *Shoudu bowuguan congkan* 首都博物館叢刊 (*Journal of the Capital Museum*), no. 8, 1993, pp. 209–17.

Zhejiang sheng wenwu kaogu yanjiu suo 浙江省文物考古研究所 (Zhejiang Province Cultural Relic Institute of Archaeology) et al, *Longquan dayao fengdongyan yaozhi chutu ciqi* 龍泉大窯楓洞岩窯址出土瓷器 (*Ceramics Excavated from the Kiln Site of Fengdongyan, Dayao, Longquan*), Beijing, 2009.

Zhencheng 鎮澄, *Qingliangshan zhi* 清涼山志 (*Gazetteer of Mount Qingliang*), repr. Beijing, 1989.

'*Zheng He yu fofa*' 鄭和與佛法 ('Zheng He and the Buddha Dharma'), *Zhibei fo wang* 智悲佛網 (*Wisdom and Compassion Buddhist Web*). http://www.zhibeifw.com/wap/r.php?id=10638

Zhongguo guojia bowuguan 中國國家博物館 (National Museum of China), *Yunfan wanli zhao chongyang: Jinian Zheng He xia xiyang liubai zhounian* 雲帆萬里照重洋：紀念鄭和下西洋六百周年 (*A Memorial Exhibition for the 600th Anniversary of Zheng He's Seven Voyages*), Beijing, 2005.

Zhongguo guojia tushuguan 中國國家圖書館 (National Library of China), *Zhufo pusa miaoxiang minghao jingzhou* 諸佛菩薩妙相名號經咒 (*Xylographs in Marvelous Images, Names, Sutras and Dharanis of the Buddhas and Bodhisattvas*), Beijing, 2011.

Zhongguo shehui kexueyuan kaogu yanjiusuo 中國社會學院考古研究所 (Institute of Archaeology, Chinese Academy of Social Sciences), 'Chengdu Fenghuangshan Ming mu 成都鳳凰山明墓' ('Ming tombs at Chengdu Mount Fenghuang'), *Kaogu* 考古 (*Archaeology*), no. 5, 1978, pp. 306–13.

Zhou Xiang 周祥, *Shanghai bowuguan cangpin yanjiu daxi. Zhongguo gudai zhichao* 上海博物館藏品大系. 中國古代紙鈔 (*Shanghai Museum collection Research Series: China's Ancient Paper Money*), Shanghai, 2004.

Zhou Xianghua 周向華 (ed.), *Anhui shifan daxue guancang Huizhou wenshu* 安徽師範大學館藏徽州文書 (*Huizhou documents in the Collection of the Anhui Normal University*), Anhui, 2009.

Zhufo shizun rulai pusa zunzhe mingcheng gequ 諸佛世尊如來菩薩尊者名稱歌曲 (*Renown Names of the Various Buddhas, the World Honoured Tathāgata, Bodhisattvas, and Worthies*) *Zhonghua Dianzi Fodian Xiehui*中華電子佛典協會 (Chinese Buddhist Electronic Texts Association). http://tripitaka.cbeta.org/P179n1612_001

Zhifo shizun rulai pusa zunzhe shenseng mingjing 諸佛世尊如來菩薩尊者神僧名經 (*Famed Sutra of the Various Buddhas, the World Honoured Tathāgata, Bodhisattvas, the Worthies and Divine Monks*) *Zhonghua Dianzi Fodian Xiehui*中華電子佛典協會 (Chinese Buddhist Electronic Texts Association). http://tripitaka.cbeta.org/zh-cn/P178n1611_001

ILLUSTRATION CREDITS

The publisher would like to thank the copyright holders for granting permission to reproduce the images illustrated in this book. Every attempt has been made to trace accurate ownership of copyright images. Errors and omissions will be corrected in subsequent editions provided notification is sent to the publisher.

All British Museum images are © The Trustees of the British Museum, courtesy of the Department of Photography and Imaging. Further information about objects in the collection of the British Museum can be found on the Museum's website at britishmuseum.org.

PRELIM PAGES

Endpapers: bpk / Museum für Asiatische Kunst, SMB / Jürgen Liepe
Half-title page: Hubei Provincial Museum
Frontispiece: © 2014. Image copyright The Metropolitan Museum of Art/ Art Resource/Scala, Florence
p. 4 © The Trustees of the British Museum
p. 6 © The Trustees of the British Museum
p. 8 © The Trustees of the British Museum
map © The Trustees of the British Museum (artwork by Paul Goodhead)
pp.16–17 The Palace Museum

CHAPTER 1 A SECOND FOUNDING: MING CHINA 1400–1450

Chapter opener: National Palace Museum Collection
fig. 1   National Palace Museum Collection
fig. 2   National Palace Museum Collection
fig. 3   Wikimedia Commons photo by Clithering
fig. 4   Wikimedia Commons photo by Camphora
fig. 5   The Palace Museum
fig. 6   The Palace Museum
fig. 7   National Museum of China
fig. 8   National Palace Museum Collection
fig. 9   Courtesy of the Library of Congress- LC-USZ62-137083
fig. 10   Wikimedia Commons photo by Yan Li
fig. 11   photo. Osvald Sirén and ©The Museum of Far Eastern Antiquities, Stockholm/ Östasiatiska Museet
fig. 12   © Yang Zhiguo
fig. 13   © Philadelphia Museum of Art
fig. 14   © Getty Images photographer: TAO Images Limited
fig. 15   Fahai Monastery, Beijing
fig. 16   © Getty Images photographer: Karl Johaentges
fig. 17   © Getty Images photographer: Karl Johaentges
fig. 18   The Palace Museum (photo. Zhang Xiaobo)
fig. 19   Courtesy of the C.V. Starr East Asian Library, Columbia University
fig. 20   TNM Image Archives
fig. 21   Topkapi Palace Museum

fig. 22   Topkapi Palace Museum

CHAPTER 2 COURTS: PALACES, PEOPLE AND OBJECTS

Chapter opener: The Palace Museum
fig. 23   After Yang 2009, p. 18
fig. 24   National Museum of Korea 국립중앙박물관
fig. 25   © The Trustees of the British Museum
fig. 26   akg-images / Universal Images Group / Sovfoto
fig. 27   The Palace Museum
fig. 28   © The British Library Board
figs 29–36 National Palace Museum Collection
fig. 37   The Muban Foundation Collection
fig. 38   Private Collection
fig. 39   The Palace Museum
fig. 40   Sichuan Museum
fig. 41   Photographed by Li Sheng and Li Xucheng of Chengdu Museum in 2003
fig. 42   Shandong Museum
fig. 43   Sichuan Museum
fig. 44   Hubei Provincial Museum
fig. 45   Shandong Museum
fig. 46   © The Trustees of the British Museum
fig. 47   Hubei Provincial Museum
fig. 48–50 Shandong Museum
figs 51–2   Hubei Provincial Museum
fig. 53   National Folk Museum of Korea
fig. 54   Shandong Museum
figs 55–60 Hubei Provincial Museum
fig. 61   © The Trustees of the British Museum
fig. 62   The Palace Museum
fig. 63   Private Collection
fig. 64   © The Trustees of the British Museum
fig. 65   © Philadelphia Museum of Art
fig. 66   © Philadelphia Museum of Art
fig. 67   Hubei Provincial Museum
fig. 68   © The Trustees of the British Museum
fig. 69   Sir Percival David Foundation of Chinese Art. Photo © The Trustees of the British Museum
fig. 70   Hubei Provincial Museum
fig. 71   Sir Percival David Foundation of Chinese Art. Photo © The Trustees of the British Museum
fig. 72   © The Trustees of the British Museum
fig. 73   Hubei Provincial Museum
fig. 74   Arthur M. Sackler Gallery, Smithsonian Institution, Washington, D.C.
fig. 75   Hubei Provincial Museum
fig. 76   Sir Percival David Foundation of Chinese Art. Photo © The Trustees of the British Museum
fig. 77   (above) © Victoria and Albert Museum, London
fig. 77   (below) Sir Percival David Foundation of Chinese Art. Photo © The Trustees of the British Museum
fig. 78   © The Trustees of the British Museum
fig. 79   (left) Shanghai Museum
fig. 79   (right) © 2014. Image copyright The Metropolitan Museum of Art/ Art Resource/Scala, Florence

fig. 80   (left) Private Collection. Photo © The Trustees of the British Museum
fig. 80   (right) © 2014. Image copyright The Metropolitan Museum of Art/ Art Resource/Scala, Florence
fig. 81   (above) Sir Percival David Foundation of Chinese Art. Photo © The Trustees of the British Museum
fig. 81   (below) © The Trustees of the British Museum
fig. 82   © The Trustees of the British Museum
fig. 83   © The Trustees of the British Museum
fig. 84   Sir Percival David Foundation of Chinese Art and the British Museum. Photos © The Trustees of the British Museum
fig. 85   Private Collection
fig. 86   © The Trustees of the British Museum
fig. 87   Ashmolean Museum, University of Oxford
fig. 88   Private Collection
fig. 89   © The Trustees of the British Museum
fig. 90   © The Trustees of the British Museum
fig. 91   © Victoria and Albert Museum, London
fig. 92   Shandong Museum
fig. 93   © Victoria and Albert Museum, London
fig. 94   © Victoria and Albert Museum, London
fig. 95   Shandong Museum
fig. 96   Shandong Museum
fig. 97   © Victoria and Albert Museum, London
fig. 98   © The Trustees of the British Museum
fig. 99   Hubei Provincial Museum
fig. 100   Hubei Provincial Museum
fig. 101   © The Trustees of the British Museum

CHAPTER 3 WU: THE ARTS OF WAR

Chapter opener: © Royal Armouries
fig. 102   Courtesy of the Royal Artillery Museum. Photo © The Trustees of the British Museum
fig. 103   Capital Museum
fig. 104   © UCLA Library Special Collections
fig. 105   © The Trustees of the British Museum
fig. 106   Photo courtesy of Shi Yijun, Wang Jinsi, Si Quanfu
fig. 107   Nanjing Municipal Museum
fig. 108   Nanjing Municipal Museum
fig. 109   Sichuan Museum
fig. 110   Courtesy of the Royal Artillery Museum. Photo © The Trustees of the British Museum
fig. 111   Ass. Prof. Dr. Bui Quang Thang, Head of the Department of Ecological Culture and Tourism, Vietnam Institute of Culture and Arts Studies (VICAS)
fig. 112   © Bridgeman Images
fig. 113   Arthur M. Sackler Gallery, Smithsonian Institution, Washington, D.C.
fig. 114   The Palace Museum
fig. 115   Wikimedia commons. Photo by Ofol
fig. 116   Shandong Museum
fig. 117   Hubei Provincial Museum
fig. 118   Hubei Provincial Museum

INDEX